The 100 Silliest Things People Say About Dogs

Alexandra Semyonova

ISBN 978-1-904-10918-1

Published by Hastings Press, England
in association with
The Carriage House Foundation
Postbus 10 308 2501 HH Den Haag, The Netherlands

www.nonlineardogs.com
info@nonlineardogs.com

Cover design: Helena Wojtczak
Cover photo: Life in a Smile by Federico Stevan

To Uk

Acknowledgments

My thanks to my brother Jason and his daughter Caroline, and to Leonie van der Lans, Willemien Buschman, and Kristen Pelleboer-Knouse, without whom I couldn't have kept going on the long project of writing a book. To Joke Mantjes, who kept me sane during one of life's most painful losses and stuck with me through the aftermath — and now still. To Sylvia Jans, who understands what it is to love dogs and has stood by me through thick and thin. To Iaira Boissevain for her cogent and careful criticisms, for giving me time when she didn't really have any, for her patience with and forgivingness of my quirks, and even more for her and energy and sense of humour. To AnteCarey Maaskant-De Groot, D.V.M., for her advice and help and for the delightful way she says it like it is. To various people who offered help and criticism, but who don't want to be named because the industry they work for won't like some of what I say here. And finally, to Helena Wojtczak for her help at the finish line but most of all just for her friendship.

Contents

INSTRUCTIONS FOR USING THIS BOOK

This is intended as a new guide to dogs. Because many widespread beliefs about dogs are not only outdated, but also bad for dogs, I want this book to be useful to the widest possible audience.

I've written this book so it can be read two ways. It can be read as a whole, from chapter one to chapter one hundred. Those who do this will, at the end, have a firm grasp of much of the new knowledge we have about dogs. It can also be used to check each belief separately. You can read the book in bits and pieces, looking up things that strike your interest, or checking something your neighbour, dog trainer or local scientist is telling you. Each chapter can stand alone and will teach you something important.

No matter which way you read it, this book will improve your understanding of why dogs do things the way they do, and it will increase your appreciation of this marvellous species so many share their lives with. This book may also even help you understand people better.

Please note that when I use the expression 'normal' dogs in this book, I mean two things. The first is, dogs who are not of the breeds we have bred for aggression and/or extremely large body size and mass. When I talk about normal dogs, I am explicitly excluding these breeds. The second thing 'normal dogs' means is dogs who have had a chance to learn about being a dog from other dogs.

Preface

The 100 silliest things people say about dogs are all based on old-fashioned ideas about Nature in general, and about dogs in specific. In this book, I debunk various myths and fables that most people still believe in, replacing them with real insight into real dogs. As you read along, you'll see your dog doing things I talk about in this book. You'll discover new things in him each day, things you never noticed before because you didn't know what they meant — or that they even had any meaning. You'll also find your relationship with your dog improving, as you interact with him on the basis of real understanding instead of the old dogmas. I hope you will feel the same excitement I felt as I made my discoveries.

Even if you've always believed in all of the myths this book debunks, you remain innocent of any wrongdoing. You probably, just like me, somehow ended up with a dog one day. And, just like me, you probably thought, 'I'd better get some advice from an expert, to be sure I do it right.' When they told you their silly ideas, they probably sounded so self-confident that it didn't occur to you to doubt they knew what they were talking about.

The same thing happened to me. After getting degrees in social and behavioural sciences, I ended up some years later with an adult dog. All I needed to do was use the same techniques I'd used in the behaviour lab — reward the behaviour I wanted, and make sure I didn't reward behaviour I didn't like. Piece of cake, perfect dog.

I wasn't exposed to all the stories dog people tell until I got my first puppy. I realised that raising a young animal, with all its species-specific developmental requirements, was a totally different thing than simply applying the laws of behaviour to an adult. Time to research dogs. I read every book I could get my hands on and talked to many trainers. All sources agreed that dogs live in a hierarchy, and that they spend all their time being either dominant or submissive to each other. They told me that even play is about determining relative rank within the group; that any request my dog made to me (to fulfill one of his needs, to play with him) was a secret attempt to increase his own rank in the hope of taking over someday. I was told I needed to make sure I was the Alpha Leader. The nice way to do this involved a number of things, which were explained to me as a sort of psychological warfare. I was told to ignore all requests from my dog. I should always go before my dog through a door, to show that I was the courageous leader. I had to eat first before I fed the dog, since the Alpha wolf always eats first and then determines who gets to eat next. The dog wasn't allowed on the couch, since the Alpha wolf always lies on the highest spot when the pack is resting. I should never approach the dog, since the submissive wolf always approaches the dominant wolf — but on the other hand, I should make sure the dog moves aside when I'm coming through, since the dominant wolf never moves aside for the lesser pack members (I sort of wondered how I was going to do this one without approaching the dog...). Even if he was lying somewhere, I wasn't to go around him, but to step over him, because otherwise I was letting him command the avenues of access to the territory. And so on and so on, about how it is absolutely crucial to maintain your Alpha rank.

This all seemed a bit far-fetched to me. I wondered why everyone started talking about wolves every time I asked them about dogs. I also kind of wondered why all had gone so well with my previous dogs, who were all allowed on the couch. But who was I to argue with people who claimed to know so much, or scientists who claimed to have studied dogs? Most of the trainers also urged me to train the pup with punishment. I definitely had to get a choke chain, get angry at behaviour I didn't like, and do things like jerking on the puppy's neck if he was leashed or, if he wasn't, throwing cans of coins or marbles at him, or squirting water in his face.

But I never used any kind of punishment. I was too experienced in the lab and knew what kinds of horrible side effects punishment has on an animal, besides the fact that you can teach it perfectly well without it. But I did believe the rest, for a while. When I saw dogs together in a park, I thought I saw all kinds of rank-establishing behaviour. But I was only observing the dogs for short intervals, of course. My doubts began when I started to have many and various dogs in the house and to observe their group behaviour for long periods of time, in groups with ever changing composition. I could hardly believe my eyes. There was no dog who always lay on the highest spot. It was always a different dog who was first to go through a door. All of them avoided collisions any way they could, usually by both dogs moving aside a little. The way they behaved around food and toys didn't follow the rules, either. They seemed above all interested in being considerate to each other and avoiding arguments where possible, not about winning. In fact, none of my own observations confirmed any of what the experts had told me about dogs.

I decided to delve deeper into the literature. I also started my own research project. After fourteen years, a totally new picture of canine reality emerged — a reality that means we have to adjust not only the layman's beliefs about dogs, but also the things science is saying about them. It turns out that many scientists have written about dogs without observing them first hand. When they have, it has been under highly artificial circumstances (in the laboratory). Only a few have attempted to observe dogs in their natural habitat. Many defined this as 'dogs not under human influence', failing to see that domestic dogs are *always* under human influence. Most observed for relatively short periods, or short intervals over a longer period — altogether a few months.

In fact, if you want to understand a social species, you have to observe a group of animals in their natural surroundings, and you have to observe them for at least one whole life cycle of an average member of the species. I suppose no one thought we had to do it with dogs, because they are so familiar. We assumed we already knew about them, and that we only needed to work out some details. Wrong.

This book is based on real live observations of real live dogs, in their natural surroundings, twenty-four hours a day, seven days a week, for fourteen years. The intensity of my study gave me the chance to discover which information was irrelevant and which was important. It was an anthropological study: besides watching them, I also participated in the dogs' social system, trying to discover and use their rules of interaction instead of imposing my human ones upon them. By allowing the dogs to teach me, I gave them a chance to contradict the myths we have built up about them — a chance to be heard, as it were. It turned out not to matter at all to the social structure who went through a door first, or who got to keep food or a toy. Those things were different every time, and are not what their social structure is based on. Nor is their social structure based on threat, aggression, or power — perhaps the most damaging myth of all. The dog's social system is based on a few simple rules of politeness that are aimed above all at not disturbing the peace.

So don't feel silly as you read this book. Despite my education in the behavioural sciences, it took me fourteen years to find the truth amidst all the nonsense. There is, however, one group that definitely should feel silly — the trainers and other 'experts' who have blown so much hot air into the world without bothering to make sure they knew what they were talking about. Knowledge about how animals learn has, after all, been available since 1938. But it is science that should be truly ashamed of itself here. At least two whole generations of scientists failed in examining their own motivations and assumptions, in looking critically at their methodology, and — thus — in being fair to this wonderful species we call dogs.

Part 1

Myths about dogs' origin and nature

Myth 1: The dog is a descendant of the wolf, and because of this we should regard him as a sort of tame wolf in our living room.

The idea of the dog as a tame wolf has a huge romantic attraction for us. We imagine the great grey wolf of the northern regions of the Earth, a powerful wild animal weighing 160–220 pounds, who spends his days hunting deer, moose or elk. We dream of our own ancestors finding (or stealing) a wolf puppy and raising him with lots of TLC. We imagine this pup growing up to be man's friend and companion, and bearing tame pups for us. After thousands generations of this, we supposedly produced the dog as we now know him. We see a direct line of descent going from our own dog straight to the mighty grey wolf we see on Discovery Channel. Wow, a wolf in our living room, what a powerful feeling!

We now know that this isn't how it happened. Our ancestors didn't tame the dog at all. The dog most likely tamed himself. Besides, the dog's ancestor isn't the mighty grey wolf of Discovery Channel. That wolf didn't exist yet when the dog began to split off into a new species — the grey wolf as he is today had yet to evolve, just as the domestic dog did. What you need to imagine is a much smaller animal, who had already split off from the wolf family line, some 200,000–500,000 years ago. This ancestor wasn't a specialised hunter like the wolf is, but rather what biologists call a 'generalist' — an animal that is not limited to one special food source or environment, but that can adapt to various situations. This smaller ancestor probably looked somewhat like the dingo and other primitive dogs who still live in the wild today. It may not have been a pack animal. In fact, pack living is rare among canids. So, like most of the generalist canids we see today, the dog's ancestor probably lived in pairs and temporary family groups, able to deal both with being together and with being alone.

So now you are picturing a smaller, more dog-like kind of animal. What did this pre-dog animal do that led, in the end, to the present day dog? And did we have anything to do with it? The answer to both questions lies in our own development as a species. Like most species, we struggled along for millions of years, our numbers limited by the availability of food. Then, about 130,000 years ago, we invented the bow and arrow. This was a great leap, but — contrary to the myth — it didn't mean that the dog's ancestor immediately joined us to help with the hunt. The dog was still just a wild animal, and like all wild canids — right up to the present, and even if they are raised in a human home — he remained totally useless to us during the hunt.

So our bow and arrow didn't mean that some wolf was suddenly able to work as a tracking and hunting dog, as the myth tells us. It did mean that our ancestors suddenly had a much easier time getting enough to eat. They started to leave small dumps behind at their encampments, dumps where there were edible leftovers for others to find. A new food source opened up for other species in the area. And when a new food source opens up in a particular environment, some animal always moves in to exploit it. In this case, a few of the sometimes hunting, sometimes scavenging, small ancestors of the present day dog were the ones who made the move. These were individuals who were attracted to a much easier (and safer) way to make a living. All they needed to do was trail along behind groups of humans and eat at the dumps we left behind. Perhaps they still ran into roaming,

human-fearing relatives occasionally when their paths happened to cross, and perhaps they sometimes still mated with these animals — but most of the pups would come of mating at dumps, between loner animals who were now getting a living by scavenging our waste. This was the beginning reproductive separation, and thus of the formation of a separate species.

So, probably about 130,000 years ago, we have a number of these dog-like ancestors who split off and entered a new ecological niche. Partially reproductively isolated in this new niche, they began to develop specifically doggy characteristics. In order to meet at the dump and thus be able to mate, these animals had to have special qualities. They had to be prepared to eat ready-made food instead of hunting (the food you give your dog is, up to this day, still made of our waste, even the most fancy and expensive brands). If they lived in groups, they had to be willing to give this up in favour of wandering around alone or in pairs (even at the dump, there wouldn't have been enough food for a large group). They had to be able to share space (the dump) with strangers of their own species who had also discovered this new source of food. And — most important of all — they had to have a less-than-average fear of humans. These animals were in the process of making a choice. They were farther from their cousin the wolf than ever, but they weren't domestic dogs yet, either. The choice that some of them made led them down the road to becoming, at this juncture, a sort of pre-domestic dog. This animal's anatomy was still adjusted to a life of travelling as they trailed along behind groups of nomadic humans. This is probably why archaeologists don't find typically doggy remains from this period. The dog's body hadn't changed yet, even though his behaviour and his brain were already changing. But before this animal could become a real domestic dog, our own species had to make its next step.

This next step came about 12,000 years ago, when we developed agriculture. Humans stopped roaming as hunters and gatherers and started living in permanent settlements. Now the pre-dog could also settle down and live permanently at the dump. Now he wouldn't run into relatives who were still hunting and still shy of humans, not even by accident. There would be no more mating with hunters, not even occasionally. His body could now adapt to a non-travelling life, besides the changes that had already taken place in his brain and behaviour. Within a very short time, the dog as we know it today was a fact. This is the period when truly doggy skeletal remains showed up. The other branches of the family continued on their hunter's way, and became the wild dogs you now see on Discovery Channel. The present-day grey wolf has nothing to do with it.

Fact: The dog and the wolf are related to each other in the same way you are related to your sixth cousin, and in the same way we are all related to some other types of primates (monkeys and apes). We share an ancestor, that's all. But the dog most definitely didn't descend from the grey wolf, any more than you descended from your cousin.

Belyaev, DK, Trut, LN, Some genetic and endocrine effects of selections for domestication in silver foxes, in *The Wild Canids*, Fox, MW, ed., Van Nostrand Reinhold, New York, 1975.

Belyaev, DK, Plyusnina, IZ, and Trut, LN, Domestication in the silver fox (Vulpes fulvus desm): changes in physiological boundaries of the sensitive period of primary socialization, *Applied Animal Behaviour Science* 13:359–70, 1984/85.

Coppinger, R, Coppinger, L, *Dogs: a startling new understanding of canine origin, behaviour, and evolution*, Scribner, New York, 2001.
Koler-Matznick, J, The origin of the dog revisited, *Anthrozoos* 15(20): 98–118, 2002.
Sibly, RM, Smith, RH, *Behavioural Ecology: Ecological Consequences of Adaptive Behaviour*, Blackwell Scientific Publications, Oxford, 1985.

Myth 2: The dog is genetically similar to the wolf, so we can expect him to behave like a wolf.

It's true that the dog is genetically similar to the wolf. But it's also true that we humans only differ genetically from a rabbit by about fifteen percent. It's also a fact that scientists (who are only human) love to chase publicity and sensational news breaks because this generates lots of research funds. Perhaps this is the reason geneticists sometimes just love to suggest that genes completely control behaviour, while in fact most of them know better. Perhaps geneticists are also partly motivated by genuine hope. After all, discovering the gene for criminal behaviour (or even wolf behaviour) would make you rich and famous, and maybe even get you a Nobel Prize.

This is, however, impossible. In a normal, healthy creature, genes determine certain structures, reflexes and potential, and then the environment does the rest. We walk on two legs because two is what our genes make us grow. Our genes determine that we have big brains, which are also designed to be able to learn to steer two legs. Whether a human ever does learn to walk, or whether she develops the IQ her brain is capable of developing are not determined by genes. These things are determined for each of us individually by the particular environment we grow up in, and by the experiences we have as we grow. A dog's genes generate four legs and smaller, less complicated brains. What the dog will do with those legs, how intelligent she ends up, and how social, are things her environment will dictate, within the parameters set by genes.

How does this work? Genes specify basic structures, processes and potential. From the moment of birth, the realisation of that potential takes place in an exchange with the environment. Urged on by incoming stimuli and by experiences the infant animal is having, the brain cells develop connections with each other (or they don't), in an ever more (or sometimes less) complex network of neurons. This is already a form of learning — the structure and organisation of the brain changing in response to the environment. It is a process that begins at birth, and it has a real, physical effect on the exact brain a mammal ends up with within her genetic limitations. We know, for example, that an impoverished environment during the first two years of life will lower a human's IQ forever because the brain develops relatively impoverished neural networks. We know that a lot of behaviour we used to think was inborn is, in fact, learned. Living in a pack is not inborn in a wolf. It is something a wolf has to learn. He has to learn which species to hunt and how to do it. You can't just dump a lone wolf into a group, or switch a group from hunting deer to hunting moose. Even the ability to raise young is learned. Behaviour is always a result of our environment interacting with the potential our genes have given us. Unless you are talking about genes that cause a physical abnormality in our bodies, a physical difference in brain structures, or a genetically determined imbalance in brain chemistry (see Myths 38 and 39), you can't just look at genes and then predict how an animal is going to behave.

But even where genes do determine behavioural potential, it's important not to forget that the dog evolved under different circumstances than the wolf. We would expect this to mean that she would be genetically adapted to a different environment, and have different genetic potential. Indeed, all dogs' jaws are smaller and weaker than any wolf's, their skulls are different, their organs for hearing are different, their cerebellum looks more like a coyote's, and all their brains are smaller and less complex than a wolf's. A domestic dog could never be as competent a hunter, no matter how she's raised. Dogs are very receptive to training; wolves are not. After birth, the dog grows up in a totally different environment than the wolf. This means that her different brain grows differently within its potential, storing other information and experiences than the wild wolf cub — that the difference between the two animals becomes even larger as life goes on. By the time she's an adult, the dog's brain and her behaviour will be radically different from the brain and behaviour of her distant cousin, on top of all the differences genes dictate. Two wolves will not behave the same way even if their genes are identical, let alone that a dog will behave like a wolf just because her genes are similar.

Meanwhile, here is something to think about. The dog and the wolf are further apart genetically than the leopard and the jaguar, which are considered two distinct species. They are a little farther apart than humans and chimpanzees. But they are closer together than human men and human women (men have about two percent less DNA than women). The Border Collie and the Pointer differ much less genetically than the dog and the wolf, yet there are important and predictable, genetically determined, differences in their behaviour. Other parts of their behaviour are, indeed, identical and/or trainable. So what is a lot of genetic difference, and what is a little? Are we nothing more than domesticated chimps? Are men really from Mars? We don't know all the answers yet.

Fact: A dog is, above all, a dog, and her genes will not make her behave like a wolf. What we need to do if we want to understand dogs is look at dogs.

Beljaev, DK, Trut, LN, Some genetic and endocrine effects of selections for domestication in silver foxes, in *The Wild Canids*, Fox, M.W. ed., Van Nostrand Reinhold, New York, 1975.

Beljaev, DK, Plyusnina, IZ, and Trut, LN, Domestication in the silver fox (Vulpes fulvus desm): changes in physiological boundaries of the sensitive period of primary socialization, *Applied Animal Behaviour Science* 13:359–70, 1984/85.

Coppinger, R, Coppinger, L, Biological bases of behaviour of domestic dog breeds, in Voith, VL, Borchelt, PL, eds, *Readings in Companion Animal Behaviour*, Veterinary Learning systems, Co., Inc., Trenton, NJ, 1996.

Coppinger, R, Coppinger, L, *Dogs: a startling new understanding of canine origin, behaviour, and evolution,* Scribner, New York, 2001.

Koler-Matznick, J, The origin of the dog revisited, *Anthrozoos* 15(20): 98 — 118, 2002.

Scott, JP, Fuller, JL, *Genetics and the Social Behaviour of the Dog,* University of Chicago Press, Chicago IL, 1974 (published in 1965 as *Dog Behaviour: The Genetic Basis*).

Smits, R, 'Genen weten niks en doen ook niks'; neurofysioloog Colin Blakemore over de samenhang tussen genen en omgeving, *NRC Handelsblad*, 19 en 20 juli 2003, Wetenschap en Onderwijs, p.33.

Van Den Berg, L, *Genetics of aggressive behaviour in Golden Retriever dogs,* Utrecht University, Utrecht, 2006. http://igitur-archive.library.uu.nl/dissertations/2006-0427-200041/index.htm.

Myth 3: Everything we know about wolves applies to dogs, too.

We've already seen a number of reasons why this isn't true. The dog's ancestor eventually became a dog because he left the ecological niche his ancestor may have shared with the wolf's ancestors probably some 500,000 years ago. The scientists aren't entirely in agreement on the exact time yet, but that's not so important. The fact remains that the domestic dog evolved in a totally different environment than the wolf. Their genetic similarity means about as much (or as little) as our similarity to various apes means.

But there is more you need to know. Even if we could apply what we know about wolves to dogs, the fact is that we don't know very much about wolves. This may surprise you. Indeed, much has been published about wolves — books, articles, documentaries on television — and most of it in such an authoritative tone. Surely we must know all about them? The trouble is that much of what people pretend to know about wolves has been based either on fantasy and speculation, or on insufficient data and poorly designed research.

Mankind has been waging a war of annihilation against the wolf for hundreds of years now, because modern man always viewed the wolf as a competitor in the hunt and a danger to his cattle. There may have been a time when the wolf wasn't scared of humans, but that was long before we developed writing, let alone science. By the time we decided to study the wolf, this animal had become so shy of us that it was almost impossible to get a glimpse of him in his natural habitat. This is, first of all, because by that time there were already damned few wolves left to study. And second of all, the ones that did survive us had learned to melt away into the forest the instant they heard or smelled us, and still do. It has been almost impossible, for more than one hundred years now, to even see a wild wolf, let alone study his behaviour — except the behaviour of fleeing from a threat to his life.

So wolves do their utter best not to let themselves be observed by humans in the wild, while science demands that conclusions be based on observations. Scientists puzzled for a while, then came up with a solution of their own. Once in a while they manage to shoot a wolf with a tranquilliser dart, after which they put a radio collar around his neck and release him to rejoin his pack. After that, the scientists can locate the group of wolves by following the signal the collared wolf is transmitting. What they generally do is go out in a plane and fly around in the hope of picking up a signal. Some days they are lucky. They locate the wolves and try to follow the group, watching the wolves' behaviour from the air. However, there is a problem with this. As soon as the plane was invented, people, as usual, abused this technology. They immediately began to kill wolves from the air. At this point, the wolf has had almost a hundred years to learn that the sound of a plane is a signal of death. Wolves who hear a plane do not go hang out on open terrain and display all kinds of natural behaviour for you. They head for cover as quickly as they can. Yet again, the only behaviour the scientist sees is flight behaviour. So Discovery Channel may make it look as if you can just walk into the woods and film a bunch of wolves from close by, but this isn't how it works. The shots you see on TV are often the product of long and careful searching and tracking, and then filmed with telescopic lenses the size of your arm. They are pieces of luck and the result of enormous patience. Lots of people who research wild wolves spend years just finding and analysing scats (wolf poop) without ever getting a glimpse of a real, live wolf.

Because of this, much of the published research on wolves has been done on captive wolves. Scientists gather together whatever wolves are, for some reason, available, and they house the wolves in a pen somewhere. Under the best of circumstances, the enclosure may be a couple of square miles. The wolves are then fed daily. Scientists can settle back and observe what the animals do, since the animals can't escape them anymore. This is, of course, a highly artificial situation. First of all, the wolves behave while being watched by their jailer. This means we watch them under heightened stress and have no idea what they'd do if a human weren't around. Secondly, it gives us no idea what the wolves would be doing if they had to go get their own food instead of hanging about all day with nothing much to do. Finally, the scientist has in fact taken a bunch of arbitrarily selected total strangers and shut them up in an unnaturally small amount of space, and is forcing them to live with each other in this small space for the duration of their lives whether they like it (and each other) or not.

This is contrary to all natural circumstances. There are a few things we do know for sure about wolves from the glimpses people have gotten of them living free in the forests. In the wild, a group of wolves travels a territory far too large for any human to enclose. Travelling is the main thing they do, filling their days with finding food. A natural pack is not a collection of strangers. A natural pack is a family, whose members know each other from birth. These family members stay together voluntarily, and each and every one of them can leave at will if he doesn't like it anymore. They can also leave to seek out a mate and form their own family. They do not have to stay together no matter what, anymore than you have to live with your own parents forever.

You won't learn much about the natural behaviour of wolves by jailing a group of strangers on a tiny surface area and watching them be bored there, except maybe that they are so tolerant and social that they still don't kill each other. Dr. L. David Mech, just about the greatest living authority on wolves, put it in a nutshell with these words: 'Such an approach is analogous to trying to draw inferences about human family dynamics by studying humans in refugee camps.'

Even where we can get a glimpse of wolf life in the wild, we are now watching a species whose habitat has been mostly destroyed. Food is now much more scarce for them than it was one hundred years ago. So is living space. So even then, we are watching wolves whose behaviour has been influenced by our presence, which has caused them a lot of problems.

Fact: The dog is not a wolf. If you want to know about dogs, you have to study dogs. But aside from this, and whether or not you could apply knowledge about wolves to dogs, the fact is that we don't have much knowledge about wolves in the first place. The stories that are told about them are all too often hunters' tales and jailers' anecdotes — basically nonsense, based on myths, fantasy, imagination, speculation, projection, lies and/or poorly designed research; or by watching them behave in a habitat that is decaying and disappearing right under their feet. It is no longer possible to study how wolves behave without some kind of human influence interfering with the picture.

Mech, LD, *The Wolf: The Ecology and Behaviour of an Endangered Species,* University of Minnesota Press, Minneapolis, 1970 (8th ed 1995).

Mech, LD, Alpha status, dominance, and division of labor in wolf packs. *Canadian Journal of Zoology* 77:1196-1203. Jamestown, ND: Northern Prairie Wildlife Research Center Home Page. http://www.npwrc.usgs.gov/resource/2000/alstat/alstat.htm (version 16 May 2000).

Mowat, F. *Never Cry Wolf; The Amazing True Story of Life Among Arctic Wolves*, McClelland and Stewart, Toronto, 1963.

Myth 4: The domestic dog is a hunting species.

We've seen that the evolution of the specifically *domestic* dog probably began when his ancestors discovered human rubbish dumps as a new source of safe and easy food. It's possible that these first dump animals were able to exploit the new food source because they were especially smart. It's also possible that they were just especially lazy. Which explanation you prefer will depend on your opinion about present day dogs.

In any case, the decision to switch from their old habits to living on human food waste was an extremely important one. The dump animals had to dare to come fairly close to humans, and to be able to eat in the presence of our smell. This led to the relative isolation from the members of their kind who did continue to roam and to shun humans. In the beginning, as humans roamed to hunt with their bows and arrows, the domestic dog's ancestor could probably trail along at some small distance, waiting until we moved on to descend upon our waste pile. This new ecological niche he'd found meant he was subject to a different kind of natural selection than the ancestor who continued to live far away from us. Our dump animal may still have supplemented his diet by roaming occasionally, but even the occasional hunting of small prey was much less important to him now. At this point, he still needed a body fit for travelling long distances since we still did, but Nature was already selecting for a brain that dealt differently with both aggression and fear.

When our own ancestors discovered agriculture and then began to keep cattle, the dog's development shifted into high gear. The great efficiency of our food production, which enabled us to fan out across the Earth, meant that we threw away much more still edible food. The dog's ancestor could now abandon roaming and hunting altogether and take up permanent abode near the dump. This meant he had to come live very close to us. We weren't leaving dumps behind and moving on anymore. The village dweller doesn't feel like walking very far with his rubbish, and it was probably still dangerous to do so, so dumps were established close to where we lived. This meant that the pre-domestic dog had to be able to eat while we were just around the corner and could show up any minute with a new load of rubbish. The fact that he could do this means that the fear parts of his brain had already changed. It also meant that he wouldn't run into relatives anymore who did still shun humans and their smell.

Reproductive isolation was now a fact. The pre-dog's genes now became subject to a completely different regime of natural selection than in the old roaming, sometimes hunting niche. This animal no longer needed to be fit for the travelling or the hunting life. The pre-dog's skeleton, muscles and brain could now start adjusting to the sedentary life. He no longer needed to kill even occasionally to eat. The ability to deliver a crushing bite, necessary to grab and kill prey, began to disappear. His jaws and teeth became smaller, as did his head and his brain.

But it wasn't just the change in food that caused the killer bite to disappear. Humans do not, right up to the present day, tolerate animals in their surroundings who are a danger to themselves and their cattle. Our ancestors probably added their own selective pressure to Nature's by killing off any of these pre-dogs who attacked humans or the animals they kept. If he wanted to be able to stay near humans and eat easily and safely at our dumps, the early dog had to get rid of aggression altogether. He not only had to refrain from attacking humans, but also from attacking our chickens, sheep and cows. Killer aggression was not only superfluous; it was now actively dysfunctional, working to reduce the early dog's chances of survival. The dog lost the inclination to kill anything at all.

Fact: The domestic dog is not a hunter. He is a scavenger. See also: Myth 5

Beck, AM, The ecology of 'feral' and free-roving dogs in Baltimore, Ch 26, in Fox MW (ed), *The Wild Canids,* Van Nostrand Reinhold Co, MY, 1975.

Beck, AM, *The Ecology of Stray Dogs: A Study of Free-ranging Urban Animals,* York Press, Baltimore, 1973.

Beljaev, DK, Trut, LN, Some genetic and endocrine effects of selections for domestication in silver foxes, in *The Wild Canids*, Fox, MW, ed., Van Nostrand Reinhold, New York, 1975.

Beljaev, DK, Plyusnina, IZ, and Trut, LN, Domestication in the silver fox (Vulpes fulvus desm): changes in physiological boundaries of the sensitive period of primary socialization, *Applied Animal Behaviour Science* 13:359–70, 1984/85.

Coppinger, R, Coppinger, L, *Dogs: a startling new understanding of canine origin, behaviour, and evolution,* Scribner, New York, 2001.

Sibly, RM, Smith, RH, *Behavioural Ecology: Ecological Consequences of Adaptive Behaviour*, Blackwell Scientific Publications, Oxford, 1985.

Trut, LN, Early canid domestication: the farm-fox experiment, *American Scientist*, March–April, 160–169, 1999.

Myth 5: But my own dog is obviously a predator, because he kills cats (or rabbits, or sheep).

When people talk about the dog as a predator, what they seem to want to say is that the dog is a hunter. In fact, a predator and a hunter are not the same thing. After all, technically speaking, a sheep is a predator (see Myth 29) — but we don't generally go talking about predatory aggression in a sheep if he bites us. It's true that some dogs do sometimes kill other animals. However, this still doesn't make the dog a hunter. A hunter is not just an animal that kills; it's an animal that kills to eat. The behavioural sequence of a true hunter that kills other animals in order to eat them looks like this:

Scent > track > watch/orient > stalk > chase > grab > kill > dissect > eat

This isn't just some arbitrary behavioural chain, it's a functional chain — a series of steps aimed at reaching a goal. The goal is to eat. You can only call an animal a hunter when he displays the whole chain, and when he does so in order to get a meal. You can't call an animal a hunter because he just so happens to look a like some ancestor who lived by hunting, or because he sometimes shows parts of the old behaviour simply because of how his body is still put together. Domestic dogs do not kill to eat. If you dump them in the woods, they will starve unless there's a popular camping site somewhere nearby where there's enough human food waste to keep them alive.

The dog evolved at the rubbish dump. He didn't need to kill to eat. Aggression not only lost its function, but it actually became a threat to the dog's survival in our proximity. The killer bite disappeared from the dog's natural behaviour pattern. Other parts of the pattern were less subject to human selection against them, parts of the chain we didn't care about one way or the other. Yet others were still useful for finding edible parts of the rubbish pile. So partly human selection, partly human indifference, and partly the demands of scavenging, operated to move the dog further and further away from whatever hunting ancestor he may have had.

This is, however, a very recent occurrence. In terms of evolution, 130,000 or 12,000 years is but the wink of an eye. Dogs are still shaped basically the same way they were half a million years ago. They still have four legs and the ability to run fast. They still don't have hands, only a mouth for grabbing things. Their sense of smell is still acute, very good for finding the edibles among all the paper and plastic. Their hearing is still acute, but it's now tuned into lower tones than the ears of true hunters (whose ears are tuned in to higher tones). Some original ancestral patterns may still be latently present in the form of reflexes. A dog may watch/orient toward something that moves, for example. But this is a pattern that goes back to an ancestor even before the reptilian–mammal split — just about all animals do it, it's not specifically a hunter's thing. A dog may reflexively snap at something that shoots by close to him, which may be a hunter's reflex — but this still isn't hunting, anymore than a monkey reflexively catching a ball coming at him is tool making.

Some of the old patterns just look like they're still present because the dog's body is shaped the way it is. Young dogs chase each other in play, but so do young cows. They are feeling the joy of using their bodies, which happen to have four legs, and they are practising social skills. When domestic dogs bite each other in play, they're not practising hunting. They're practising not biting too hard. When they grab something or pick something up with their mouth, it's not because they are hunters with an urge to bite — it's just because they don't have any hands. When they look like they're stalking a mouse, they're probably just curious, since dogs like to know what's in their living space. The stalk and stare stance is just the way their body is put together, although to be honest we don't do it much differently ourselves when we want to creep up on something. Our dogs might want to chase the mouse away, but they probably aren't thinking of killing it, and most of them certainly aren't planning to eat it.

So what about our cat- and sheep-killing dogs? Let's look first at the dog as he probably was in the very beginning, at least 12,000 years ago. To do this, we have to go to villages in the Third World, where these original mongrels can still be found hanging out in the village or around the dump. They are direct descendants of the original dog, but so are our own dogs. So what's the difference? The difference is that humans have never messed around with the village dogs' genes to make them into gun dogs, fighting dogs or fashion dogs. These village dogs have been selected purely by the necessities of the ecological niche they live in — natural, not human, selection created them. That is, aside from rather insistent human help in wiping out aggression altogether by killing dogs that scared or attacked humans and their cattle, children or chickens. We can assume that these Third World village dogs represent the original, *natural* dog. These natural dogs don't display the hunting sequence as explained above. If they show these behaviours at all, then it's only separate, isolated parts of the chain. They engage in these behaviours mostly during play, and there is no real aggression involved, same as the great majority of our own dogs. Mostly, these dogs wander around in villages or watch humans who come to the dumps, staying in the background, lazing around in the shade, not hunting or biting anything at all. Flight is their first reaction to anything that is perceived as a threat (unless they are cornered, of course).

If we now move over to look at the dumps near big cities in the industrial countries of South America, we get a different story (described by the Coppingers in their book *Dogs*, and by various friends of mine who have lived in these countries). Here, besides various small, modest dogs of the kind we call mongrels, we also find larger dogs that we can identify as belonging to official 'breeds' (ones that have been very recently created by modern humans). These are city dogs who have either escaped their owners or been abandoned by them. Unlike the mongrels, certain of these city dogs do display the killing bite. Now this is no wonder, and here's the reason why. These are countries where the machismo culture still rules. The South American dumps are full of pit bulls and rotweilers. These are breeds in which humans have worked hard to revive the killing bite, putting together concentrated and precise breeding programs to produce killer dogs. These human selected and bred dump dogs will even threaten humans who come to look at the dump, and they are, unlike the mongrels who are also hanging around, truly dangerous. This contrast gives us the key to why some people have a problem with their own dog killing other animals, which they then mistakenly attribute to 'hunting' behaviour.

For about the past hundred years or so, since the very first official breed registers were established, we have been messing around with the natural dog in a very intense way. Once we understood how inheritance worked, we began reviving various parts of the dog's latent behaviour chain to suit our own preferences. We did this by selecting for differences in body and brain as we bred dogs. Indeed, genes only specify potential, but by messing around with them we have messed around with potential. I will explain how this works later, in Myths 38 and 39. For now, it's enough to say we created the Pointer, exaggerating the 'orient > watch' and the start of the 'stalk' parts of the hunting sequence, to get a dog who freezes up at the beginning of the stalk. This is the pointing position. The Border Collie is bred for the watch and the stalk. She 'gives eye' and approaches the sheep in the stalk position, posed for the pounce. She may even nip at their heels, but without attacking. The retriever is bred for the grab bite, and executes this bite softly and without progressing to the killing bite. The pit bull has the killing bite and the shearing dissection bite, but without the preceding parts of the sequence (no stalking, freezing up, nor any warning at all).

If your dog is killing cats or rabbits, it's probably a breed in which breeders have been too enthusiastic about reviving the grab bite by breeding for a changed brain. We often see this in various hunting dog breeds, as well as in breeds that are commonly chosen for police work (e.g. the German Shepherd, the Belgian Shepherd Malinois), and in breeds that we have specifically moulded for real killer aggression (e.g. some terriers and the so-called bull-and-terrier breeds). It is the interference of the modern consumer in the dog's genes that has created dogs with one or two selected and highly exaggerated reflexes. In their romance with the wolf, these people tell themselves the dog is displaying parts of some wolfish hunting chain. They forget that many of these behaviours had acquired a different meaning and function as the dog scavenged the local dump. Scenting and tracking is just as necessary to find edible bits of garbage. Running is just as good for escaping as for chasing something. All animals have to bite and chew to eat, even the vegetarian ones. So even if these behaviours are leftovers of some hunting ancestor, these dogs only show various parts of the sequence, and these parts have gained a new meaning and function. However, showing fragmented parts of a hunting sequence does not make a dog a real hunter. A real hunter will display the whole sequence, and she will display it only when it's functional and useful to do so. Our own breeding behaviour hasn't revived the ancient natural chain. Rather, we've taken advantage of this scavenger's shape and her play behaviour, applying artificial selection to create dogs who show separate and exaggerated behaviours, which we then kid ourselves has something to do with some wild 'predator'. All we've done is create abnormalities. Often, a distortion of the dog's body has gone along with this. All of these dogs would still be hopeless at the real hunt and would probably die of starvation if they had to make a living of it.

Aside from our consumer interest in her genes, there are also other reasons why your dog might be killing other animals. If your dog is not a pit bull or one of the others we've bred for exaggerated size and/or aggression, and if you allow her to develop normally by playing with other dogs while she's young, she will learn to control her bite with great precision no matter how excited she is. This is a thing all natural dogs learn, as a matter of course, since there are no humans around to keep them from interacting with other dogs during their puppy days. If you overprotect your puppy, not allowing her to play often and long with other dogs, you prevent her from learning to control her bite. She can bite too hard without even knowing she is doing it, and without meaning to do any harm. She just has no idea what she can do with her teeth. This is not because she is a hunter, but rather an educational deficiency.

Punishment can also be a reason for a dog to kill cats or other animals, even if she isn't of a breed that we've made into killers. If a dog is often punished in the presence of other animals, she will eventually start to become aggressive towards those animals. Dogs don't generally associate punishment with their own behaviour. Rather, they tend to blame punishment on something that just happens to be nearby when the punishment takes place. In other words, your dog won't understand that you are punishing her for growling at the cat, or chasing the cat away from her treat, or for being too interested in the sheep. What the dog perceives is that you often punish her when the cat's around, or whenever the two of you get near sheep. Now, it is a proven fact that punishment very often arouses aggression. When you put these two facts together, we get a logical result. The punished dog will try harder and harder to chase the damned cat away before you notice the cat and start acting all mad again. All you see is that the dog is still chasing the cat, and that it's getting worse, so you punish her even harder. The cat becomes more and more aversive to the dog, and the aggression, which punishment quite normally evokes, becomes more and more uncontrolled. If the dog now gets a chance to chase a cat (or a sheep), she may very well kill the other animal. This does not mean the dog is a hunter, because even rats and mice, prey species who have never hunted, display the same aggression when punished in the laboratory. A dog who kills other animals is often the result of the owner inadvertently training the dog to feel aggressive towards other animals.

So now we have several situations in which a dog escapes and then comes back later, after having killed a cat, or a rabbit, or a sheep. She may leave the dead animal behind, or she may come back to you carrying the whole dead cat or rabbit in her mouth. You think you are dealing with an instinctive hunter.

But let's look yet a little closer. If you go back and look at the hunting sequence, you may notice that something is missing in your dog's behaviour, namely the last two parts of the real hunting sequence. Your dog does not rip apart the cat she caught, nor does she eat it. The pit bull (and the other aggressive breeds) will often execute ripping, dissecting movements during an attack. But they also will often continue to attack long after the other animal is dead, and then they suddenly calm down and walk away. You will not see a real hunter do either of these things. The dog who suffered an educational deprivation in her youth just doesn't know she's biting too hard. She isn't intending any harm at all, let alone having hunting intentions. The punished dog is not naturally aggressive. Her reaction is punishment-induced aggression, which has nothing to do with hunting. She just wants to get rid of the cat, if possible for once and for always, so the punishment will stop.

It does sometimes happen that a dog who has been allowed to play with other dogs while growing up, and who has never been punished around other animals, will escape and play ravage with a herd of sheep. Even so, these dogs are not hunting; they are playing. The dog will chase a sheep, grab it, possibly wound it badly or kill it. Then the dog will switch to chasing another sheep who is trying to run away, executing the sequence all over again. To this dog, the game is only interesting as long as the other animal is still moving. Eating is not the point. The dog that kills the sheep still hopes to see dinner waiting in his food bowl when he gets home. This makes the game and its motivation essentially different from what a real hunter does. The real hunter isn't playing when she chases another animal. She is involved in a serious activity, namely, food acquisition. The real hunter has to put a lot of energy into merely surviving, and she is therefore careful about her energy expenditure. Hunting is done as efficiently as possible. The wolf takes a single prey and eats that prey with hair and hide. It is this very fact that enables biologists to know whether it was a wolf, or indeed a dog, who attacked the herd in the night.

Fact: Your pedigreed dog is not a product of Nature, but rather a product of the consumer society. Our interference in her genes has disassembled her in a sense, removing a number of typically doggy characteristics, adding a number of human-desired and exaggerated ones that Nature never would have chosen, and actually making her less of a real, natural dog. We have been able to do this because the dog *descended* from an animal that sometimes hunted. She has the same basic body shape and has some of the old structures in her brain in a diminished or changed form. But this is not at all the same thing as saying the present day domestic dog *is* a hunter. A present day domestic dog who kills has other reasons for doing it. Her behaviour is either a distorted and non-functional magnification of separate behaviours that struck our fancy, or it is due to lack of education or cruel education. It has nothing at all to do with the serious business of getting food or with the natural behaviour of the domestic dog as a species.

Fact: The domestic dog is a scavenger, including your killer dog.

Myth 6: Dogs have an instinctive bite inhibition, which automatically makes them unable to bite if the other surrenders in a fight.

This myth is told with much flair. Dogs are supposedly as chivalrous as human knights of old used to be. If two dogs are arguing (with their teeth of course, as dogs sometimes will seem to do), they are supposedly trying to really hurt each other. (More about this nonsense in Myths 12 and 13.) During such an argument, the underdog can supposedly save his own life by flopping over onto his back. Just as King Arthur would not cut off the head of the errant knight kneeling in remorse before him, neck exposed for the sword, the top dog is supposedly instinctively unable to go in for the kill once he sees the other dog's exposed belly. According to this myth, all signs of 'submission' cause an automatic, inherited, chivalrous inhibition of the dog's bite to turn on, so that he can't inflict damage on the other dog even though he still wants to.

This is all very romantic, but it isn't true. Worse, if you believe this myth, you may end up creating a dangerous situation by the way you raise your dog. What are the facts?

It is true that a normal dog's brain is designed, at birth, to enable him to grow into a creature who is very reticent about using aggression. This capacity is seated in various neurological structures, and in the brain's chemical housekeeping. Both of these are indeed partially determined by genetics. However, a dog is most definitely not born already controlling and inhibiting his bite. He is also not born with any knowledge about the meaning of the signals and gestures that dogs use to communicate. These are both things he has to learn. And it's the way in which he learns these two things that ends up making him reluctant to use any kind of aggression at all.

A pup is not finished yet when he is born. His muscles and his jaws are small and weak. His brain still has to do ninety percent of its growing. This combination of weak jaws and an incomplete brain are one of Nature's great designs. The puppy has time to learn all kinds of things long before he is capable of inflicting real damage on anyone. Because his brain is in the early stages of formation, everything he learns now will become actually, physically anchored in the actual, physical connections which are now growing among the neurons in that brain. If he learns now to control how hard he bites and what all the canine signals mean, this knowledge will be anchored forever in his brain's physical structure. He will be able to have instant and precise reactions for the rest of his life, without having to think about it.

'But', you may ask, 'why are puppy teeth so darned sharp if the pup still has to learn to inhibit his bite? Isn't that so he can inflict damage despite his weak jaws? And why do puppies do so much biting if not to practice aggression?' Answer: Those sharp puppy teeth aren't meant to inflict damage; they are meant to inflict pain. In doing so, they serve a specific and important function in the pup's development of bite inhibition. Puppies start to play biting games with littermates even before they are able to walk steadily on their feet. The sharp teeth make sure that even at this weak stage, the pup's bite will be painful to his playmate. The pup stumbles over to a sibling and delivers a play bite. This sibling yelps (a pain reflex, not learned behaviour) and moves away. The biting pup is amazed and impressed by the results of his play bite. Apparently his teeth are very dangerous. He also finds out that biting ends the game, and that the other pup shuns him for a while. The next time he wants to play, he'll be more careful. He'll make sure his play bite is only a grab, without any pressure behind it at all.

If the pup makes the same mistake with an adult dog, something else happens. The adult dog lashes out, acting like he's attacking the pup. He jumps all over the pup, bumping the pup off balance, growling like he's going to kill the pup, and snapping *in the air* back and forth on both sides of the pup's head and neck as the pup lies there under this tidal wave of violence. The pup sees the huge adult teeth whizzing by, back and forth around his head and neck, just missing him each time, and he begins to yelp with fear (a reflex, not learned behaviour). The adult dog stops his feigned attack, maybe growls a little more at the pup, but then he walks away.

A little later, the puppy tries to approach the adult dog, but the adult dog isn't in the mood yet. He freezes up and stares at the pup, perhaps he curls his lip to expose some front teeth for a half a second. The pup sees this, but he doesn't as yet attach any meaning to it. He keeps approaching. The adult dog lashes out, biting just once in the air about an inch in front of the pup's face. Then the adult pauses, watching to see what the puppy will do now. The puppy's tail has dropped, and is now pressed against his buttocks (a reflex, not learned behaviour). He sees that this time the adult dog isn't jumping all over him immediately. But the puppy remembers what happened just a few minutes ago, and he doesn't dare move, so fleeing isn't an option here. So he chooses to try out a behaviour that was always safe and pleasant, back in the days when he couldn't pee or poop unless his mother massaged his belly with her tongue. The pup flops over onto his back and waits. Now, the adult dog has seen this gesture before, and he knows that it is a signal that says, 'I have no bad intentions'. The pup has, by accident, done the right thing. The adult dog breaks eye contact, maybe sniffs the pup's groin, then goes to lie down a couple of yards away. The puppy waits a while, but nothing else happens. He finally dares to try to walk away. He finds out that he can now safely do this.

These are the learning experiences. The puppy doesn't know his teeth are especially sharp, or that he can't inflict real damage yet, so these experiences teach him that his teeth are very dangerous. If he's not careful with those teeth, bad things happen. Either no one wants to play with him anymore, or he gets a horribly scary reaction. He is learning to feel an aversion for using his teeth carelessly, because he is finding out he has to be worried about what it may unleash upon himself.

The puppy has also learned something about yelping. The other puppy yelped before he ran away. So a yelp predicts that the other won't play with you anymore for a while. On the other hand, when the pup yelped himself, the adult dog stopped snapping his jaws in the pup's face. Apparently, yelping yourself stops something that scares you. The puppy has learned that a stare and a curled lip have predictive value: the other dog will lash out if you keep approaching. He has found out that lying on his back will get a different reward than back when his mother licked his belly: the irritated adult dog shows some calm interest in the pup's belly, then moves off. The puppy has now had the experience that when the other looks away, it means you can stand up again without being snapped at. The pup is starting to assign meaning to various signals and gestures — both in himself and in the other — which, up to now, just seemed like random behaviour to him. These gestures and signals are gaining predictive value about what the other might do. They also start to be an instrument the puppy can use himself, in order to influence the reactions he gets from his surroundings.

This is how a puppy learns to be able to take part in social traffic safely by the time he is an adult. He learns to be reticent about starting arguments. He learns to be extremely careful about how hard he bites, limiting himself in fact to pressureless grabs. He learns to recognise social signals and use them. It is important that the puppy has all these experiences early on, before he loses his sharp little milk teeth. By the time this happens, his jaws will already be strong enough to inflict real damage. By that time, the adult dogs won't be so forbearing with him anymore. He'll be coming into puberty, and start temporarily having trouble controlling his impulses. If he hasn't developed a firmly anchored, reflexive bite-inhibition by then, it will become dangerous for him to play with other dogs. If he is biting too hard, he is dangerous for other dogs — they won't be able to teach him without great risk to themselves. They may react so violently to his too-hard biting that it becomes dangerous for him to play with them. A dog reaches an age where it is too late to learn. He will go through the rest of his life with a handicap.

If you make sure your puppy has all these experiences before he loses his milk teeth, you will be making sure that these important elements of social behaviour are actually anchored in the physical connections between his brain cells. Your adult dog will inhibit his bite even when he is extremely excited. He won't bite too hard in an argument with a playmate, nor when you accidentally step on his foot and he lashes out in a pain reflex. Neither you nor the other dog will ever have more damage than a bit of dog spit on your clothing. Your adult dog will instantly recognise and respond to the subtlest of signals given by the dog he is playing with (or arguing with). He will be able to avoid arguments you didn't even see coming (and don't know you missed). He will be trustworthy when it does come to an argument, neither going on too long, nor inflicting wounds during the 'fight'. He will be better able to protect himself because he can see when the other dog is feeling uncomfortable, and he knows how to reassure him.

Please note: These are not things you can teach your pup. Only other dogs can teach him these things.

<u>**Fact:**</u> Dogs are not born with an instinctive bite inhibition. They are not born knowing the rules of King Arthur's Round Table. They are not born knowing their native language any more than we are. These are all learned behaviours. It is our responsibility to make sure our puppy gets the chance to learn these things during the proper developmental phase, by exposing him to lots of other puppies and socially skilled adult dogs.

Maturana, HR, Biology of language: the epistemology of reality, in Miller, GA, and Lenneberg (eds.), *Psychology and Biology of Language and Thought: Essays in Honor of Eric Lenneberg,* Academic Press, NY, 1978, pp 27–63. http://A/Maturana1.htm (2002)

Maturana, HR and Varela V, Autopoiesis and cognition: The realisation of the living, in *Boston Studies in the Philosophy of Science,* Cohen, RS and Wartofsky, MW (eds.), Vol. 42, Dordrecht: D. Reidel Publishing Co. 1980.

Myth 7: Dogs are pack animals.

The idea that dogs are pack animals is a result of nonchalantly believing that dogs must do everything wolves do. The little we do know of how wolves behave in the wild shows that even a wolf is not magically, innately a 'pack animal'. Most – but not all – wolves live in packs. These packs are closed groups. They are, in fact, families, consisting of parent animals and their offspring of the past several years. Living in packs is not genetically inherited behaviour in wolves. It is learned behaviour. Whether a wolf lives in a pack is dependent on many factors in a wolf's life. The circumstances under which he is socialised as a young pup will determine whether he is able (and willing) to live in a group. The specific environment he grows up in will determine whether a pack can be formed, for example by whether there is enough food available to support more than a single lone wolf. Human occupation might make group living impossible. A lone wolf can hide more easily and thus survive where a group might not; or a wolf may start life in a pack but end up alone, because his pack mates have been slaughtered. Various accidental events during his life will play a role. He may leave his birth group but never run into a lone female to mate with. Famine or disease might wipe out large prey, forcing a group to break up, with each animal hunting and living alone on prey too small to share. When wolves do live in a pack, it is a closed family group, in which strangers are but rarely admitted. New families are formed when a young wolf reaches maturity, when (if) he leaves the group to find a mate of his own and raise his own puppies. Among the canids, a 'pack' is, *by definition*, a family group, whose members hunt together and defend a territory together. Okay up to here, except we were all so sure the dog is a sort of tame wolf that we forgot to take a look at real dogs.

But not everyone was so careless. A few researchers have taken the trouble to study dogs, going out to follow free-living dogs around and watch what these dogs do. One study of free-ranging urban dogs showed the following:

- More than half of the dogs wandered around town alone.
- About 26% of the dogs had a special buddy they hung out with for a while.
- About 16% of the dogs travelled in groups of three, in which members came and went with time.
- Less than 2% of the dogs moved around in larger groups.

Where there is even a group at all — and that is in less than half the cases — scientists do not describe the group as a 'pack'. Rather, they refer to 'a group of dogs'. The group is not a family. It is evanescent. Even the groups of two are not always the same two. A group is neither closed nor permanent and stable. New dogs can join, sometimes a dog or two leaves (or dies). At the spots where dogs gather to sun a little, or at the rubbish dump, or in the alleys where the waste bins are, large groups of strangers can hang out together without any problem at all. A group of dogs is a temporary gathering of friends and acquaintances, in which basically solitary animals enjoy each other's company for a while before all go their own way again.

Now, this isn't such a surprise. The grey wolf lives in a group partly because her existence is so unbelievably hard. She generally lives on large prey that she

can't catch and kill alone. She has to wander far and wide to find prey, then expend large amounts of energy to bring it down. She then has to travel long distances to bring food back to her pups. Raising offspring demands an investment that no lone wolf can afford. Even so, it is not unusual for 80–96% of the pups to die before they reach the age of ten months.

The free-living dog lives an entirely different life. She lives on garbage that doesn't run away and doesn't have to be killed with the help of a group. She doesn't have to wander great distances in the hope of running into prey (city dogs wandered a range varying in size from two to ten football fields). In fact, free-living dogs turned out to spend about eighty percent of the day playing, sleeping or lazing around. In her natural habitat (this is, somewhere close to humans), the domestic dog doesn't have enemies that group living would help defend against. The main causes of death for her are cars, poisoning and shooting by humans, or slow decline due to heavy parasite loads. A group offers no reproductive advantage, neither for protecting the pups, nor for bringing them food. The mother protects her pups mostly by bearing them in a hidden place. After that, she nurses them. When they are ready to eat solid food, the pups start to search the rubbish dump themselves, taking care of themselves at an age that would totally amaze a wolf. In urban areas, about half the pups reached the age of one year without the help of a group. In rural areas, the survival rate was much lower, but this was mostly due to human efforts to find and eradicate litters. Pack living serves no purpose for the domestic dog, so, like most canids, she doesn't bother with it (see also Myth 8).

These are all facts revealed by the few scientific studies that have been done of free-living domestic dogs in their natural environment (cities, Third World villages, rural areas around the world). However, we don't need to consult science to find these facts. All we really need to do is put aside all the blinding dogmas we've learned, so we can actually see our own dogs for a change. When we take our daily walk with her in the park, we usually run into at least a few new dogs. Our dog has no problem with this. In fact, we go to a park specifically to allow her to meet new dogs because we see how much she enjoys it. Dog walkers take out large groups of dogs, often with a different group composition each day. They make a living at this, so apparently it works just fine. When two dog walkers run into each other in a park, the two groups of dogs merge into one large, merry gathering, no problem. When they split up, the dog walker might have to go physically retrieve a dog who leaves with the wrong group because she found a great new friend there. Sometimes we have to call our own dog quite a few times before she will leave play with a new acquaintance to rejoin us. This is a demonstration, right before our very own noses, that dogs live in open, flexible groups, not in packs. Shelter dogs are another example. Shelter dogs have been ejected from the group they originally lived in for some reason — but this doesn't mean there is no choice but to kill them. Re-homing remains an alternative, precisely *because* dogs are not pack animals, and *because* they are both able and more than willing to form close relationships with total strangers. None of the things mentioned in this paragraph would be possible if the dog were, in fact, a pack animal.

Fact: The whole reason the domestic dog does so well living among us humans is that she adapted herself to a different life than the pack life. Dogs are semi-solitary creatures. They wander alone around the rubbish dump or the back alleys, looking for food. When dogs do form groups, the members are not related to

each other, didn't grow up together, met each other as adults and formed their easy friendships. The groups are fleeting collections of acquaintances. Of course a dog becomes attached to other dogs she knows well — but she has no aversion to strangers, and is glad to turn them into friends.

Fact: Dogs are anything but pack animals.

Beck, AM, The ecology of 'feral' and free-roving dogs in Baltimore, Ch 26, in Fox MW (ed), *The Wild Canids,* Van Nostrand Reinhold Co, MY, 1975.

Beck, AM, *The Ecology of Stray Dogs: A Study of Free-ranging Urban Animals,* York Press, Baltimore, 1973.

Mech, LD, Alpha status, dominance, and division of labor in wolf packs. /Canadian Journal of Zoology/ 77:1196–1203. Jamestown, ND: Northern Prairie Wildlife Research Center Home Page. http://www.npwrc.usgs.gov/resource/mammals/alstat/intro.htm (version 16 May 2000).

Mech, LD, *The Wolf: The Ecology and Behaviour of an Endangered Species,* University of Minnesota Press, Minneapolis, 1970 (8th ed 1995).

Mech, LD, Whatever happened to the term Alpha wolf?, /International Wolf, Winter 2008./ http://www.wolf.org/wolves/news/iwmag/2008/winter/alphawolf.pdf accessed January 2009.

Semyonova, A, The social organisation of the domestic dog; a longitudinal study of domestic canine behaviour and the ontogeny of domestic canine social systems, Carriage House Foundation, The Hague, The Netherlands, 2003. www.nonlineardogs.com.

Thomas, EM, *The Hidden Life of Dogs,* Orion, London, 1994.

Myth 8: The dogs who live with me in my home in a permanent group can be referred to as a pack.

Many of us have more than one dog. This means that we have a non-fleeting, permanent group of dogs living with us in our house. This doesn't mean that this permanent group of dogs is a pack. It's usually an accidental collection of unrelated dogs, just like the free-living groups mentioned in Myth 7, although they may have grown up together. And the selection probably wasn't made by the dogs, but by us. But even if you are a professional dog breeder, and even if all your dogs are related to each other, your group of dogs still isn't a pack. This is because dogs as a species are semi-solitary animals who are great at making friends, but who don't form packs the way wolves do.

In fact, most people who have more than one dog don't encounter problems when they walk their groups of dogs in a park. The group is perfectly capable of interacting with other dogs and having great fun doing so. This is the *normal* state of affairs among dogs. If your dogs have a problem with visitor dogs in your house, or if they are antagonistic to other dogs in a park, this still doesn't mean your dogs are showing pack behaviour. It could mean that they are not adequately socialised. Dogs are not born with canine social skills. Although they are genetically predisposed to learning them, we have to give our dogs (who are basically our prisoners) the opportunity to do so. Some of us don't know we have to do this, others are too frightened of what grown up dogs might do to the pup, yet others just don't have anywhere they can take their pup to allow it to interact with other dogs in the puppy phase. A dog who doesn't get the chance to learn social skills in his youth may feel apprehensive when he meets new dogs. He may be clumsy about making new friends. When dogs feel apprehensive or afraid, they will sometimes express this by showing hostility. It could also be that you did allow your dogs to learn and practice their social skills, but that one or more of your dogs has had a traumatic experience with a strange dog. The trauma might have taught him (or them) that offence is the best defence. A third possibility is that you often get angry at your dogs in the presence of strange dogs — for example, for lunging while on leash, or for 'fighting'. If this is the case, your dogs have learned that other dogs are bad news. They want the new dog to leave before you start acting so grouchy again.

The problem with thinking of dogs as pack animals is that it makes us misunderstand our dogs. It can lead us to behave in ways dogs don't and can't understand. This pack idea can frighten people so that they don't socialise their puppy the way a dog needs to be socialised if he's to live happily in our world. It can cause us to attribute the wrong causes to behaviour, which prevents us from finding the right cure for a problem — or rather, the right way to help a dog who is having trouble. It has even led some people to believe that it is normal for dogs to try to kill other dogs, while in fact this is pathological behaviour in a dog.

Fact: The formation of closed groups and the inability to interact with strange dogs are, in the domestic dog, abnormal behaviours, and are a result of abnormal circumstances — of us humans frustrating natural processes. You can't generalize about dogs on the basis of abnormalities, nor does abnormal behaviour mean that your dogs are living in a pack. Rather, it means that they are, for some reason, having trouble with their social skills.

Myth 9: Dogs are territorial.

'Territorial.' Here's another piece of terminology that has been transferred straight from talking about wolves, who are wild animals, to talking about dogs, who are domestic animals. The problem with transferring terms like this is that it creates the illusion that we already understand behaviour. Then we think we don't have to examine the behaviour anymore. After all, it already has a label, right? We don't realise that the label is actually preventing us from seeing what's in the bottle. We often paste a label on something that really consists of many smaller behaviours, each with its own triggers and causes. In addition, we then forget that understanding a wolf is not the same as understanding a dog. We end up attributing wolf causes to dog behaviour. This tendency to use labels and then let them blind us causes all kinds of problems for the dogs who live with us. This is why it's important to clear up some of this terminology, to abandon much of it, and at the very least to look at what is really going on with dogs before we paste a label on what they are doing.

When dog people transfer the word 'territorial' to dogs, they often do it without understanding what biologists mean when they talk about territories among wild animals. A territory is a geographical area that an animal consistently defends, mostly against others of its own kind (conspecifics). Most animal species aren't territorial, but even when they are it's important to look at what's behind the label. Some animals will defend a space only at a certain time of year or a certain time of day. Some defend only against same-sex conspecifics. In addition, a territory isn't just some area where an animal so happens to live. A territory is related to food acquisition and reproduction. Under natural circumstances, a territory is determined by how much food a wild animal needs and how available that food is. Wild animals can't afford to waste a lot of energy, so a wild animal's territory is usually exactly the area that is sufficient — given the animal's needs and the density of food resources — to feed the animal (and possibly a mate and offspring). Where food is scarce, territories are large. Where food is abundant, the territories claimed by wild animals are proportionately smaller. In the breeding season, many animals will claim a small nesting area around the place where they bear their young, to protect the young during the vulnerable neonatal period. This nesting area is usually located within the area that is necessary for food acquisition, but not always. It's usually just large enough to assure that the neonates won't easily be subject to surprise attack by an enemy. Territories are defended most of all against conspecifics, who are direct competitors for the same material resources.

According to the experts, wolves, who do look very much like some of our dogs, are territorial. Wolf packs generally don't welcome new or strange wolves into their territories. This is partly because food is scarce and worth defending. It's also partly because wolves are what we call 'neophobic' — they don't like unfamiliar things. This is not surprising. Life in the wild is dangerous, so it's important to a wild animal to have as much predictability in life as possible. A wolf pack is a family whose members know each other from birth. They all know each other well, and pretty much know what to expect from each other. They recognise other wolves as wolves, but not as familiars whose behaviour is predictable. So this larger thing called 'being territorial' really consists of several smaller components — the wish to protect offspring, the need to defend scarce resources, and the general fear of the unfamiliar and unpredictable.

But the dog is not a wolf, and he lives under completely different circumstances. One of the reasons the dog was able to become a *domestic* dog at all was because he was able to hang out at our rubbish dumps together with strangers of various species without getting aggressive. Besides this, most free-living dogs in the world lived in a relative abundance of food at our dumps until about thirty years ago, when poverty among humans began to increase radically all over the world. Dog population control takes place through infant mortality, cars, humans, parasites, and disease, not by starvation. Good at sharing space with strangers, and with enough food around, the present-day dog did not evolve into a creature who automatically claims a territory. We can't know what kind of behaviour increasing poverty will lead to in the dog, but thirty years is not as yet enough for the dog to evolve already into a different kind of creature. As things stand now, the only thing all dogs seem to claim is a sort of personal zone. This is a circle with a radius of about three to four feet around the dog. Inside this portable zone, he moves around the dump without bothering about strangers. The dog might keep more distance from a stranger than from a familiar dog, but he does this without trying to claim the whole dump as his own. Free-living city dogs tend to travel around within a relatively small range, but this range is also not a territory. A city dog will defend a vestibule or a clump of bushes where he sleeps, but he does not defend his travelling space. Even in agrarian regions, where food is less abundant, dogs who know each other do not defend their ranges or their dumps from strangers. Again, it is only a sleeping or birthing spot that is defended. Familiarity plays an important role in how dogs behave toward other dogs. Once dogs have met a stranger several times elsewhere, the stranger can often join the group at the sleeping spot. Dogs do not claim a territory as defined by biologists.

'But', you may say, 'my dog won't tolerate strange dogs (or even strange humans) in the house, and my dog psychologist told me this is territorial aggression'.

Despite what the dog psychologist says, our well-fed city dogs are not territorial the way wild animals can be. Our well-fed city dogs, in fact all domestic dogs, are learning creatures and creatures of habit. If a dog is used to running into other dogs somewhere, he won't get all upset about it. If he runs into another dog in a place where he's not used to seeing other dogs, this seems strange to him (and probably a little worrying). Whether a dog will tolerate strangers within his yard or house also depends on his experiences in the past. If a dog is used to seeing strangers drop by, and if he has pleasant experiences with strangers, he won't object to them. If he is not used to seeing strangers, or if he has had unpleasant experiences with them, he can react with anxiety or antagonism. This is not territorial instinct, but rather a conditioned (i.e. learned) reaction, be it positive or negative, to a specific stimulus (a visitor). If it were instinctive, your dog psychologist wouldn't be able to treat it. People who own wolf hybrids can tell you that. Regardless of how they socialise or train their pet, it is never safe to bring strangers into the house without confining the animal where he can't get to the visitors. But your dog is a dog, and because of this, he most certainly can learn — with your help — to welcome visitors in the house.

But those are legal visitors. What about the burglar? Most dogs will react angrily to a burglar, even if they otherwise welcome legal visitors in the home. Isn't this the expression of a territorial drive? The answer is no. The dog who welcomes visitors will be used to things happening according to a certain routine. First of all, the visitors generally come in through the door. You are present, and you routinely do certain things. You greet your visitors in a friendly way, take their coats, settle them in the living room, go to the kitchen to get some drinks for everyone. If a 'visitor' suddenly comes in through a window, the dog will notice that this is not the usual routine. And dogs tend to think a change in routine is a bit strange. You aren't around to signal to the dog that, aside from the visitor's point of entry, the rest of the routine is going to progress as usual. Even the friendliest dog will feel unsure about what is going on. And the more uncertain a dog feels, the more likely he is to react in a hostile way. This reaction is not a defence of territory, but rather the dog defending his own personal safety in what is, to him, a scary situation.

There are also other factors besides habit that play a role in a dog's behaviour toward strangers. When dogs meet someone new, be it another dog or a human, and be it indoors or outdoors, there is always a process of trying to figure out who the other is and how the other is going to behave. Some dogs have more self-confidence about this and some have less, depending on their life experience. A dog will do subtle tests, to find out whether the stranger is going to obey the normal social rules. He looks for signals that the stranger is going to behave peacefully, eschewing aggression. He approaches, and in doing so he finds out how much space the stranger needs to feel comfortable. Among dogs, in their own dog system, the dogs can start to play after a first check. In play, dogs learn more about a stranger. They learn whether the stranger will respect signals to keep a little more distance, whether the visitor knows s/he should respect the dog's personal zone when asked to (or whether s/he's a boor who tries to steal your ball anyway), and so on. Dogs discover each other's personal preferences and personal boundaries. If the stranger's manners aren't entirely right, and it comes to a conflict, then this also provides a crucial piece of information. In a purely ritual 'fight', arguing dogs find out whether a stranger has learned to control his bite so they can have a disagreement without wounding each other. This whole thing is a process of mutual orientation and getting to know each other, so that dogs can build trust with a new acquaintance. In the end, they can share a space, knowing they are safe in each other's company. How long this process takes and how much tension it involves depends entirely on both dogs' personal history, personal preferences, and social skills.

If a meeting takes place outdoors in a park, the only things that are lying around are sticks and stones and (perhaps) some human litter, and maybe the tennis ball you were just throwing for your dog. There's lots of space for increasing distance if either dog feels the need, and there is a flight path open in case things get out of hand. When a meeting takes place within the home, there are a lot more valued objects around (such as the dog's toys, his food bowl, various chewies etc.). Space is limited, and so are escape routes. Your dog may feel much less sure of himself when meeting a stranger in the presence of all his valued objects, in a limited space where the stranger might not be able to keep enough distance even if he wants to, and where neither of them can just get the hell out if need be. He may react with hostility, needing to guard his valued objects and his own physical safety against this stranger whose reactions are unknown to him. The fact that he does this in the house does not mean he is being territorial the way a wild animal is. He is defending his safety and his sources of pleasure in life in a situation *where there are no escape routes*. His reactions aren't a result of instinct, but of the simple fact that dogs need more space than our living rooms to feel good establishing relations.

This — and not some territorial instinct — is why it is so much easier to allow dogs to meet each other outdoors. This is why an insecure dog does so much better if he's allowed to meet a human visitor out on the front pavement with you before you all go into the house together. In both cases, the dog gets the chance to assure himself about the stranger's reactions and social behaviour before he has to share a confined space with the stranger, which space is densely packed with all kinds of valued objects, and from which there is no flight route.

The dog who barks out the window at other dogs who pass is also reacting to a feeling of insecurity. There are various possible reasons for this. Some of these dogs have limited social skills and just feel insecure whenever they see another dog. Some have been the only dog in the street for a long time, and just aren't used to seeing another dog walk by. Others have had a traumatic experience with another dog. Since the other dog is just passing by anyway, your barking dog gets to see the stranger disappear. This yields him the powerful reward of anxiety reduction. This all has nothing to do with food acquisition, nor with a physical territory being claimed. In fact, I've known plenty of dogs who do this out of boredom; it's not even anxiety, just entertainment.

Fact: When a dog will not tolerate visitors in the house, it is always a result of his personal history. The treatment is to teach him that he doesn't have to feel anxious with strangers. Pasting a wolf label on a dog's behaviour only prevents us from seeing what is actually going on and helping him to get over his problem. What really is not going on is, in any case, the defence of a territory as such.

Practical examples

The Coppingers

Raymond and Lorna Coppinger have watched free-living dogs all over the world. In their book *Dogs: a startling new understanding of canine origin, behaviour, and evolution* (2001) they are very clear about the fact that they never had a problem sharing a dump even with feral domestic dogs. The dogs stay just out of reach, maintaining the personal zone with its radius of about three to four feet. The only exception they found to this was at a dump in Argentina, where there was a group of abandoned rotweilers and pit bulls. This was the only case in all their travels when they did not feel safe approaching dogs at a rubbish dump. This was, however, not because these dogs were territorial. It was, we can assume first of all, to do with the way their evidently macho owners had socialised these guard dogs before dumping them. Secondly, as we have seen in Myth 5, pure-bred dogs do not represent the dog as a natural species. We cannot look at pedigreed dogs and learn about the natural dog. The very fact that these dogs 'of high breeding' (Coppinger, p.322) were the only dogs who got hostile at rubbish dumps is, rather, evidence that this is deviant behaviour in a dog.

In the same book, the Coppingers describe dogs who do defend a stretch of beach near a hotel against other dogs. These were feral dogs living in an area where there was only a very limited amount of food. In a case like this, where a food resource area is defended, the behaviour does match territorial behaviour. But this is not due to an inborn drive dogs have, rather it's a product of the circumstances they live in.

Dogs in Rural Italy

In a study of dogs in rural Italy, MacDonald and Carr (1995) maintain that the dogs they observed did defend territories. In fact, the study is mostly illustrative of how far pre-formed ideas can influence what a researcher sees. The village dogs observed did not actually live in groups, nor did they routinely travel together. Each dog had its own little range it wandered around in. However, these individual ranges tended to overlap and be wandered by more than one dog, all of whom knew each other. If a dog did venture out of his own neighbourhood, resident dogs would bark at him until he retreated back into the space he usually travelled. MacDonald and Carr label this barking as aggression, even though a physical confrontation never occurred. They note, further, that most of these barking matches took place around range boundaries, or where ranges overlapped near food sources. From this (space + food), they draw the conclusion that the dogs were showing territorial behaviour. Observations of dogs not living in the villages showed a different pattern. These dogs tended to travel in company (most often in pairs), again sticking to a range that overlapped with the ranges of other groups at a food source (the dump). 'Aggression' consisted here, too, of barking matches, though the barking matches at a dump often did not result in the departure of any dog. Occasionally, the non-village dogs are claimed to have killed strange dogs that wandered into their range. Again, the conclusion is that the dogs are showing territorial behaviour.

The striking thing is that Boitani et al (1995) describe the same group of dogs very differently. Here, all dog-kills are attributed to either humans or wolves. In general, dogs were observed to stick to their own familiar range, whether or not they encountered strangers during an excursion outside it. We are also told that the dogs are surprisingly tolerant of other, unfamiliar, dogs as they feed at the dump. We are told that barking matches with strangers take place not at the boundaries of the range or at the dump, but near the core resting areas. Puppy mortality was high (mostly due to human interference), so maintenance of the population was largely dependent on recruiting new strays into groups of familiars. Later the same authors suddenly and surprisingly conclude that 'aggression' takes place throughout the dogs' ranges, and that dogs are clearly territorial.

So which observations are we to believe, and how does one conclude from tolerance, dump-sharing, and occasional barking that dogs are territorial after all? This may be a result of hoping, perhaps unconsciously, for confirmation of familiar labels. There are also lots of tables showing how activities have been quantified. But in both studies the authors admit that it was impossible to find out where the dogs came from, or to know their history. In addition, the dogs observed were largely Abruzzos, an Italian breed that was traditionally used for cattle guarding, and the more recently introduced German Shepherd (see Myth 30 for comments on this breed). This background would lead us to expect the breeding to involve artificial (human) selection for behavioural traits (for example, wariness of strangers), and that humans would encourage this tendency in raising their dogs (who would later become stray or dumped dogs). This is an area where many dogs are kept chained up in yards, or raised in isolation so they will end up guarding the herd or the yard — not exactly the optimal way to socialise a dog to meeting strangers. Many suburban dogs who live with people have the same problem. Are they territorial, or are they just completely unsocialised? The differences between village and city dogs vs. rural and suburban dogs suggest that a dog's learning history is crucial, rather than some innate territorial drive in dogs.

In the end, attempting to find the 'natural behaviour' of dogs by seeking out situations in which stray dogs supposedly do not live under human influence doesn't work. It ends up ignoring the fact that many strays are a result of our genetic manipulation, and that most stray dogs were raised by humans rather than by other dogs. It may be that some dogs show territorial behaviour under certain circumstances, but it's important to look at what's really going on before you just paste the label on. It is certainly not true that domestic dogs as a species are innately 'territorial.'

Myth 10: Dogs live in a dominance hierarchy, with the Alpha dog at the top as the absolute leader.

One of the things we hear most about dogs is that dominance is extremely important in organising their groups. The story goes that their interactions are all about gaining and maintaining status. The dog with the higher rank dominates the dog with the lower rank, who submits. Dogs are always trying to climb up the ladder, because they know higher ranks bring bigger advantages in life. This whole story is, yet again, based on tales about how wolves organise their packs. This is the one myth about dogs that virtually everyone seems to know — not only beginning dog owners, but even people who have never had a dog and wouldn't want one. I rarely meet people who don't believe in this myth.

Therefore, it will probably surprise you to hear that we now know (thanks to Dr L. David Mech) that even *wolves* do not live in a dominance hierarchy. To live in a dominance hierarchy, and to base your behaviour towards others on who has which rank, you have to be able to do quite a bit of abstract thinking. You'd have to have a map of the social structure in your head, in which you are comparing various ranks with each other and assigning these ranks to yourself and others. Neither the wolf nor the dog has the large frontal lobes in the brain that would enable them to think in such abstract terms. A dominance hierarchy also requires a stable group that is organised in a rigid structure. Dogs do not live in stable groups. They live semi-solitary lives, which are enriched by fleeting friendships. As we will see in Myth 11, the groups dogs do form are not at all rigidly organised. The structure of dog groups is, rather, highly flexible, which is the whole reason they are so good at absorbing infinite numbers of strangers. And the final strange thing about this myth is that no one has ever yet been able to find a real dominance hierarchy within a group of dogs, no matter how hard they looked or what kind of statistics they applied. The whole idea is utter nonsense.

So what is going on? How could science make such a blunder, and how did this myth end up being so firmly rooted in our minds?

If we want to understand this, we have to go back a little further in history and look at ourselves. It is common knowledge among historians that humans have always projected the structure of their own societies onto the animal kingdom. The ancient Egyptians, for example, lived in a society governed by a royal family, whose members were demigods. Divinity, and links to divinity, were very important in organising Egyptian society. Many Egyptian gods were portrayed as animals, and this was projected back onto the animals in the mundane world, assigning various divine characteristics to various animals. In the Middle Ages, when our societies were organised into nobility versus impoverished, vulgar peons, people also divided the animal kingdom into noble versus common animals. The noble animals were believed to have the same qualities as human nobility. They were beautiful, graceful, clean, courageous, wise, chaste, loyal, chivalrous, and so on. The common animals were like human commoners. They were seen as ugly, clumsy, cowardly, cunning, promiscuous, sneaky and so on. The lower animals were ruled by, and they respected, the noble animals. The human nobility had exclusive rights to the owning and hunting of noble animals, while the human peons had to limit themselves to peon animals. This distinction between noble and common animals still exists among hunters to this day, where the hunting of noble animals still enjoys more status than, say, rat-catching.

Although we now like to think of ourselves as more rational and less superstitious, the fact is that our projections onto animals did not stop when the modern age arrived. With the rise of industrialism, we reorganised our own societies to operate on the basis of competition rather than birth. We still find it interesting to have a title of nobility, but you aren't really Someone unless you are capable of competing on the basis of personal prowess and skills for a place on our social ladder. Social status is not based on magic or on accidental parentage, but on our personal ability to dominate in open competition with other human beings. A trust fund does help, of course, but this is only because it gives us a head start and an edge in our competitive enterprises. We are willing to look up to someone like Donald Trump, who began with thirty million and made more of it by competing ruthlessly with his peers; but there is no creature more despised than the trust fund child who devotes his life to spending Daddy's money and hoping we will be in awe of him merely for having it. In our society, someone must lose in order for someone else to win, and we adore the winner. We believe that he is naturally superior to the loser in some way.

How very accidental that, just as we were rearranging our societies according to this model, someone just so happened to discover that the animal kingdom works according to the principle of competition, too! How very accidental that this insight came at the end of the nineteenth century, just in time to reassure us that the rather unpleasant world we were creating was the only possible outcome of natural laws! See, see, even animals are constantly engaged in ruthless competition, in which only the strong and dominant survive. We are now beginning to understand that this was a projection (see Myth 14), but we do still live in a competitive market society, and this makes it difficult for most of us to let go of the old ideas.

But, besides the question of whether competition as such is a natural law, there is another problem. Though our market society is, indeed, obsessed with winners and losers, it is not organised in a strict and rigid dominance hierarchy. In fact, the more our societies are based on open competition, the less of a dominance hierarchy we have. We have human rights and civil rights and freedom of speech, and we don't have to do what rich people tell us to do. If Donald Trump shows up at your door, you can tell him to go jump in a lake, and there's nothing he can do about it.

So where did this idea of a strict dominance hierarchy among animals come from? In fact, this particular idea is a much more narrow projection than the general projection of competitive organisation. The dominance hierarchy is an anthropomorphism (the projection of human qualities into a thing or an animal) that has its roots in a very specific time and place in our history. It is also one of the most tragic things for animals that 'science' has ever produced, because the idea of a dominance hierarchy is commonly used to justify all kinds of strange and cruel practices towards dogs. It is the justification for seeing rebellion in everything a dog does, and for cruelly crushing that rebellion. It's okay to beat him, kick him, shock him, strangle him, because all of this will teach him his rank. Then once he knows his rank, he will automatically obey and do everything we want him to do. The cruelty this idea has generated will no longer surprise you once you have absorbed the following: the idea of a strict dominance hierarchy among dogs was introduced into science by a Nazi (yes, you read that right, a Nazi): Konrad Lorenz.

Most people don't know that the entire science of animal psychology got its start in Hitler's Germany. This happened in Berlin on 10th January, 1936, when the German Society for Animal Psychology was founded under the auspices of, and sponsorship by, the Nazi government. Konrad Lorenz was co-editor and an important contributor, writing many articles for the Society's journal, *Zeitschrift für Tierpsychologie*. Unlike some others who stood at the roots of animal psychology as a science, Lorenz never had problems with the Nazi authorities. On the contrary, he joined the party as soon as he could (1938), and the Nazis liked him so much that he was appointed professor of psychology at the University of Königsberg in 1940. The admiration was mutual. Lorenz worked at the Race Policy Bureau. In 1942, he participated in examining 877 people of mixed Polish–German descent, selecting who would and who wouldn't go to a concentration camp to be murdered. He believed firmly in superior and inferior races and consistently expressed great contempt for the latter. He believed in a strict, hierarchical society, in which an absolute authority ruled to whom all owed obedience. And, just as humans had always done before them, the Nazis — including Lorenz — projected their ideas about human society onto the animal kingdom. This is illustrated by the Nazi Cult of the Wolf.

It just so happens that the Cult of the Wolf played a very important part in Nazi ideology. The wolf was held up as an example, to show that the Nazis were merely trying to reorganise society according to noble, natural laws. Projecting, and without bothering to read any science or to gain any real knowledge, the Nazis (and Lorenz) depicted the wolf as a noble, wild, hardened, ruthless animal who possessed all kinds of wonderful Nazi characteristics. The wolf lived, just like the Nazi, in a closed and elite group. He was, just like the Nazi, absolutely loyal to this group, ready to unquestioningly sacrifice his life for the sake of the group if the need arose. The group's structure was just as hierarchical and rigid as the structure of the Nazi Party. Each wolf had a rank he strictly adhered to, submissive to those above him, ruthless to those beneath him. Most important perhaps, the wolves were led by a sort of Führer: the Alpha Leader. The Alpha Leader was a strong, always male wolf, whom all the other wolves worshipped and obeyed at all times, and who was fiercely desired by all the female wolves (yes, even the Nazis had sexual fantasies). And now come all the other things we are told about dogs. The Alpha Wolf receives deference in all things. He is always the first to eat and the first to go through a door. He is always up front in any kind of procession, and he always gets to sit or lie higher than the other wolves. The other wolves hurry out of his way when he is coming through. They are constantly giving off submissive signals in his presence. The Alpha Wolf can bite anyone he likes without getting bitten back. He is so utterly sure of his authority that he can, when in the mood, behave mercifully towards his inferiors — for which these inferiors are then infinitely grateful and worship him all the more. The similarity to Adolph Hitler can hardly escape us.

In general, it is taboo among scientists to personally attack the author of a theory, but this taboo does not (and cannot) apply when the author ignores all evidence to project his purely personal prejudices onto the thing he is studying. Such behaviour leaves us no choice but to address the personal background that led to such prejudices.

Lorenz specialised in studying birds. His ideas about wolves had their sole source in the Nazi Cult of the Wolf, not in science. His ideas about dogs were shaped by — as he later put it — the false gods he'd adopted as a young man. He informally observed his own dogs in his living room while he took part in Nazi activities. He first published *Man Meets Dog*, which was based on these observations, in 1949. There were as yet no published studies of the domestic dog, thus nothing to contradict Lorenz as he daydreamed just four years back to his Nazi Cult of the Wolf. He watched dogs who had been raised only by himself or given to him by his Nazi friends, and who only left the estate he lived on in his company. Lorenz's dogs were all Chow mixes and Norwegian elkhounds. He in fact had no idea about how dogs other than his own behaved, or how his own would have behaved if they had been properly socialised. But that didn't matter. Lorenz limited himself to popular publications about dogs — an arena in which everyone is free to present their own opinions as fact. It was an arena that permitted Lorenz to ignore Schenkel, who was at the time the great authority on wolves, and who strongly protested some of Lorenz's ideas about dominance and submission among them. It was an arena in which Lorenz has been caught in more than one blatant lie, but also an arena where lying has no consequences. Here, Lorenz had total freedom to continue (consciously or unconsciously, it doesn't matter) spreading the Nazi view of nature — and he used this freedom persistently until the day he died. The idea about dogs living in a dominance hierarchy very like the Nazi Party, and that dogs spend the whole day thinking about power, is nothing more than Konrad Lorenz's fictional legacy to us.

In a sense, Lorenz admits this in his book *Man Meets Dog*. He writes, 'In humans, the bonding with ideals only happens once: beware the man who, in an impressionable period of his life, gives his heart to false gods.' Indeed, after the war, Lorenz adamantly refused to repudiate his Nazi ideas. He was awarded the Nobel Prize in 1973, as co-founder of the 'science' of animal psychology. The prize made him powerful in the scientific world, a power he used to suppress contradiction of his theories as long as he lived. Confronted with this, our brave scientists chose to then just ignore Lorenz's past. (See Myth 99 for explanation of this cover-up.) It was only after his death in 1989 that most of Lorenz's theories were finally abandoned as invalid. The main one that still survives is his theory about dogs and dominance, and it's time to get rid of this one, too. How many of us truly want to treat our dogs as if we're a Nazi dictator?

Fact: The idea of dogs in a dominance hierarchy with an absolute Alpha leader at the top has its origins in Nazi ideology rather than in the real behaviour of dogs. This may be a shocking and rather uncomfortable thing for all of us to acknowledge, but this fiction about dogs has caused so much suffering that it is high time to call it for what it is and to dump it. The quicker we do this, the less shame on us.

Carson, G, *Men, Beasts and Gods: A History of Cruelty and Kindness to Animals,* Charles Scribner, NY, 1972.

Cohen, E, Law, Folklore and animal lore, *Past and Present* 110: 6–37, 1986.

Dahles, H, Game killing and killing games: An anthropologist looking at hunting in modern society, *Society & Animals*, Vol.1, No. 2, 1993.

Darnton, R, *The Great Cat Massacre and Other Episodes in French Cultural History,* Vintage, NY, 1985.

Deichmann, U, *Biologists under Hitler*, Harvard University Press, Cambridge MA, 1996.

Hills, AM, The motivational bases of attitudes toward animals, *Animals & Society,* Volume 1, Number 2, 1993.

Konecki, KT, Pets of Konrad Lorenz. Theorizing in the social world of pet owners, *Qualitative Sociology Review*, Volume III, Issue 1, April 2007.www.qualitativesol iologyreview.org, accessed July 2008.

Lorenz, K, *Mens en hond (So kam der Mensch auf dem Hund)*, Uitgeverij Ploegsma, Amsterdam, [1949] 1957. In English: *Man meets Dog*, Routledge, London, New York, [1949] 2002.

Mech, LD, Alpha status, dominance, and division of labor in wolf packs. *Canadian Journal of Zoology* 77:1196–1203. Jamestown, ND: Northern Prairie Wildlife Research Center Home Page. http://www.npwrc.usgs.gov/resource/2000/alstat/alstat.htm (version 16 May 2000).

Sax, B, What is a 'Jewish dog?' Konrad Lorenz and the cult of wildness, *Society & Animals*, Volume 5, Number 1, 1997.

Worster, D, *Nature's Economy: A History of Ecological Ideas,* Cambridge University Press, NY, 1995.

Myth 11: Retake: Dogs live in a dominance hierarchy.

We have now seen that this is a rather evil human projection. Now we come to the question of what dogs actually do, if they don't engage in dominance all day long. If dogs don't live in stable closed groups (which they don't), and if they are constantly having to meet strangers (as they are), and if the groups are constantly evaporating, changing and re-forming, then how do these groups arrive at any kind of stable or even workable organisation?

The answer is, in a nutshell, that dogs live in what we call an 'autopoietic, complex, self-organising system, which will tend to move away from chaos and towards any one of many available stable states within its state space.' Now this sounds complicated and technical and hard to grasp, because it is full of jargon. But as with most things, it is not so complicated at all if only you remove the jargon, which we will now do.

A system is a collection of parts, but it is not any old collection of loose parts. A stamp collection is not a system. To form a system, the parts have to be somehow connected to each other. Because they are connected, they constitute a whole that is distinguishable from the surroundings. But tying a bunch of tin cans together still doesn't make them into a system. A system has parts that move in relation to each other, in order to perform some function or reach some goal. A coffee machine is an example of a system, whose parts move in a coordinated way and in relation to each other, to perform the function of producing a cup of coffee. A car is a system. The parts are set in motion and work together when the function of the car has to be fulfilled — getting some load from point A to point B. However, neither of these machines is complex or self-organising. They are not complex because there is only a single arrangement of parts to choose from. If a spark plug falls out or you put water in the petrol tank instead of the radiator, then the whole thing stops working. It's no use trying out putting the coffee filter under the pot for a change. There is also only one equilibrium to choose from: a certain mixture of petrol and oxygen (or coffee and water), the right octane (or voltage), the timing of the sparks exactly right, various gaps just exactly so wide and belts just so tight. These systems are not self-organising. They are put together in a factory by some power outside themselves, according to a design that someone else thought up. If their balance gets lost, these systems are not able to restore the lost equilibrium themselves. Some outside power has to take them apart and put them back together again, restoring them exactly to the state they were in when they came from the factory.

A self-organising system is one that is capable of creating some kind of order inside the system without outside help. The parts move on their own and they can be arranged in various ways. They move around with respect to each other until the system arrives at some kind of equilibrium. When the parts move, they don't move randomly. They follow certain rules. These rules are internal to the parts themselves, something in their own nature that limits their movements and behaviour. One example of a self-organising system (hereafter: SOS) is a bunch of atoms in a bell jar. The atoms are connected to each other by the fact that they share a physical space in which they continuously collide with each other and exchange energy. Their system is distinguishable from the outside world — they aren't colliding with any atoms out there just now. The goal of this system is to spread the available energy around evenly. The atoms will move around, obeying the laws of thermodynamics, until this even division is reached. At this point, the system has arrived at a stable state. There are many arrangements of atoms that will work. It doesn't matter if a particular one is over here or over there. If you heat the bell jar, the atoms will begin to move again until the energy is again evenly spread around. They do this without external help, moving around according to their own internal rules, colliding and rearranging themselves until a new equilibrium (this is, a stable state) is reached.

A second example of an SOS, one that starts to look a little more like dogs, is a room full of people at a party. The collection of parts (i.e. people) in the room constitutes a small social system, for as long as the party lasts. It is bounded by the walls of the room, and distinguishable from the outside world full of non-invited people. Inside the room, each person is a part in the system. These living parts of the system move around, following certain internal rules, until everyone in the system is in a comfortable position. This works a little differently than a bell jar full of atoms that have no feelings. In an SOS that consists of living beings, one of the factors that affect the search for balance is each living creature's feeling of well-being. This makes our party a *complex* system: equilibrium is being sought on more than one level at once. Each system part (each party-goer) attempts to find an inner balance of feeling good, while at the same time not disturbing the balance at the level of the party as a whole.

The goal of this social system (our party) is to provide maximum enjoyment for a maximum number of guests at the same time. The system is not in equilibrium until everyone has a drink, a good place to sit, and a conversation partner they like. At this point, the inner balance of all guests is stable, while the social system itself is in balance as far as the goal it is meant to achieve. All the parts will remain where they are as long as this balance is maintained.

This lasts only so long, until someone's drink is empty, or until conversation partners get bored with each other. At this point, there is a dip in the individual well-being of a number of system parts, which also means a dip in the larger system's fulfilment of its own goal. Some system parts may start to move around, looking to repair the dip — refilling a drink or shifting conversation partners. But it doesn't have to be a dip that causes change. It can also happen that some new and interesting guest arrives. Some of the party-goers will see a chance here to increase their internal state of well-being yet more, compared how it is with the person they are talking to. They may shift positions so as to go talk to this new, interesting guest. Here, it's not a dip triggering change. Instead, it's the chance of yet more fun that gets some parts moving. They can gain this increased enjoyment without causing the whole system to crash, and in fact, their own improved fun level will move the larger system even closer to its goal of maximum fun for maximum guests. Some of the parts in our SOS will, thus, start moving around, taking up new positions in relation to each other, until their dips are restored to the previous level, or until their fun is even more maximised — upon which the system has found a new equilibrium on all levels. There are many various arrangements of party-goers that will serve the function of maximal fun — there is more than one equilibrium to choose from, both on the level of the individual and on the level of the whole.

The movement of parts is not, however, arbitrary. It is governed by internal part variables (since people enjoy different things), by external factors (like which chairs and drinks there are to choose from), and by certain rules. All of our participants follow certain rules as they seek new balances. These rules are, in this case, the rules of politeness at parties. For example, the evening must progress without embarrassing scenes or heated arguments. You don't throw someone off his chair by brute force, there are certain subjects you do not bring up, and you do not conspicuously join the conversation group that includes the man who just found out yesterday that you are having an affair with his wife. These are rules that limit the behaviour and movements of the system parts as they continually seek equilibrium on the individual and the social levels.

The rules are internal to the parts, imparted to them and made into part of who they are during their production (i.e. during their upbringing by other human beings). The party-goers follow these rules voluntarily. If everyone behaved in an egotistical manner, seeking only to maximise their own internal well-being position (e.g. when the lover did give in to the temptation to show off to the husband, or if someone was just tipped off her chair onto the floor), the whole system (the party) might deteriorate into a non-fun free for all. No one wants this to happen. People who break these rules risk getting thrown out in order to maintain system stability, because after all, the whole point of the system is to maximise fun for as many guests as possible, and not just for one selfish boor. So we know that too much selfishness will make things unpleasant not only for everyone else, but also for ourselves. We ourselves gain by participating in keeping the system stable (i.e. civil) and are willing to make smaller sacrifices in order to get this gain.

As we maximise our positions according to our own internal states, juggling variables only we can know about (tired legs, thirst, boredom), while yet allowing the rules to limit our behaviour, the system as a whole organises and reorganises itself without interference from any central, organising authority. In fact, we absolutely want the system to *self*-organise by our making our own choices and following our own internal rules as we move around in the party's social landscape. We want the party to reshuffle itself again and again into a comfortable equilibrium for all system parts, by those parts being free to move and rearrange *themselves* as inner states (thirst, boredom) and outer circumstances (a new guest) change. It is extremely irritating to us if our hostess insists that we talk at length to her unmarried son or daughter, or if she tries to make us sit in a certain spot, drink her favourite drink, or eat more than we want to.

Now to get back to dogs. Every time multiple dogs — and that means even just two — share a physical space, they immediately constitute an SOS, which will immediately start to move away from chaos by seeking an equilibrium. The dogs' SOS is very similar to our party. It too is a complex system that looks for delicate equilibriums on more than one level simultaneously, taking many invisible variables into account, and with many different equilibriums to choose from as it self-organises. When a dog sees a stranger, his inner equilibrium might go off balance — his adrenaline level might rise, his feeling of safety might suffer a dip, or his curiosity might be aroused because he expects an increase in his well-being. These are internal variables that depend on his experiences in the past with strangers. Either way, he wants to restore some kind of internal balance. At the same time, he will want to know that the larger, social balance — the peace in the group — is still safe. The domestic canine SOS has the same goal as our party: maximal well-being and safety for all the parts (in this case dogs) who are sharing the physical space at that particular moment. Just like our party, each part will execute a search to maximise its own inner well-being and stabilise its own part state, while at the same time maximising (or at least preserving) the stability, peace and fun of the larger social landscape the dogs occupy together. And, just like our party, they do this without reference to any central, organising authority.

So when dogs meet each other, they immediately start looking for the return of both the internal and external equilibriums that have been disturbed by the sight of each other. But if they don't know each other, there may be some danger involved. After all, a dog always carries his weapons with him, and you don't always know if the other guy is going to follow the social rules, or whether he is going to understand your signals and react normally to them. So the first thing dogs have to do is check out whether the other dog is going to use his weapons, and whether he understands and uses the common language. (More about these signals in Myth 12.) After some exchange of signals, it becomes sufficiently clear that there is a common language and that neither dog is going to get violent right away. Both dogs can now at least predict the other's behaviour in the domains of language and aggression. This is the crucial minimum of predictability that has to be established before the interaction can progress safely to the next stage.

It can be that this next stage is moving off to follow their humans. The next time these dogs meet they will still know about each other and the meeting will be less tense. It can also be that the dogs stick around to play with each other. In this case, the next stage of exploration starts: learning about each other's personal preferences and boundaries. As the dogs play on a field, they discover various things about each other. The first dog is very anxious the keep the stick his owner just threw and wants the second dog to stay several feet away from it. The second dog likes contact games rather than a ball or a stick. They can't talk to each other, so the dogs have to find this out by trial and error. The first dog growls when the second one so much as looks at the stick. The second dog can conclude, 'Okay, that's important to him and he wants me to keep some distance.' The first dog sees the second one stop or move away, and then he knows, 'All right, he understood my signal, and he values peace in our relation enough to let me keep my stick.' The second dog makes all kinds of 'come chase me' gestures, which show the first dog that this is the kind of game he wants. Secure enough now about his stick, the first dog might leave it for a moment to indeed play a round of chase along the border of the field. If the second dog bumps the first one during this game, he might get a snarl. This tells him that the first dog is not comfortable with such close contact. He might drop his tail, fold his ears back, move away a little — he's saying, 'Okay, I got your message, and I didn't mean any ill.' Or he bumped into a third dog during the chase, and these signals are saying, 'Oops, didn't see you, sorry.' These dogs are not being dominant and submissive. They are simply exchanging information about their respective inner states so that they will become or remain predictable to each other. Predictability about each other's likes, dislikes and personal boundaries allows them to find or maintain equilibrium in their relations with each other. When all the dogs in the physical space have found some equilibrium, then the larger social system has also arrived at one of its possible balances. The dogs play cheerfully, sharing space, taking each other's preferences and boundaries into account, dashing past each other at exactly the right distance each dog needs, no problem.

These relations generally have to be established one on one. Because dogs learn about each other by exchanging signals, they have to look at each other to learn. It is looking at the other that causes your feelings specifically about him to arise and change your inner state, which you then signal. It is by looking specifically at you that the other dog sees the signs of your internal state. So a dog can only concentrate on one relationship at a time. This is one of the reasons a dog will freeze up and stand totally still when he is being smelled by a whole group of other dogs. By freezing up, he is giving a non-violence signal, but is saying nothing more. He keeps his mouth shut for the moment, as it were, because you can only have complicated conversations one-on-one. If he is very socially secure, the dog might just flip onto his back for the whole curious crowd ('I just know everyone will be charmed by the sight of my belly'). This is a safe signal to send out to a collective, one that can't offend anyone or lead to difficult conversations. If he does this, the whole group gets the important message, some predictability about the new dog in one go ('He knows our language and has no violent intentions'). The preservation of the general safety in this dog's presence is immediately clear to all.

What we usually see happen is that the more self-assured dogs sniff the frozen newcomer for a moment, then just walk away. Often, one dog will stay near the newcomer. This is because he still doesn't feel sure enough about the newcomer to share the space with him. His inner state is still out of balance (maybe he's had bad experiences in the past, and his adrenaline level is still a little high due to this new dog showing up). He is still looking to restore his inner equilibrium, and wants more information. To get more specific information, the dogs will have to look straight at each other, and this is just not possible in a group. But now the others are gone, and our insecure dog stands there growling. I call this growl a threat gesture because the growl means the dog perceives a threat to his safety or well-being. With this threat gesture, he is basically telling the new dog that he feels unsure of himself, and is asking for reassurance so his inner state can settle down. If the new dog gives a calming signal, for example turning his ears outward and lowering his tail just a dot, he is saying, carefully, 'You don't need to worry, I'm no threat to your safety or well-being.' The first dog's adrenaline might drop a little, and so does his tail, while he stops growling ('Okay, I feel a little less worried now'). When the second dog sees that the newcomer feels less tense and thus less likely to lash out defensively, the second dog can safely take the non-threat signals a little further. He folds his ears all the way back, drops his tail completely, and starts to move a little. The first dog feels yet more reassured, and gives signals to express this. The second dog sees the decrease in tension and feels safe breaking eye contact to smell the other dog's lips or backside, or even to make a little play jump. This signalling of decreasing tension goes back and forth, until both dogs have restored their inner equilibrium. To put it differently, the dogs each begin to trust each other, which enables them to relax and share a physical space. Don't worry — 'trust' is not anthropomorphism here. Even among humans, trust is nothing more than the feeling that the other is sufficiently predictable that your internal state is not disturbed by fear of danger in his presence.

After this, in play, or in walking further together, the dogs explore each other's personal boundaries. Just like our party-goers, each dog has an internal state of well-being that he wants to preserve. This well-being can be affected by many variables, depending on the dog's history. A dog's behaviour and choices in seeking maintenance of well-being have nothing to do with some personality trait that is written in stone (e.g. 'dominant' or 'submissive'), but are the result of the dog's experience in the past. The choices are also influenced by his internal state from moment to moment (tired or not, hungry or not, full of adrenaline or not). Some dogs have learned that a tennis ball is the most wonderful play opportunity they will ever get, so they are fierce about keeping the tennis ball. Other dogs don't see any meaning in the tennis ball and will give it up willingly to another dog. A dog's personal zone is larger or smaller, depending on his experience in the past with intimate contact. The dog on a diet is obsessed with the bread someone strewed around for the birds. The castrated dog doesn't much care about the female in heat who just showed up. And so there are many different well-being positions in life, which are all highly personal, and which each dog will try to preserve. The outside observer can't always see these variables, but this is no reason to pretend they aren't there. That we can't see them doesn't matter, as long as we know, watching the dogs, that they are trying to preserve a certain internal balance, exchanging one thing against another according to their own insights (not ours!) about what serves them best at that moment.

As they are balancing their internal equilibrium, one of the things dogs keep an eye on is the equilibrium in the larger, social system they share with the others. If this system becomes unstable, it is, just like our party, unpleasant — and perhaps dangerous — for all present. When two dogs have an argument, it's unpleasant for both of them — adrenaline levels shoot up, they have to expend a bunch of energy, and it always feels kind of scary because you never know absolutely for sure what the other guy will do. So social stability is one of the variables that affect dogs' inner well-being, and they are very good at keeping an eye on it.

This is why dogs are so sensitive to social space. Again, they learn as they go. Two dogs are racing around the field, playing tag. One of them runs very closely past a third dog, who is lying there chewing on his tennis ball. This third dog jumps up and does some protest barking and air snapping, then returns to her ball. The running dog looks to us like he didn't even notice this, but in fact he picks up on this social-space information on the move and without batting an eye. If we keep watching, we see that the next time he passes, he does this at a greater distance from the chewing dog. Even in wild play, dogs pick up on what's going on in the larger picture and change their behaviour to accommodate and keep the system stable by not perturbing the other dog too much.

This is also why dogs are willing, to a varying extent (depending on their personal histories), to make trades or give things up to each other in order to restore a threatened or lost social balance. Two dogs who have just met both run after a ball someone throws. As they approach the ball, one of them starts to growl. The other dog can't know what kind of history is behind this, but he knows the growl is a sign the other feels worried about the outcome and that the relationship could now become unstable — a conflict might arise. So he slows down and lets the first dog get the ball. After all, he has plenty of tennis balls at home, and to him the ball is an excuse to play the running game. The growling dog notices this. The next time they go for the ball together, he doesn't growl, but he gets the ball again just the same. Later, the second dog's owner is giving him a treat. This dog is on a diet and is always hungry, so this time *he* growls when the first dog approaches. 'You can have the ball, but you sure can't have my food.' The first dog moves off a little and watches from a greater distance. The hungry dog notices this. The next time treats are handed out, he may still keep an eye on the other dog, but he might not feel he has to growl. He's seen that the other is willing to keep a little more distance around food. (It just so happens that in this other dog's home, tennis balls are scarce, but food isn't.) The two are each learning what is and isn't important to each other's internal well-being equilibrium. They take this into account in their interactions, and thus keep the social system stable.

This is not a dominance hierarchy, but a system of mutual trade-offs. One dog is willing to trade a little playing space for peace on the field. Another dog will give up a ball, another food, receiving the resource 'peace' in return. This is a complex SOS, which seeks equilibrium on multiple levels at once. The dogs are not trying to 'dominate' each other, but are seeking compromises, to bring all levels of the system into acceptable equilibriums at the same time. Dogs do not try to selfishly maximise their own well-being anymore than our party-goers did (see also Myths 14, 15, and 16). And you can't tell what's truly going on just by watching the visible physical resources. In the first place, as we have already seen, social stability is one of the factors that affect dogs' inner well-being. Arguments (social instability) decrease everyone's well-being by making all feel less safe. In the second place, and this is something scientists seem to have forgotten, dogs greatly enjoy each other's company. The very presence of the other adds to a dog's personal well-being. So when a dog 'sacrifices' something (e.g. the tennis ball), this isn't really a sacrifice. The dog is making a choice, an exchange, between two things he values. In such a case, we can only conclude that the dog apparently values the avoidance of a conflict, or preservation of the good relations with the other dog, more than he values the thing he gave up.

So the behaviour we have been taught to call 'dominant' is in fact merely an exchange of information, upon which the dogs then make choices. It is a search for a mutually satisfying balance between two dogs. It is not up to us to determine that one dog has 'won' and the other has 'lost.' In doing so, we fail to take their own variables into account (which are the only ones that matter!). In fact, the dog that gives up a thing thinks he is making a satisfying, and in his own eyes winning choice, given his own valuation of all the available options and taking all the multiple equilibriums into account that he wants to preserve. Assigning more value to a thing that is taken by force is a truly typical *human* projection! This projection has led scientists to miss another reality. If we watch un-blinded by labels and projections, then we see that dogs most often get hold of an object by the handy use of charm, calming signals, and distraction tactics. There's not a dog in the world who then values the object less because he got it this way. And it is another human projection to call these tactics 'submissive', when in fact they are an expression of greater social skill. It is, generally, the socially unskilled dog or the distressed dog, who reverts to force to take a thing, and it reveals much about us (and nothing about dogs) that we would consider such a dog 'superior' or assign leadership qualities to him.

With our picture in place of dogs exploring each other's boundaries and making compromises to reach inner and outer equilibriums simultaneously, we can now describe the rules the dogs follow as they do this. During my fourteen-year study of dogs, I was able to discover these rules and test them exhaustively. These are dogs' own rules, not ones thought up by a human — although humans greatly improve their relationships with dogs if we obey these rules (which we don't always do). In any case, every socialised dog carries these rules inside himself, just as our well-brought-up party-goers have internalised the ones they learned growing up. Dog rules are, however, different from human rules, and there are not so many of them. Here they are:

1) **We will not use aggression in social interactions, but will limit ourselves to signals and avoid damaging each other.** This is *the* main rule dogs depend upon. It is extremely traumatic for a dog when another dog does not honour this rule and attacks for real. (And don't try to tell us that humans have this rule too, or we will know you never watch the evening news.)

2) **We will respect each other's personal zone and not enter it without permission.** This rule is important, but it is less important that Rule Number One. It isn't so much traumatic as somewhat threatening when a dog disobeys this rule. When this happens, you may see some snarling and snapping, or maybe even a short, ritual 'fight' (which isn't really a fight — see Myths 12, 13, 33 and 34). This is a rule we do share with dogs, though we disobey it more often. (The dog who disobeys this rule is just as pathological as the human who engages in sexual harassment on the work floor.)

3) **We will be considerate of each other's personal preferences once we have learned them.** How far this consideration goes is, as we have seen, dependent on each dog's internal state at a particular moment, balanced against the wish to maintain both relationships and social peace. (See Myths 14, 15 and 16 if you think your dog doesn't obey this rule.)

With these three simple and elegant rules, internally carried by each part of the domestic canine social system, the dog system is able to achieve one of the many possible equilibriums with amazing flexibility and speed. Each dog ends up with the things he values most at that moment while social peace is preserved, and the dog who consistently does not obey the rules get thrown out of the system (which chasing away can be a collective enterprise). We cannot determine some kind of hierarchy among the dogs in this balance (unless we are willing to project), because we cannot know how the *dogs* are valuing the things they add and subtract from their position in the whole. All we can do is observe that each dog has reached a position he is happy with. This position is not reached by brute force, but by voluntarily seeking compromises. It doesn't interest a dog in the least whether some other dog has 'more'. In fact, dogs don't even have the brain structures that would enable them to think the concept 'more' or 'less', conceiving of and comparing sizes or quantities. This kind of math is quite beyond them. All a dog knows is that he has his own personal 'enough' (more on this later, in Myth 14). Therefore, this dog SOS works excellently well. A dog group can absorb practically unlimited numbers of dogs quickly and flexibly, as long as everyone follows the three simple rules.

At the beginning, I said that dogs live in a complex, autopoietic, self-organising system. Now we understand 'complex' and 'self-organising'. But what does 'autopoietic' mean? It means, quite simply, that the system is capable of producing and repairing its own parts. You don't have to take an autopoietic system to the garage, or buy new parts for it. It is self-perpetuating and self-maintaining. Autopoiesis occurs when a system consists of living creatures. A dog bears pups without external help, and dogs all around the world raise pups — if humans don't interfere — into functioning system parts who know and voluntarily follow the rules. As we have seen in Myth 6, the ability to take part in the social system is learned, not inherited. Dogs do this part production quite well all by themselves.

A dog must interact with other dogs while he's a pup so as to learn the rules, otherwise he may end up having trouble participating in social interactions. An adult dog who didn't play enough with others in his youth may need finishing (as a part) if he is to function in a social system. Another dog may have a traumatic and damaging experience, and end up needing 'repair' to be able to function again in the dog social system. We may need help repairing our dogs, but dogs are quite capable of repairing such a part themselves without outside help. They will help the traumatised dog get over his fear, providing him with reassuring social experiences. It's actually quite touching to watch how socially skilled dogs react to fear in another dog — we could learn a lot from them. The socially clumsy (or incomplete) dog gets snapped at and snarled at, until he tempers his clumsy behaviour and starts to act more politely. The other dogs aren't 'dominating' him, but are providing this incomplete part with some learning experiences he missed out on, and he is learning as he goes. As long as the hooligan refrains from using aggression (i.e. delivering one or more uninhibited bites, thus inflicting damage on other system parts), he will be able to learn from other dogs how to take part in the system.

Thus there are two production processes, which make sure the system is producing and repairing its own parts. One of them is the biological process of bearing and raising offspring. The second production process is learning. Learning is crucial both to the production of socially functioning offspring and to the repair of parts that don't function optimally for some reason.

So learning is an important production process in the dog SOS. Learning takes care of the production of functioning system parts and repair of damaged or incomplete parts. Their ability to learn enables dogs to take the deviant signals into account that they encounter, for example, from a dog whose tail the humans have cut off or bred to be permanently curled up on his back. Their learning ability, their readiness to seek compromise, and their three simple rules enable dogs to absorb members of other species into their social system. A dog can learn how to interpret the signals, and thus predict the behaviour, of a parrot, a cat, a human, if only we allow him to go through the right learning experiences. He is then able to use these signals across the species-boundaries, to seek equilibrium and construct an SOS with all kinds of non-dog species. It's actually miraculous — or maybe not, given the context the dog evolved in.

Dogs live in a flexible and complex self-organising system which is capable of seeking and finding equilibriums on multiple levels at once (all the dogs in equilibrium while the social system also finds a balance). The system produces and repairs its own parts. There are three simple rules that determine the system's movements by the individual parts independently and voluntarily following those rules, without some central authority guiding things. The system functions to find the maximum available safety and well-being of all the present participants. There is no hierarchy. There is only a whole range of possible balances, both for each individual participant and for the system as a whole. Each equilibrium is arrived at as the dogs seek compromises, weighing various choices, and seeking a balance between their own well-being and the stability of the social landscape (which is also an element in their well-being). A dog who can't compromise can't take part. His behaviour destabilizes the social system, making it unsafe or uncomfortable for other participants. Dogs aren't preoccupied with power, but rather with building mutual predictability and trust, so the system can balance in one of the many acceptable equilibriums it has to choose from. These 'acceptable equilibriums' are situations in which each dog present has a well-being position he is satisfied with. Giving up a ball or a bone to preserve the relationship and the social peace does not mean the dog has 'lost.' It means that he has made a trade-off, shifting from the well-being position that included the ball to a position that included something else he decided was more important.

The ability to follow Rule Number One, no aggression (i.e. no uninhibited bites and no attempting to inflict real damage on others), is essential, however. Aggression makes a dog unable to function as a part of any dog social system. He will always be attempting to sabotage the entire system. His presence makes the social system unsafe for all the other participants. He can't be repaired, because this is too dangerous — he will be trying to destroy other system parts rather than to learn from them. The dog does not exist who is willing to risk his internal equilibrium to such an extent that he may cease to exist as a living system himself! (See re: exceptions to this in Myths 38–40.) Dogs who do engage in aggression, or who will risk their existence as a living system in order to fight, are not products of nature. They are a result of human tampering with dogs. Repair is impossible, and the owner has the responsibility to keep the dog away from other dogs.

Fact: The domestic dog's social system is, thus, much more complex — but also much more elegant and intelligent — than a mere 'dominance hierarchy.' This 'dominance hierarchy' model is clumsy and anthropomorphic, and does not do justice to dogs.

Semyonova, A, The social organisation of the domestic dog; a longitudinal study of domestic canine behaviour and the ontogeny of domestic canine social systems, Carriage House Publishing, The Hague, The Netherlands, 2003. www.nonlineardogs.com.

Myth 12: Dog body language is all about dominance and submission.

We have now seen (in Myth 11) that dogs live in a complex and flexible self-organising system, and that this system has many acceptable balances to choose from. As the dogs move within their system, each dog also has many satisfying options to choose from. Dogs are not interested in competition the way people are (see Myth 14). In fact, such things as momentary hunger, thirst, and adrenaline levels, past experiences with tennis balls and other dogs, how many tennis balls happen to be lying around at that particular instant, the desire to keep the relationship with the other dog, what the other dog seems to want — myriad factors and choices — are playing a role as a dog decides what to do from second to second. Dogs are always balancing and compromising between many internal and external variables as they search for a mutually satisfying balance in a social interaction. They measure this by their own criteria, not by ours, and each dog's personal criteria are different.

So dog body language is not about dominance and submission. Rather, it functions to inform the dogs about each other's inner state (call it mood, emotion, momentary motivation, as you like), so they can take each other's inner state into account as they interact. Their language is about information, predictability, knowledge of each other, and finding compromises that both dogs are all right with.

If we want to understand what dogs are truly saying, we have to put all the old ideas aside. What we do need to remember is that a dog is always armed when he meets another dog. We also need to remember that some dogs have had good experiences with other dogs (or with humans), while others have had mixed or bad experiences. A dog can feel unsure of himself when he meets a stranger. If we take this into account, we see that all the signals we have been told to interpret as 'dominant' really mean something else.

The dog who enters an interaction with threat signals (high tail, high posture, staring, curling a lip, growling, hairs bristling on the back, stiff gait etc) is in fact telling the other dog that he feels worried about the other's intentions. Uncertainty. It is entirely possible that the threatening dog is completely sure of his ability to keep the other at a distance by the use of force — but this confidence in his prowess in not the cause of the threats. The cause of the threats is *lack of confidence about what the other dog is going do*.

This may seem paradoxical to those of us who are used to thinking in terms of 'dominance' and 'submission', but there is strong evidence for it. Dogs who frequently and chronically threaten are often greatly helped if we give them anti-anxiety medicines during a behavioural therapy (Simpson and Simpson 1996). If it were all about 'dominance', and if anxiety about the other dog's teeth were the only thing holding a dog back from being a total dictator, we would expect a reduction in anxiety to lead to even more bullying — but this turns out not to be the case. A second set of proofs is found in a longitudinal study (Semyonova 2003), in which it turned out that dogs threaten the most in the period after an unpleasant or scary experience with another dog (or a human). Dogs also threaten more often if they have just generally had too few pleasant experiences in their history, or too many bad ones. In the field of behavioural therapy, it turns out that dogs stop threatening their owners only when they learn to trust what their owners are intending to do. Trying to dominate a dog generally makes his threat behaviour worsen, unless the owner is willing to beat the dog so severely that he becomes paralysed with total fear (but that isn't 'dominance', it's just terrorising an animal). The dog will still bite if cornered, as any animal will, and the dog leads an unhappy life. A threatening dog is just plain worried about what the other is going to do, so he gives off a signal that says, 'please don't come any closer'. This is not dominance. The only solution is to work on showing the dog you are trustworthy and not dangerous.

The dog who behaves 'submissively' isn't being submissive at all. This dog is anxious to make contact because he enjoys social traffic so much. He is telling the threatening, unsure dog (or human) about his own inner state, saying that he has no scary, evil or strange intentions. He is telling the other that he will respect the rules of politeness. He is trying to reduce the other's worry, by saying, 'I'm not going to bite you', or 'I won't steal your ball', or 'I won't come into your personal zone until you give me permission'. Because these signals are meant to take away the other dog's anxiety (i.e. to calm the other dog's inner state), we call them calming signals. This is a better description of what the signals aim at doing than calling them 'submissive'. These signals all require that a dog have enough confidence to put himself in a vulnerable position. Averting your gaze, making squeaky puppy-noises, trying to look smaller, exposing your neck or belly — it takes confidence to use these signals, enough good experiences in life to believe that other won't attack suddenly. It is, in fact, this dog who is taking control of the situation. He is taking the worried dog by the hand, as it were, and comforting him, trying to reassure him that contact can be safe and pleasant.

The threatening dog is revealing that he hasn't had many pleasant experiences (or fears a bad one now), that he has less social self-confidence, and that he needs a little distance. He asks for distance and reassurance, and the other dog gives it to him. To put it more precisely, the threatening dog is indicating that his inner equilibrium is lost, because (for example) his adrenaline level is very high. The confident dog knows by experience that certain signals will help restore the other dog's inner equilibrium. (Of course, he isn't thinking this abstractly — he just has experience that if he gives off a calming signal, the other dog responds by reducing his threats a little, allowing our calming dog to come a little closer.) Indeed, the threatening dog receives this information about the confident dog's lack of bad intentions and he relaxes a little. Perhaps he drops his tail a few inches and turns his ears a bit. The confident dog approaches a little closer, continuing to give off calming signals. The threatening dog signals that his inner state is yet a little less mistrustful. This goes back and forth until the threatening dog has gained enough confidence that he can allow real contact. The calming dog has had success in returning both the worried dog and the social system they occupy together to equilibrium. Of course, it can also happen that the worried dog can't conquer his anxiety, not even with so much help, and that the confident dog decides to just leave him alone and go do something else.

Fact: Dogs use their signals to exchange information about each other's inner state and each other's intentions, so they can take these into account as they interact. It's all about conquering anxiety and establishing trust. 'Dominance' and 'submission' are purely human projections.

Longitudinal studies

One of the problems in the study of dog behaviour is that scientists only look for a very short time. Often they create experimental situations, put some dogs in these situations, test some responses, then draw their conclusions. Sometimes they observe dogs for a somewhat longer period. But this is usually still several fairly short sessions spread over several weeks or months. The researcher doesn't see what the dog is doing or experiencing between sessions. Often these are shelter dogs, dogs who are brought to a behavioural clinic at a university, or adult dogs researchers are watching 'in the wild'. The trouble with this kind of observation is that you come in in the middle of the movie, go to the loo six times during the show, and then leave before it's over. You can't really know why the characters are doing what they do, what the plot is, what parts you've missed, and you miss the ending.

A longitudinal study is a study that covers a very long period of time, so that you can see how things develop over the years. Preferably, you also have to make sure you can watch the thing you're observing at least most of the time, so you don't miss important events. This is the only way to really find out what is really behind behaviour — by watching how it arises in the course of a dog's life and how it changes as the dog has various experiences.

The short-looking scientist sees a dog growling at the vet and resisting being touched. This scientist declares that the dog is dominant and wants to control the interaction. But if you've been watching for a longer time, you might know that the last vet this dog saw punched the dog in the head and then kicked him because the dog had air-snapped in a pain reflex. The dog is now scared of vets.

Behaviour suddenly looks very different if you have been around watching for a while. When you have been watching long enough to know what kind of experiences a dog has had in the past, then you draw entirely different conclusions.

Bolles, RC, Species-specific defence reactions and avoidance learning, *Psychological Review* 77:32–48, 1970.

Borchelt, PL, Voith, VL, Dominance aggression in dogs, in Voith, VL, Borchelt, PL, eds, *Readings in Companion Animal Behaviour,* Veterinary Learning systems, Co., Inc., Trenton, NJ, 1996.

Burgoon, JK, Buller, DB, Woodall, WG, *Nonverbal communication: The unspoken dialogue,* McGraw-Hill Companies, Inc, NY, 1966.

Dunbar, I, Bohnenkamp, G, *Preventing Aggression,* Center for Applied Animal Behaviour, Berkeley CA, 1985 (3rd ed June 1986).

Maturana, HR, Biology of language: the epistemology of reality, in Miller, GA, and Lenneberg, E. (eds.), *Psychology and Biology of Language and Thought: Essays in Honor of Eric Lenneberg,* Academic Press, NY, 1978, pp 27–63. http://A/ Maturana1.htm (2002).

Mazur, J, Conditioned reinforcement and choice with delayed and uncertain primary reinforcers, *JEAB* 63: 139–150, 1995.

Miczek, KA, Weerts, E, Haney, M, Tidey, J, Neurobiological mechanisms controlling aggression: Preclinical developments for pharmacotherapeutic interventions, *Neruosci Biobehav Rev* 18: 97–100, 1994.

Overall, KL, *Clinical Behavioural Medicine for Small Animals,* Mosby, Inc., Missouri, 1997.

Powell, D, Francis, MJ, Francis, J, Schneiderman, N, Shock —induced aggression as a function of prior experience with avoidance, fighting, or unavoidable shock, *JEAB* 18: 323–332, 1972.

Rugaas, T, *Calming Signals*, Legacy By Mail, Inc., Carlsborg, WA, 1997.

Semyonova, A, The social organisation of the domestic dog; a longitudinal study of domestic canine behaviour and the ontogeny of domestic canine social systems, Carriage House Foundation, The Hague, The Netherlands, 2003. www.nonlineardogs.com.

Simpson, SS & Simpson SM, Behavioural pharmacotherapy, in Voith, *Readings in Companion Animal Behaviour,* Voith, VL & Borchelt, PL, eds., Veterinary Learning Systems, NJ, 1996.

Myth 13: When two male dogs meet, the first thing they want to do is establish their relative ranks with each other.

We have all seen male dogs facing off in what looks to us like a threat match. The popular story, and even the scientific dogma, is that they are trying to establish who is dominant, i.e. who has the higher rank here. But we have seen that dogs don't live in dominance hierarchies. They live in flexible, self-organising systems, which are sometimes very fleeting. We know that the dog SOS seeks equilibrium by juggling a multitude of variables, and that the only way to find a hierarchy is by projecting human values onto the choices dogs are making (see Myth 11). So what is this canine face-off truly all about?

When two dogs don't want to have anything to do with each other, they have a quite simple way of achieving this: keep your distance and don't bother to make contact with the other guy. When dogs do make contact, this is a choice. (This is assuming you haven't shut them up together in the bathroom.) It means they are interested in each other and want to establish some kind of relationship. They are voluntarily entering each other's personal zone.

They both know this may be dangerous. Dogs are always armed. Not all dogs follow the social rules. So the bluffing dogs are, in fact, testing the three following rules.

1) We will respect each other's personal zone and not enter it without permission. This is the first rule that comes into play when dogs meet each other. Socially skilled dogs do not enter the other dog's personal zone without permission. (The grand exceptions to this are the aggressive breeds, the insufficiently socialised dog, and the adolescent dog.) You might not have noticed it, but our two males were already conversing long before they ended up facing off opposite each other. From the moment they saw each other, in fact. Before they were anywhere near each other, both males had already signalled that they weren't going to attack immediately. Each dog has also already signalled that he feels unsure of the other. This is what the whole slow approach on stiff, high legs means, including any growling and baring of teeth. Nevertheless, by approaching each other, they are both indicating that they do want contact. So, long before they are in the actual face-off, they have given each other permission to enter the personal zone, to see if they can establish a relationship.

As they stand there growling and other ado, they are learning about each other's inner state. The fact that both of them just stand there growling is proof that both are still refraining from attacking. At some point, *the most socially confident dog* will decide he's had enough proof that he's fairly safe in the other's presence. This more confident dog will be the first to give off a calming signal, perhaps dropping his tail a little and relaxing his stiffened legs somewhat, or turning his ears outward. These are reactions to the returning equilibrium in his own inner state (for example, that his adrenaline level has begun to drop as he starts to feel safer). This helps the other dog's inner state calm down a little, so this second dog's bristling hairs might smooth out, or he reciprocates by dropping his tail and turning his ears. His legs relax some, so both dogs' elevated attitude is now gone. The dogs progress to sniffing each other's body parts (usually anus and genitals). They may walk a few steps away from each other. They may deposit urine somewhere for each other to smell. You won't always be seeing these signals, because they can be quite subtle.

Sometimes it looks to you like the dogs just suddenly stopped facing off and started playing with each other, and you think you're lucky. You're not lucky. The dogs have simply, but skilfully, used their signals to establish a minimal level of trust.

But it's not *always* so simple. Sometimes dogs feel a need to test the most basic of all dog rules.

2) We will not use aggression in social interactions, but will limit ourselves to signals and avoid damaging each other. This is the main rule, upon which all social traffic among dogs depends. To understand how this works, we first have to distinguish between real aggression and so-called ritual aggression. Aggression is aimed at inflicting maximal damage on the other, perhaps at killing him. Aggression is the delivery of one or more uninhibited bites — when a dog sinks his teeth in, uses the full power of his jaws, or rips, shears, and tears, and is trying to cause serious wounds. 'Ritual aggression' is, in fact, not aggression at all. It is symbolic. The dog keeps his jaws open and waves his teeth around. He might grab a fold of the other dog's skin and pull on it a little — but he does this without causing wounds. He's not biting, he's pinching. It's inaccurate to call waving the teeth around and delivering pinches 'aggression'. These actions are nothing more than signals the dog are exchanging. These signals look awful to us, but in fact they are delivering a very important message: 'Even now, as upset as I am, I'm being careful about how I use my teeth on you.' We are petrified, but after the whole thing is over we can't find a single wound.

Even ritual fights are very rare among dogs, but we need to understand what is going on when it does reach this point between (usually) two males. Usually dogs manage to build trust with milder signals. As they began the face-off, the two males showed each other they wouldn't attack immediately simply by not doing so. But the fact that one of the two still isn't relaxing may mean he's socially unskilled. He's not showing the usual readiness to indicate non-threat as quickly as possible. This is abnormal behaviour in a dog. His continuing tenseness means he still may go so out of balance that he lashes out at some point. At the same time, he's not choosing to just leave the shared physical space. This can be very upsetting to socially skilled dogs. The socially skilled dog is confronted with another dog who is obviously insecure and touchy, but who also wants to stay. If the tense dog stays, touchy as he is, who knows what he might do later? The socially skilled dog is not willing to make the trade-off of leaving himself. The joy of playing with all the others on the field is too great, so leaving is not one of the approximately equal well-being options he can choose from. The touchy dog also wants to stay, apparently not feeling so threatened by the other dogs who are present. He's chosen the dog he feels most insecure about to have the face-off with. This might be the biggest other male around, but it might be some smaller dog who happens to look a little like the terrier who attacked him three weeks ago.

It may also be that *both* the dogs are just generally so socially insecure that they don't dare just trust the 'No Aggression' rule. It can be that both dogs have had a bad experience with another dog who looked like the one they are facing off with. At the same time, they are choosing not to walk off and just go on their lonely ways. Both dogs still have hope (based on past experience) that a balance can be found and that this will be rewarding in the end. If they didn't have this hope, or if they thought a confrontation would lead to disaster, they'd have avoided each other in the first place.

In both cases a situation arises where each dog feels a need to test the other — to see the other either leave or give off a non-threat signal that shows he's finally relaxed enough that he won't be dangerous.

A dog can't just wait and see. The dogs' inner states are so far from equilibrium (so full of adrenaline and other stress hormones) that some kind of inner balance has to be restored before they can do anything else. The social system (even if it consists of only these two dogs) is also too far out of equilibrium. There are two dogs present whose well-being is suffering quite a dip. All this loss of equilibrium feels dangerous to dogs, who simply can't share a physical space with another whom they feel very worried about. After all, how can you just go off and play while there's a constant fear the other will suddenly attack while you're not looking, or bite you because you whizz by too close? Both the inner states and the social system have to be in balance, this is how the dog system works. If the balance can't be found with both present, then it'll have to be restored by one of the dogs leaving the shared physical space. So two dogs feel unsure of each other, but both want to stay. It will be the more insecure dog whose inner state goes so off balance that he loses it and lashes out at the other dog, and there they go.

Now we have what us humans call 'a fight'. But it isn't a fight, it's communication. The dogs make a lot of noise, wave their teeth around, bat at each other's faces, maybe grab hold of the loose skin around the neck and shoulders, tug a little, let go, wave their teeth around some more, grab hold again. This all yields important information. For example, each dog shows the other that he has learned bite inhibition in his youth (see Myth 6). They also prove to each other that they will actually use this bite inhibition even in a tense and heated moment. By mutually proving this to each other — and sometimes the proof can only be found in the eating — the two dogs can, ultimately, start to feel safe in each other's presence. In the 'fight', they give the ultimate proof that they will be careful with their teeth no matter what. What usually happens is that one of the dogs decides he's had enough proof, so he gives off a signal that he's done testing. The other dog also knows he hasn't really been bitten during all this, so he responds to the signal by cutting it out, too — thus showing he does know these calming signals and what they mean. Suddenly the 'fight' stops. The dogs now have enough information about each other to feel sure that sharing a playing field together will not result in a dangerous situation.

The dogs have not established respective ranks. They have done some trust building. Hopefully, you have allowed them to do this without 'saving' them from each other. When you do 'rescue' them from their conversation, they will just resume the conversation the next time they meet, because the thing still needs to be said before they can feel okay about sharing space.

I have to give one warning here, though. This chapter is about normal, socialised dogs. Not all dogs are normal or socialised. You should be extremely careful about exposing your dog to breeds that have been specifically bred for aggressive behaviour. These dogs are unable to engage in ritual conflict resolution because humans have bred a brain abnormality into them that makes them literally unable to control their fighting behaviour (see Myths 38–40). This may not be their fault, but they will kill your dog all the same. And there are other dogs, not specifically bred for aggressive behaviour, who have just never learned to inhibit their bite or to seek social compromises. These dogs are just as dangerous as the aggressive breeds. When you think your dog is in real trouble, e.g. if you see the other dog making a shearing or tearing movement with that piece of skin he's grabbed, or *if your dog begins to scream*, then you should rush over to help him. The best thing to do is to grab the attacking dog's hind legs (not your own dog's!) and lift them into the air. Most attackers will react as if you hit the 'off' switch. Ask the owner of this dog to leash his dog, and do not let go of those legs until he has done so.

That said, we can get back to normal, socialised dogs. There is a third rule these dogs test, usually in play after the first acquaintance has been made.

3) **We will be considerate of each other's preferences once we have learned them.** Sometimes two dogs will have a threat match about a ball or a stick that is lying around and that they both spotted at the same moment. This occurs very occasionally between two dogs who already know each other, but usually it is dogs who have just recently met for the first time. Both dogs want the tennis ball. To understand what happens next, we have to refrain from reverting to labels and analyse what is in fact going on.

A dog's desire to have or to keep an object is a result of past learning experiences — e.g. he has learned that the tennis ball can be a source of pleasure. But not all dogs know this about tennis balls (or sticks, or whatever). One dog is on a diet, the other just ate. One dog's owner is always making a point of taking things away from him, the other's doesn't do this. And so on. Each dog will have his own particular valuation of all the objects that are lying around, and his own particular touchiness about it. At the same time, we have to remember that the preservation of relationships and social peace is, to dogs, a great good. As they look at an object the other dog also wants, it's not just about the object. They also have to make a decision about disturbing the peace or damaging (or even losing) the relationship with the other dog, whose company they were just enjoying so much. Each dog will have his own valuation of these social resources, just like with physical objects, and this will be dependent on the dog's personal history, just like with the physical objects.

If we remember this, then the way we describe behaviour changes. The dog who decides to walk away and surrender the physical object has not forfeited rank nor 'submitted.' He has simply weighed all the various factors and all his various preferences, and decided that some other combination was worth more to him than the combination that included the tennis ball. He has maximised his inner well-being according to his own values, values we can't judge for him. We can't decide for him that he has 'lost,' because in his own eyes the real losing move would've been to lose the trust and friendship of the other dog. By seeking a compromise — both with each other and between all the various factors that affect their own well-being — dogs shift their respective well-being positions, so that both dogs are satisfied with the outcome. The more often two new acquaintances have sought these compromises with each other, the more they know about each other's preferences, and the more easy and pleasant interactions will be.

Fact: The face-offs and symbolic 'fights' (which are merely exchanges of signals) between two male dogs are not about rank and dominance. They function to generate predictability and trust in various crucial areas of interaction. In a threat match, each dog tells the other he feels worried. Each dog demonstrates his trustworthiness by not really biting, even in an escalation. These matches also serve to learn each other's preferences and boundaries, what each dog needs to feel comfortable, so this can be taken into account in future interactions.

Semyonova, A, The social organisation of the domestic dog; a longitudinal study of domestic canine behaviour and the ontogeny of domestic canine social systems, Carriage House Foundation, The Hague, The Netherlands, 2003. www.nonlineardogs.com.

Myth 14: Competition is a natural law. Dogs organise their groups via competition.

This is a human projection. We live in a so-called Free Market society, which is based purely on aggressive competition. Just like the knights of old (and the Nazis), we now project our own social organisation onto all of Nature. We are told that competition is the only efficient way to organise anything, that only the strongest and best survive, and that our competitive society is a natural phenomenon. But if competition is such a natural phenomenon, then why do we need a whole army of expensive marketing psychologists to keep the whole thing going? If open competition will produce the best choices for us, then why do companies go to so much trouble to hide information about what they are really offering us? And if this is such an efficient and natural way to organise things, then why do we have more and more trivial material junk, but less and less general well-being? Why is everyone so stressed out and unhappy, and why are so many more people poor now than, say, fifty years ago?

The answer is: because the whole idea is a fiction, and basically represents a failure of education — because we've been through this already, at the beginning of the twentieth century. The whole ideology leans heavily on Charles Darwin, who wrote that all creatures are involved in a struggle for life, and that in this struggle the fittest will survive. Darwin explains at great length that 'fittest' refers to the creature that is best adapted to the environment it lives in. This creature will have the best chance of surviving long enough to bear and raise young, thus passing on its genes and the adaptation to the environment. People read this sloppily, and thus began to project. They concluded that competition in 'the struggle for life' meant a direct confrontation between animals (just like us), and that the 'fittest' meant the animal who was best able to win a confrontation by the use of violence (just like us). They applied their own human standards, and decided that the 'winner' was whichever animal was able to accumulate the most resources. Gosh, the whole animal kingdom is just like us!

In fact, Darwin writes about adaptation by means of better camouflage, the ability to exploit a new source of food, the ability to use energy more efficiently, to bear young at a slightly more favourable time of year, and to *avoid* (not conquer) those who want to eat you. Darwin's 'struggle for life' is not about armed conflict, nor about acquiring more resources than you really need. It's all about setting up a safe little spot and a small, personal 'economy of enough' in the ecosystem the animal lives in. This is, in fact, even true of humans — which is why we need the never ending stream of advertising to fool us into thinking it's not enough yet.

Competing for ever more resources is, in other words, not a natural law. Never has been.

Animals are not subject to the propaganda we are subject to, so they obey natural laws. Unnecessary competition and conflict is a waste of energy. Those who waste energy are less fit than those who don't, so an animal lives in her own little economy of enough and is satisfied with that. Animals don't enter into armed conflict with each other unless their safety is threatened. Animals don't enter into direct competition with each other unless their little economy of enough is threatened. These are the real natural laws.

Fact: Dogs are, like all other non-human animals, not out to greedily compile the *most* resources. They aren't even aware of whether someone else has more, as long as their own little economy of enough is intact. Social peace (as opposed to constant competition) is important, because it conserves energy and increases the safety of life. Dogs are normally not at all competitive. Rather, they organise their groups by maximising safety in social interactions, seeking compromise and social balance, and keeping their relationships with other dogs intact. This is why their social system works so well and is able to absorb unlimited numbers of other dogs.

Beckerman, LP, 'The non-linear dynamics of war', Science Applications International Corporation, ASSET Group, www.belisarius.com,1999.

Crist, E, 'Neo-Darwinism', www.imprint-academic.demon.co.uk/SPECIAL/03_15.html, March 2002.

Darwin, C, *On the Origin of Species; a Facsimile of the First Edition*, Harvard University Press, Cambridge MA, 1964 (original 1859).

Friedan, B, *The Feminine Mystique*, Penguin Books, Harmondsworth, Middlesex, 1965.

Midgley, M, 'Gene-juggling', www.royalinstitutephilosophy.org/articles/midgley_gene_juggling.htm, May 2002.

Sibly, RM, Smith, RH, *Behavioural Ecology: Ecological Consequences of Adaptive Behaviour*, Blackwell Scientific Publications, Oxford, 1985.

Worster, D, *Nature's Economy: A History of Ecological Ideas*, Cambridge University Press, NY, 1995.

Myth 15: The dog who can take and keep the most resources is the dominant dog.

This myth pictures animals as four-legged humans. Our societies were, in the first half of the twentieth century, regulated by competition and violence, including two world wars, so we assumed it must be that way in the animal kingdom, too. Scientists went and counted how often a particular captive wolf won an aggressive confrontation with another captive wolf, and voila, there was a dominance hierarchy. The definition of 'the dominant wolf' was the one who could deal out the most violence with impunity, while not having to be on the receiving end himself. (Yes, it was, of course, always a male wolf.) But alas and alack for our clever scientists, wolves living in the wild turned out only rarely to have aggressive confrontations with each other. It also turned out that the oldest wolf (who should've been the 'dominant' wolf) had the least arguments of everyone. He wasn't receiving any violence, but he wasn't dealing much out, either. Now, scientists hate it when their statistics get screwed up, so they were in quite a tizzy. What now?

We had entered the post-World War Two period of peace, so violence began to seem less relevant to scientists. We had also entered a period of accumulation of wealth, in which some of our members who didn't look so strong at all were coming out powerful winners. So, after some amount of puzzling, scientists decided it wasn't violence that determined dominance in Nature after all. It must be 'resource holding'. We had to look at which wolf got to control the most resources, things that keep us alive and allow us to pass on our genes. The question arose as to which resources had to be counted. And, since most scientists are young men, it ended up being the kinds of things young men are worried about obtaining: above all, food, sex and comfy sleeping spots, and in second place such things as the front-row seat (since front row seats are of great importance to the ultimate survival of the scientist — see Myth 99).

But it still didn't work, in particular when they tried to apply it to dogs. Whether the scientist counted aggressive encounters or resource holding, the 'dominance hierarchy' turned out to produce quite a different diagram than the rigid linear hierarchy of the Nazi Party and science itself. There were triangular hierarchies (A over B, B over C, and C over A), sometimes whole circles and spirals, a criss-cross of arrows going in every direction to show who was dominant over whom. Very messy. Another problem was that these 'hierarchies' were anything but stable. If you take a group of dogs apart and separate them for a while, then put them back together in the same space, then count food, sex and resting spots again, well, you get a whole different set of triangles, circles, spirals and arrows, which seems to have little or no relation to the one you had before.

Scientists had, in fact, proved that there is no such thing as a dominance hierarchy in a group of dogs (though of course they didn't see this). To them, the whole thing just looked totally unstable and unpredictable. How could a stable social organisation ever result? So scientists turned to puzzling about what was wrong with their statistical methods. If only they could find the right statistical method, they thought, they would find the hierarchy dogs must live by.

The real problem wasn't the statistics. The real problem was that scientists were counting the wrong resources. Because of their own attitude toward life, they had missed a number of resources that others do find important. In other words, there is more to life than food, sex and the best spot to sit. Not all resources are quite so vulgar, and not all resources are material. For example, safety is a highly valued resource to most animals (see Myths 11–13). And safety is heightened for all when the rule is to compromise rather than to fight. Another resource — to dogs, at least — is the relationship with the other in and of itself, whether or not it yields some material gain. Dogs enjoy each other's company immensely and are very anxious to preserve relationships and to be allowed to participate. The company of other dogs improves the quality of their life. And anything that improves the quality of an animal's life is (in her own eyes, which are the only important ones) a resource. So we must consider relationships to be a resource a dog is also trying to keep, as she considers what to do about other valued resources.

Once you take these invisible resources into account, you get a more accurate picture of what is going on. What you then see is not a hierarchy, but a system that makes complex choices as it constantly works its way back to equilibrium. Competition would mean the loss of a number of valuable, though invisible, resources — resources that can only be conserved by mutual compromise and trade-off in material things. By thinking only in terms of competition and hierarchy (i.e. projecting), scientists totally missed what was really going on. The canine system is capable of moving parts around in all kinds of combinations and positions without losing its equilibrium. The system is flexible and capable of adapting quickly to momentary circumstances, which is quite another thing than unpredictable and unstable. Rather than competing, the dogs are each on one end of a well-being seesaw that they each want to keep balanced. They make trade-offs with each other, so that the 'weight' on both sides of the fulcrum stays balanced enough to keep either side from touching the ground. It's not unpredictable at all. In fact, if you know the dogs involved, you can quite easily predict which choices they will make, as can dogs once they know each other.

Fact: Dogs don't live in a hierarchy and aren't interested in controlling each other's behaviour beyond demanding ordinary politeness (which usually just means respect for their personal zone, however big or small they need it to be with this particular other). You can't tell anything about their system just by looking at the exchange of physical objects. Your dog is not interested in competing with you, nor with another dog, about material goods the way humans do, because — lacking extreme conditions — relationships and safety are very often a much more important resource to her. If you take all the invisible resources into account, you get a different and better picture of what dogs are really doing.

See also: Myths 10 and 99.

Semyonova, A, The social organisation of the domestic dog; a longitudinal study of domestic canine behaviour and the ontogeny of domestic canine social systems, Carriage House Foundation, The Hague, The Netherlands, 2003. www.nonlineardogs.com.

Myth 16: But *my* dog is competitive, because he always wants what the other dog has.

The wish and the ability to search for social equilibrium are not innate qualities. These are things a dog learns in the course of his life. All newborn mammals are egotistical and impulsive. The neonate just does whatever occurs to him to do. He learns by experience. He does something and finds out — to his utter amazement — that by his behaviour he causes a change in, or elicits a response from, his surroundings. He tries out all kinds of behaviour and learns by trial and error what the environmental change or response will be to different things he does. As he goes along, he learns to take this into account before acting. As he plays with siblings at the nesting site, he learns that egotistical behaviour can lead to conflict, and that conflict does not always end well for him. He may lose the thing he wanted, or something painful happens, or something scary. He discovers that his contentious behaviour leads others to avoid him. He loses the pleasure of their company — the chance to sleep all comfy and warm in the pile of puppies, to play with the others, and so on. In adolescence, his hormones start raging through his body and he loses much of the control he'd gained over his immediate impulses. He goes through a repetition of the learning process, experiencing yet again what happens if he causes instability in the social system. Others decline to play with him, and — if he continues too long with his obnoxious behaviour — the adult dogs chase him out of the group. They don't feel like dealing with constant disruption, want only peace and stability in the social landscape, and there he is all by himself again. By the time he reaches adulthood, the dog has learned that compromise is the way to go. Compromise yields him the most benefit. His life is safer (greater chance that meetings with new dogs will go smoothly and peacefully; less chance of being wounded in an argument with a dog who turns out to be a human-bred psycho, or who also hasn't learned to compromise; less pointless energy expenditure in general), his inner state is more stable (less anxiety and/or pain), and his well-being is increased (welcomed by other dogs). He is now ready to participate in the domestic canine social system as a mature member. He is a finished and functioning system part.

Not all dogs get the necessary learning experiences.

There are dogs who are taken from their mothers and siblings at the age of seven weeks, and then kept from other dogs. The anxious owners pick up their puppies every time an adult dog approaches. These owners make sure their sweet darling always gets his toy back when some other dog has somehow fairly taken it. They protect the puppy when some other dog growls at him, and discipline all adult dogs who try to interfere with the puppy's behaviour. These puppies never learn what happens if they don't learn to control their impulsive behaviour. Once they are grown up, they still just dive at anything they want, thinking they have a right to take it, even if it is in the personal zone of another dog. They often end up in conflicts about possession.

'Goodness me', says the owner, 'he certainly is a greedy dog'. Meantime yet again taking the toy away from the other dog to give it back to her little, greedy darling. These dogs aren't competitive. They are impulsive, and they never got a chance to learn the rules.

Then there dogs who live with humans who believe in the dominance hierarchy, and who think that they must constantly be dominating their dogs. As they grow up, these dogs learn that the other will never be willing to compromise. Their parent figure is always taking things away from them, chasing them from resting spots, insisting on being the only one to decide about beginning or ending play, about the route to walk, about everything in life. The dog learns that even hinting at a wish of his own makes the other engage in all kinds of threat behaviour or punishing behaviour. These dominating humans punish their dogs for protecting their personal zone during play with other dogs, because the human sees dominance in everything the dog does. He believes that allowing his dog to protect his personal zone from another dog will make his dog think he can dominate the human, too. By his own behaviour, the human teaches his dog that others are competitors and oppressors. He generates great anxiety in the dog about the security of life, and about what will be taken away from the dog next.

By the time this dog is grown up, he can be touchy if another dog approaches, in particular if he happens to have a favourite toy in his personal zone. After all, the dog's owner has taught him that he will never be left in peace with his modest 'enough' (see Myth 14), and that loss is always imminent. But he will not only be touchy about possessions within his personal zone. Because things are constantly taken away from him, and because he is never allowed to express a longing, the dog has too little satisfaction in life. He lives in a state of eternal emotional famine. This is similar to the laboratory situation — the human has artificially heightened the dog's motivation to possess a thing. This artificially heightened motivation can make it difficult for him to resist the impulse to invade another dog's personal zone to get a thing he desperately wants but gets too little of in life.

'Gosh', says the owner, 'he certainly is greedy.' But in the meantime, this owner will punish the dog again, at the very least by taking the longed-for object away from him, thus preventing his dog from finding out that the other *dog* would have been willing to compromise. These dogs are not competitive, they are oppressed, and they suffer a kind of sensory deprivation on the emotional level.

Fact: If you skipped to this myth, then you apparently have a problem with your dog. In that case, someone has either taught your dog that he doesn't have to seek compromise and equilibrium, or else someone has taught him that the other won't. A dog, including your dog, will not be competitive unless humans teach him to be.

WHAT IF YOU ALREADY HAVE THIS PROBLEM WITH YOUR DOG?

This book is not a how-to book, but it can tell you where to go. Jean Donaldson's book, *The Culture Clash*, gives excellent advice on how to retrain your dog so she won't be so touchy about material possessions.

Myth 17: It's unnatural for dogs to have to live in an urban environment.

A lot of people think a dog will be happier in the country than in an urban environment. They reason that a country dog has more space to run free, more time off-leash and more opportunity to do the things dogs do naturally. They picture a dog living a free and interesting life among all the countryside greenery.

This is a romantic idea of what a country dog's life is like. The time is long gone when the farmer used to spend the whole day walking his fields with his dog at his side. Farming is now a highly industrialised business. The countryside is laced with a network of roads that make a free roaming dog's life dangerous (and often very short). The fact is that many farm dogs live a life of loneliness. They are kept tied to a chain or confined to a small yard, sometimes wearing a shock collar that will keep them in this yard. The dog has explored the tiny area she lives in 600,000 times already, and is bored to death. She sees a human when someone comes to feed her, or when her hut is cleaned out (if she has one). She never sees another dog. She lives without company and without anything to occupy her time. The farmer thinks the dog must be happy, since she's outside all day. In fact, you might as well keep a dog on a small balcony in the middle of a metropolis.

A dog is often a little better off with urban dwellers whose house has a yard. She gets to be in the house at least some of the time, where she has company and something to do. But there's a disadvantage to this life, too. When people have a yard, there's the temptation to put the dog in the yard instead of playing with her, giving her some attention or taking her for a walk. She can play out there in the yard, people think. In fact, the dog has explored the yard 600,000 times already, she never sees another dog, and she spends her time there lonely and bored. Or she amuses herself by digging holes, and ends up living at the end of a chain, just like the country dog.

Then there's the urban dweller in a small apartment on the fourth floor. Most of these people do not keep the dog on a small balcony. Many of these people work full-time, leaving the dog to spend a lot of time alone — but that's no different than the country dog or the suburban dog. This urban life has advantages. The city dweller has no choice but to keep the dog in the house, which means dog has company whenever the human is at home. The dog has to be walked several times a day, if only to go to the toilet, so she gets at least this chance to explore new smells. Many city dwellers are aware that a dog should get 'green time', and since they don't have a yard, they regularly take the dog to a park. The dog gets to meet other dogs and play with them, which (besides the enjoyment it provides) keeps her social skills honed. Because the city dweller has no choice but to spend time on the dog, the city dog often has a much better life than the country dog or the suburban dog.

Humans might object to dogs in the city because they opine that there's too much dog crap on the pavement, which insults our aesthetic senses. But this is a different question altogether than whether the dog, herself, suffers from pooping on a pavement. The fact is that the dog's natural environment is anywhere people are. She can do well in any human habitat, depending on what the humans do with her. How many trees are around is not so important.

Fact: The urban dog is often much happier than the dog who lives in a green environment.

Myth 18: Pedigreed dogs are better than mixed-breed mongrels.

Many people still believe that a pedigreed dog is somehow better than a mixed breed mongrel (a.k.a. 'Heinz 57' dogs). These people also believe that man created the dog in the first place. Having read this far, you now know that it was actually Nature that gave us the dog. Or rather, that the dog gave us himself as a present by deciding to join us. We didn't have anything to do with it, aside from inventing the bow and arrow, and later agriculture, thus getting ourselves more food. The dog's ancestor came to our dumps with the whole natural range of his species's genes in his possession. At the dump, a process of natural selection started, which ended up producing an animal who was excellently adapted for living nearby humans. This dog's body was the right size for whatever climate he lived in, how well he needed to be able to conserve heat or get rid of it quickly, and to the local availability of food. He stopped hunting and became a scavenging species. His jaws became smaller and weaker. Aggression dropped out of his behavioural repertory. He developed a social system based on finding compromises, and his sensitivity to social signals and body language enabled him to learn and use the signals of other species than his own in social interactions. In the end, he became an animal who is capable of establishing relationships with strangers of many different species. He was perfectly adapted for sharing human habitats. We didn't have to help him, and we had other things on our minds, anyway.

As our affluence grew, we began to have enough time and resources to start thinking about luxury goods. We turned the dog into one of these. Humans started to select and breed dogs, sometimes for a special task, sometimes for a certain outward appearance. To get the kind of luxury dog we wanted, we had to narrow down his gene pool. We did this by choosing dogs who had, for example, an especially long and narrow snout, or exceptionally long or short legs, and having those dogs mate with each other. In the end, we narrowed some of the gene pools to such an extreme that a whole breed might originate from just a few founder dogs. But even in breeds where we didn't do this, unhealthy genes often crept in and infected the entire breed. Progressive retinal atrophy, various problems with their skeletons (hip dysplasia, unstable knees and elbows, self-fusing vertebra), the extremely short life span of the Great Dane, these are just a few examples of the problems many pure breeds tend to have. Pedigreed dogs are vulnerable because humans have chosen to fool around with their genes.

But it's not just their bodies. In some breeds, humans have also chosen to exaggerate various segments of the ancient hunter's behavioural chain. We've put the stalk > chase back into the Border Collie, scent > track > orient back into the Pointers, and the grab > kill bite back into the pit bull, just to name a few. In doing this, we have limited the behavioural repertory of these breeds. The original dog spent about eighty percent of his day lazing around. The Border Collie can't do this; he has to work, and if you don't let him then he pesters you all day to do something with him. Or he runs down to the local playground and tries to herd the kids there (this is often mistaken for aggression). The Pointer has been so strongly bred for the point that he gets instant tunnel vision when he sights or scents, for example, a bird. These dogs easily develop an ADHD-like restlessness, and many of them have trouble concentrating on anything but a tracking task. The pit bull can't develop relations with other dogs without a fatality resulting sooner or later, and the killing bite surfaces all too often suddenly and at unexpected moments and directs itself at humans. And so on. Each pure breed has not only its own particular hereditary diseases, but also its own particular behavioural peculiarities.

By our breeding practices, we have moved these dogs away from the perfect balance the original dog had found for dealing with us. Sometimes this interferes with the pedigreed dog's happiness, when he's put into an environment where what he needs is more original-dog characteristics. This happens when people choose a dog because they like the external appearance of the breed, but have no use for the specialised breed behaviours. Sometimes this interferes with our human happiness, when what we really wanted was a naturally doggy dog. This is also a result of falling for looks alone, and then discovering to our dismay that you can't have the looks of a breed without also having the — often inconvenient or heartbreaking — breed-specific behaviours.

The mixed-breed mongrel, on the other hand, is either a direct descendant of the original dog, in a line humans have not interfered with, or else he is a mix of two or more human-created breeds. In any case, the mongrels have a broader range of genes than the pedigreed dog. This makes them less vulnerable to hereditary problems and diseases. Their behavioural repertory is broader. Mixed breed dogs are more like the original natural dog, whose only specialisation was the ability to live closely with us. They are more likely to be able to feel happy leading a life as a household pet, and less likely to behave in ways that shock us or drive us crazy. But this doesn't mean they are 'better' than pedigreed dogs. If you want a dog to help you herd sheep, a 'Heinz 57' will be of less use to you than a dog bred specifically for sheep trials. Ditto if you need a dog to help you hunt, or to win bets for you in illegal dog fights.

Fact: Whether a pure bred dog or a mixed-breed mongrel is 'better', depends entirely on what you want from a dog.

Part 2

Puppies

Myth 19: You can use a puppy test to pick the right pup from the litter.

This myth was very popular for quite a while. People thought you could test a puppy and find out what her personality would be like when she grew up. The test consists of several parts. Does the puppy approach you without being coaxed, or does she seem shy? Once she's made your acquaintance, does she follow you around the room, or does she seem totally uninterested in you, despite having smelled your hand? Does she resist when you suspend her in the air on one of your palms, or does she just hang there passively? What does she do if you lay her on her side and won't let her get up? If you throw a wad of paper, does she go get it and bring it back to you? One of the rules was that you had to test a puppy when she was *exactly* seven weeks old. If you were even one day later, then learning would start to influence the outcome of the test, and you wouldn't be testing her innate personality anymore.

And that is the punch line, the reason the whole thing was a load of nonsense to start with.

There is no moment when you can measure a mammal's behaviour free of learning. We now know that learning starts the instant the mammal leaves the womb, and perhaps even before that. When a pup is born, she has inherited the sucking reflex without having to learn it. However, if she doesn't find a nipple and start to suckle within a few minutes, thus supporting the reflex with a learning experience, the reflex will disappear forever. She is born with a reflex to wave her head back and forth, and to crawl in ever broadening circles. This maximises her chances of running into her mother's belly (and the nipples) in time to keep the suckle reflex. Finding the nipple is already a learning experience, teaching her that creeping toward warmth and her mother's smell is a good thing to do. She is also learning, within seconds of being born, to associate the smell of another dog with pleasurable experiences. This is reinforced perhaps a few hours later by the experience of sleeping in the warm pile of siblings. Later, as her ears and eyes open, her muscles slowly develop mass and strength, her milk teeth come in, and play begins with her siblings, she starts to have all kinds of other experiences that will be teaching her about her surroundings and how to interact with them. By the time a puppy is seven weeks old, she has already learned a vast amount. Whether or not she approaches you, or lies there passively in your palm, or lets you pin her down without panicking, will all depend on her learning experiences up to the moment you walked into the room.

In Myths 6, 11 and 12, we have seen that all social skills, even including the use of a dog's body language, are learned. Everything the pup learns ends up anchored in her brain. But at seven weeks, none of it is, as yet, permanently decided, because her brain still has to do eighty percent of its growing. If you put the pup in a different environment (in this case, your own home), she will immediately begin to learn about the new environment and to adapt her reactions to it. This means that the way you treat her will play a big role in how her brain grows, and thus what kind of adult dog she becomes. Not heredity, but you, determine whether or not she will trust humans, whether you are a pleasant or unpleasant factor in her life, whether she understands and willingly complies with your requests, and so on. None of this is written in stone, not even in an adult dog. Behaviour is always generated in and by a back-and-forth process with the environment a mammal lives in. The breed you buy (if you buy a pedigreed dog) will give you a predictor for a number of innate tendencies you can expect, but as for the rest of the dog's personality — the puppy test will only tell you what the pup is like at the moment you give her the test.

Fact: A puppy test doesn't predict the future. The best way to know what kind of grown-up dog you are going to end up with is to take an honest look at yourself.

P.S. And by the way, the puppy test is also an experience she will learn from, so if you are determined to do such a test, at least try to do it in such a way that you don't traumatise the pup!

Myth 20: The primary socialisation period lasts exactly twelve weeks.

Once upon a time (in the late fifties/early sixties), there was a very famous research project about the behaviour of dogs. This famous research showed that there is a certain predictable pattern in the development of a puppy's behaviour. It turned out that a pup does not show a fear reaction to new things he runs into before the end of his sixth week of life. During the seventh week, the fear reaction begins to show up, but it takes some time to develop. It isn't until the end of the twelfth week that cautiousness for new things overshadows the pup's innocent openness, and his tendency to be inquisitive and explore. This is the moment when he starts to be scared of and avoid novel things.

The researchers thought there was an evolutionary logic behind this. After all, the puppy stays within the nesting area in the first six weeks, which area his mother won't allow enemies to enter. In his seventh week, the puppy is physically developed enough that he begins to wander somewhat further — so Nature (or, if you like, evolution) made sure he would, from this moment, begin to be ever more careful. Nature did this by causing the fear reaction to awaken at precisely this stage of the puppy's life, reaching completion at twelve weeks, when the pup is big enough to start making real excursions into the big, bad world.

Up to here, the story is valid. However, people once again engaged in sloppy reading, and the nuances the researchers had written down got lost. This story is now passed on as if the pup has a sort of switch in his head that is either 'on' or 'off', with nothing in between. We are told that the switch turns off at *precisely* twelve weeks. If he hasn't learned to deal with the vacuum cleaner by then, well, forget it.

In fact, this research showed that dealing with new things *slowly* gets scarier for the puppy after his sixth week, with the scales tipping at twelve weeks. However, twelve weeks is nothing more than a general average the researchers found. And this average applied to pups who lived in an impoverished research environment, to boot. It wasn't as bad as a laboratory cage, but it was not full of all the stimuli and experiences your own puppy will be having in your home, either. The researchers also did not describe this average as an on-off switch, but as a moment when the emotional seesaw has passed the balancing point and gradually begins to tip toward the other side. And as we all know, we can easily influence the movement of a seesaw by loading things on one end or the other, keeping it in balance for a much longer time.

The primary socialisation period is, according to this famous but misquoted research, easy to stretch out at least to the end of a puppy's sixteenth week. You do this by acting gently and with wisdom. You can't just suddenly turn on the vacuum cleaner and begin to do the carpet at a furious pace. If you do that, you throw a concrete block on the 'fear' side of the seesaw. What you *can* do is store the vacuum cleaner in the middle of the living room for a while, so the older puppy can explore it as a silent, stationary object, and get used to its shape and smell. Once he's done that, you can practice turning the thing on for a sec (just a sec!), after which the pup can explore the machine again and find out it's still not dangerous even though it just made such an awful noise. After a while, he won't experience the noise as a sign of possible danger anymore. You separately practise acting like you're vacuuming (with the machine turned off), so the puppy can get used to the fact that the thing moves around sometimes. After a while, the puppy will know that it's still the same old non-dangerous object, even if it does move. Finally, you test how far he is by doing five seconds of real vacuuming. By doing it this way, you stack aspects of the vacuum one by one on the 'safe' side of the emotional seesaw for your puppy. Allowed to get used to each property of the vacuum cleaner one at a time, he will be able to deal with the whole conglomeration in the end, and to stay relaxed when you vacuum the living room.

The same goes for a busy shopping area. You take your older puppy/young dog for walks in the shopping street early in the morning, before it gets busy (property: place). At the same time, you gradually get him used to music in your living room, starting with the volume very low and slowly progressing to very loud (property: loud noise). Later, you can take him to the shopping area when people are starting to show up to shop (property: bustle). In the end, he will be able to deal with a busy street. The same goes for visitors in your home. You don't just dump the puppy in the middle of a crowded, noisy birthday party. First you get him used to one visitor, who just so happens to have dog treats in his pocket (property: strange humans). Then you get the puppy used to two, then three, then six visitors, who all treat him kindly just like the first one did (property: large numbers of strange people). You gradually get him used to loud music in the living room when no one is around (property: loud noise). Eventually, he will be able to deal with a party (as long as it's not the kind of party that would scare any dog out of his wits).

This procedure is applicable to all kinds of things in life.

Fact: The primary socialisation period is, in fact, a product of the growth of the puppy's brain. If you have ended up with an older puppy, don't despair. His brain doesn't suddenly stop growing at the end of his twelfth week. If you are willing to act intelligently and kindly, you can make sure his brain still learns to deal with new things, still growing the right neural connections after his twelfth week without connecting it all up to the fear areas of his brain. All you need to do is patiently put him through a series of habituation exercises, watch his reactions and take it slow enough that he doesn't feel afraid at any step along the way.

Coppinger, R, Coppinger, L, *Dogs: a startling new understanding of canine origin, behaviour, and evolution*, Scribner, New York, 2001.

Scott, JP, Fuller, JL, *Genetics and the Social Behaviour of the Dog,* University of Chicago Press, Chicago IL, 1974 (published in 1965 as *Dog Behaviour: The Genetic Basis*).

Myth 21: My puppy absolutely must be kept away from other dogs until his vaccinations are complete.

This is a myth because it is an oversimplification of a delicate question. It's neither an absolute truth nor an absolute falsehood. Rather, it is a question you need to evaluate on the basis of your particular situation. A wise decision will depend on where you live, whether there's a disease going around, and how many of the people in your neighbourhood (or at your park) keep their adult dogs' vaccinations current.

Here are the facts you need to weigh:

1) The primary socialisation period lasts about twelve to sixteen weeks. The pup isn't much afraid of new things during this period. She will, later in life, experience everything she is exposed to during this period as a normal part of life and the universe: the vacuum cleaner, the bustle of traffic or a busy street, fireworks — as long as her first exposure isn't traumatic. In Myth 20, we saw that the primary socialisation period can be stretched. However, this is a phase in which your puppy is learning a lot more than just staying relaxed while you vacuum. This is the time when adult dogs will be teaching your puppy to prefer peaceful compromise to the use of aggression and helping her practice her body language and other methods for reaching these compromises. If we want these skills to become firmly anchored in her growing brain, it's important to expose our puppies to socially skilled adult dogs as early as possible. While she's very small, socially skilled adult dogs will not enter into a real conflict with a puppy, but will limit themselves to behaviour that amounts to parental guidance. This can sometimes look harsh to us, but the risk of a puppy being wounded or traumatised is minimal. By the time a pup has had her third and last vaccination, the period of being indulged is already starting to pass. Adult dogs will expect her to have learned one thing and another already, just by virtue of her age, and they can react more angrily to a lack of social manners. They still won't hurt her, but the heatedness of their responses can be traumatic for an older puppy who has never been with an adult before. Because her first experiences are scary, the puppy can end up being socially insecure for the rest of her life. She can even become anti-social. This means that her well-being will be permanently diminished, and it can cause much sadness and trouble for her owner.

2) Some canine diseases can cause permanent damage, while others are fatal. You do have to take the risk of disease seriously. At the same time, you can't get a disease unless you are exposed to the bacteria or virus. For example, we won't get cholera from a fly on our food, because there are no cholera bacteria around for the fly to pick up — at least, not an American or British fly. So none of us go get cholera vaccinations, unless we are planning to travel to a country where there is cholera, or unless our neighbours came back from their world tour with cholera. Your pup is not at high risk for getting a disease unless the disease is already present in the places you take her. The best person to consult about this is your vet, who should know which diseases are cropping up in the area you live in. If there are dogs coming in with the diseases we vaccinate for, then you should indeed isolate your pup until she is well protected, and let the primary socialisation period pass. As we saw in Myth 20, it is possible to recoup the necessary experiences for her later,

though it will be a bit more work. You will then have to go look for dogs close to her own size, so her first experiences with adult dogs won't be overwhelmingly frightening if she gets some reprimands from them.

3) Adult dogs whose vaccinations are kept current have antibodies in their bloodstream. When they are exposed to a disease, their bodies quickly clean up the virus or bacteria. There is much less risk that a vaccinated dog will transmit a disease to another dog. This gives us another alternative for our very young puppies. We can choose to let them play with a select group of dogs who we are sure are vaccinated.

Veterinarians are trained (and obligated) to care above all for your dog's physical health. This is why they often advise us to isolate a puppy until her vaccinations are complete. However, we also have an obligation to care for our pups' mental health and social well-being. If you take the trouble to get more detailed information from your vet, you will be able to weigh the risks and make a good decision without being guided only by fear. But before you do this, read our next myth, too.

Myth 22: No matter what, I have to make sure my puppy is exposed to other dogs during his first twelve weeks.

Just as the vet will think above all of your puppy's physical health, many a trainer or animal behavioural therapist will tend to concentrate only on your pup's mental and social development. There is a risk that you will be advised to expose your puppy to adult dogs *no matter what* before he is at the end of his twelfth week. A professional blind spot is the word here.

The first twelve to sixteen weeks of your puppy's life are very important for learning things he will need for the rest of his life. But mind and body are in fact an integral whole — you can't have one without the other. What we need to do is find a balance in taking care of both.

It would be an exaggeration if you were to get yearly cholera and yellow fever vaccinations while never leaving the European continent, and otherwise to avoid all contact with other humans. But on the other hand, it would be a form of insanity to travel to a cholera or yellow fever area without getting the shots first. It would also be unhealthy to visit your neighbours, who just came back infected from a cholera or yellow fever country without some kind of protection. If a canine disease is going around in your city or neighbourhood, or even if a case has recently occurred, then the best thing is to limit your puppy's contact with other dogs. Your vet can tell you whether it is safe to let your puppy play with vaccinated adults, or whether it's better to isolate her completely for the moment.

The diseases we vaccinate dogs for are all serious to fatal. Many are viruses and can't be cured with medicines. You can't ignore the need for protection, no matter what your trainer or dog psychologist says. After all, you can't socialise a dead puppy. Instead of just blindly doing one thing or another, the best thing is to consult with your vet, and to make a well-informed decision about balancing the care for both your puppy's physical and mental health.

Myth 23: You housetrain a pup by rubbing his nose in it when he has an accident in the house.

This is an old-fashioned myth that many of us are brought up with. Many people know better at this point, but many well meaning people do still believe in this myth. Since I still run into it very often, I have to mention it in this book — for the sake of puppies.

Dogs (and cats) have a natural tendency not to dirty their core living area — the places where they play, sleep and eat. This natural protection against the transmission of disease and parasites is already present at birth. In the first four weeks of his life, a pup can't relieve himself until his mother pushes him onto his back and begins to lick his groin. This massage stimulates the bladder and colon to empty themselves, and the mother consumes what they produce, thus keeping the nest clean. The pup isn't able to relieve himself independently until the end of his fourth week, when he's become strong enough to crawl away from the sleeping area to do so. From this point on, the pups start to deposit their waste further and further away from the nest they sleep and play in. For the rest of his life, an adult dog will not dirty his sleeping area (unless he is confined and ends up with no other choice).

This doesn't mean the pup will know he's not supposed to poop anywhere in your whole house. The house looks huge to him, with places everyone lives in and places no one spends time in. This is the reason why most pups will look for a spot at the edge of the room or in a corner somewhere — in his innocent puppy mind, he is following the rule of not dirtying the central living space. So he is acting in good faith, and before you get angry with him, please try to solve the following riddle:

> You are on holiday in Russia, and you have just been to the toilet in your hotel's lobby. You are on your way out of the lobby. The cleaning lady runs after you, grabs your sleeve, and starts yelling at you in Russian. Everyone is staring at you as the angry cleaning lady leads you back to the bathroom. Once there, she stands there talking angrily at you and gesturing at the toilet cubicle you just used. You have obviously done something wrong. Was it the empty roll of toilet paper you failed to replace? Was it the light you didn't turn off? Did you perhaps leave brown stripes behind, or were you supposed to use some other cubicle altogether? Before you look at the answer at the end of this chapter, think about how this would make you feel. You meant no harm, and you do your best (next time replacing the empty roll or turning out the light, and using a different cubicle each time you go), yet this keeps happening to you every time you use the bathroom. You just can't figure out what mistake it is you're making. In the end, you become afraid to use the bathroom in the hotel at all, or you try to do so only when you've checked to see that the cleaning lady isn't around.
>
> Once you've let it sink in how this would make you feel, you are allowed to look at the answer on the following page.

A pup means well, but he needs our help to know what we want him to do (it's no use yelling at him in what is, to him, Russian). What you need to do is carry him outside frequently, so he gets the opportunity to do the right thing. When he does do the right thing in the right place, you reward him instantly with some delicious titbit and lots of squeaky-voiced praise. Besides taking him out about every two hours, you also need to carry him outside an extra time just after he eats, when he's just woken up from a nap, and just after a session of enthusiastic play (these are moments when most pups will suddenly feel a need to go). If he has an accident in the house, the best thing is to ignore it. Rather than getting angry with him, just clean it up — and see it as a learning experience for yourself, that you need to be more alert to the signs that he's feeling the need. When you can't keep an eye on him (not to punish a mistake, but to see his signals and help him do the right thing before it's too late and he loses it), you can confine him to his sleeping area — his crate, or a large cardboard box he can't climb out of. He will do his best to hold it, reluctant to dirty an area just big enough for him to lie down in. But don't leave him there too long, because if he is forced to dirty this tiny area and then lie in it, he will start losing the natural tendency to try to keep the living area clean! Our intention here is to help him avoid mistakes, and to be able to reward the right thing as frequently as possible. If you do this, it won't take more than two or three weeks for him to understand where he's supposed to go.

But we aren't finished yet. Knowing where he's supposed to go is one thing, always being able to do it that way is another. A puppy's sphincters aren't fully developed yet. He won't always have the strength it takes to hold himself. His brain is also still growing, including the parts that control the sphincters. To his dismay, the pup finds that his body sometimes does what it will, and that he can't hold it no matter how hard he tries. A lot of pups make it through the day all right, when they're taken out every few hours, but still aren't able to hold it all night yet. He may start to squeak or squeal in the middle of the night. Try not to get irritated. Remember that he's small and helpless, he can't get out of the box, can't open the front door himself, his body can't hold it so long yet, and he is asking for your help *so he can do what you want him to do.* Again, if you force him to dirty the area he sleeps in, you may be creating a dog that will never be housetrained, because his growing brain will be storing the wrong signals. So help him, even in the middle of the night. It won't be forever. Within another week or two he'll be able to get through the night, and by the time he's three months old, you'll have the Totally Housetrained Pup.

Fact: When you punish a pup for accidents in the house, you're actually punishing him for being small and helpless. Never forget that your puppy is a baby, and that he genuinely does want to do the right thing. He needs our help, and doesn't deserve our anger.

Answer to the riddle: I bet you couldn't guess this one. In Russia, no one flushes toilet paper down the toilet because this tends to block the generally ancient plumbing. The cleaning lady knows you did it wrong because (if everyone is lucky) the paper doesn't go down after the first flush. It floats around in the hole a while first. Toilet paper *must* be deposited in the wastepaper basket next to the pot. It's considered bad manners and very inconsiderate to do it any other way.

Myth 24: You can tell which puppy is the dominant one by putting a bone between them and watching which of the two pups gets possession of it.

Scientists seem to just love this one. They believe, quite strangely, that they can find something out about dogs and their social relations by creating a totally artificial situation and then watching what happens. When one of the two puppies ends up with the bone, the scientist thinks he has discovered a property in the puppy. When the pups do (or maybe don't) engage in this forced competition for a bone, the scientist hollers 'Eureka!' and thinks he has discovered something about how dogs organise their social groups.

In fact, the whole situation is an artificial human creation, and the result of this experiment says absolutely nothing about either of the pups or about dogs in general. Let's look at the facts.

First of all, the experimenters never tell us about the puppies' socialisation history. Of course not. If you want to keep up the pretence that you are exploring innate qualities, you have to avoid talking about learning (and hope no one notices), because admitting that learning is relevant would invalidate your experiment before you even get started.

But learning is relevant, which brings us to the second fact. The puppies live in an impoverished environment — the laboratory. If you present an interesting new stimulus in such an impoverished environment, both the animal's motivation to explore it and his emotions will be artificially heightened. Because of this, you will observe atypical behaviour.

Laboratory dogs are generally housed in separate cages. They are occasionally placed together for an experiment. So we are talking about dogs who don't know each other very well, and who will each feel unsure of what the other will do. We are also talking about dogs whose social skills are not well maintained, due to living in isolation most of the time. If you put two such dogs together, you will observe social *dis*organisation. If the dogs are puppies, then you are talking about young, highly impulsive creatures, whose social skills wouldn't be developed yet even in a natural environment. Their behaviour will be an expression of impulsiveness and lack of social skills, and of a need to explore, try things out, and experiment with behaviour. You will not be seeing any innate qualities, but rather observing a learning process. And you most certainly won't be finding anything out about the social organisation of adult dogs.

So we create an artificial situation, and place two atypical dogs in it, who both live in a permanent state of deprivation. The dogs are bored to death, they may never have seen each other before, we know nothing about their life history, and there is only one bone. The fourth, very sad (and devious) fact is that the puppies are often starved for a while before they are put together with the bone, to make sure they will engage in a conflict about it.

In fact, the whole idea is utterly ridiculous and — if we're honest — unscientific. You could just as well draw conclusions about human beings by watching us only during famines and wars, and omitting to observe or mention human societies that simply function. Or you could just as well take two starving humans whose life history you don't know, place them at a table with one plate of food, and then declare you have discovered innate qualities in them, and that you now know how humans organise their societies. Or watch a couple of two-year-olds arguing over a toy, and declare that you now know how our Western democracies work.

The studies of dogs in their natural surroundings all show that dogs normally will not engage in this kind of conflict with each other. Most dogs prefer keeping the peaceful relationship to fighting over a bone. You have to create an artificial situation, and then also refuse to consider the dogs' histories, if you want to pretend you have discovered something called 'dominance' in a dog. In fact, 'dominance' is a human projection. Humans may go to great lengths to create situations in which dogs will exhibit somewhat human competitive behaviour, but this is a human construction — an artefact. It doesn't help us understand canine behaviour.

Fact: The Two Puppies With a Bone test is a complete waste of time, and it tells you absolutely nothing about either pup's future personality.

Myth 25: You can teach puppies to share with each other by making them eat together out of one bowl.

This is a myth that some (lazy?) breeders like to believe in. This myth is not only incorrect, it can also be damaging.

One of dogs' basic social rules is, 'We enter each other's personal zone only with permission.' There is also the subsidiary rule: 'You're allowed to keep what you have in that zone.' Socially skilled adult dogs don't normally take things from each other by force. If it's in your zone, it's yours until you relinquish it. These rules are not instinctive or innate. Dogs have to learn them. Puppies generally learn these rules with great ease. This learning starts the moment the pup is born. Each pup finds a nipple on Mum's belly, and gets all absorbed in eating his meal. If another pup comes along and displaces him, the pup finds another nipple just a couple inches away. Once the pups are big enough to accompany Mum to the dump, they find that food is spread about everywhere. They don't need to steal from each other to survive. (Remember this: the biggest causes of death among free-living dogs are cars, parasites, and being shot, poisoned, or otherwise killed by humans — not starvation.) Given the puppy mortality rate (between fifty and ninety-five percent), they are outnumbered by adults, who will teach them about social distances right from the start. The seed is planted for peaceful social interactions even in the presence of food, for willingness to compromise, and for the willingness to respect the other dog's personal zone.

If we make the puppies in our household eat from one bowl together, we disturb this natural learning process. We create a situation in which the pups do have to compete, one in which they do have to take food from each other in order to eat at all. We force them to enter each other's personal zone without permission and take what the other has in order to survive. While they are very small, they might not notice this, because they all fit easily around the bowl at once. However, once they get big enough that it gets hard to fit all their heads in the bowl at the same time, then eating starts to become a kind of war. This situation lays the foundation for two serious problems later in life.

First, there will be a problem with other dogs. The pup learns, at the shared food bowl, *not* to respect the other's personal zone. He *must* push into the other's personal zone in order to eat — i.e. to keep from dying. The other puppies have to do the same. The fact that there's only one bowl makes compromise impossible. Because the puppy's brain is growing its basic structures and neural connections now, he will also be forming his basic orientation in life. He will end up oriented to competition instead of compromise. He will not hesitate to enter the other's personal zone if there's something there he wants. He will expect the other to do the same to him. As an adult, this dog will be constantly getting into unnecessary conflicts — either because he pushes into the other dog's space and meets resistance, or because he's paranoid the other dog will and lashes out in advance. The poor customer who bought the pup doesn't know the breeder believed in this myth, and ends up wondering what he did to deserve such a difficult dog.

Second, there may well also be a problem with humans. The puppy learns, at the shared food bowl, that the presence of others while he eats forms a threat to getting enough sustenance. The activity 'eating' ends up anchored in the pup's brain as a stressed and competitive business, a fight for physical survival. Someone else around while he eats becomes a learned signal that loss is imminent. And the anticipation of losing a necessary life resource arouses aggression. The puppy will be in an aggressive mood around food, because food is associated with the need to compete with others and with a fear of loss. This dog will, as an adult, remain tense and sensitive when he's eating. He may defend his food fiercely against anyone who happens to walk by. This behaviour tends to expand itself to inedible objects because the dog is constantly worried about his personal zone. He growls about a sock he happens to be lying near, or a Kleenex someone left on the floor, and his human is totally baffled. He wonders what caused this behaviour, and why the dog lashes out at him about a sock, since he's never taken anything away from the dog.

Fact: It is a big mistake to make pups eat together from one shared food bowl. They won't learn to share the way we want our children to, quite the contrary.

P.S. If the pups eat from separate bowls, you can monitor whether each is getting enough to eat and whether one of them is off her food for some reason.

Note: Always watch how the breeder feeds the pups before you decide to buy one.

See also: Myth 88 about how to feed puppies safely.

Possession and the personal zone: Touchy dogs

Socially skilled adult dogs normally don't take things away from each other by force. However, we've all seen dogs at dog parks who don't seem to know this rule. The ball a dog's owner brought to the park rolls away a good distance and ends up outside his personal zone. Some other dog grabs the ball and runs off with it. Or the dog's owner throws the ball and a second dog manages to speed in and get to the ball way before the first dog has dog-legal possession. In both cases the first dog pursues this second dog, very angry, determined to get his ball back, if need be by force. This can be very surprising to the second dog, who does know the rules and resists having them broken. It can lead to quite upsetting-looking fights. What is going on?

In my experience, dogs who do this have inadvertently been taught to do so by their owners. Put more precisely, their owners have prevented them from learning and accepting this dog rule. The human takes a ball to the park and is, herself, possessive about the ball. After all, it cost her two pounds and a trip to the shops, and she brought it to play with her own puppy. When another dog manages to get hold of the ball fair and square, according to the dog rules, this human goes over to the other dog, takes the ball back, and gives it back to her pup. She does this every time the pup loses possession of the ball. She also does this if the puppy loses a stick he was playing with. After all, it was his stick, and it's so unfair that the bigger dog grabbed it just because the pup can't run so fast yet. This human taking things back from another dog is step one, where the pup learns that he always gets his ball, toy or stick back. Step one also means the pup never learns to deal cheerfully with the frustration of losing the object fair and square, or to seek some peaceful and dog-legal means of regaining possession.

Step two is that the other dog is quite surprised to have something taken out of his dog-legal possession just like that. He looks around in amazement and sees that the pup now has it. The dog's brain isn't complex enough to understand that this is the human's fault and that the pup doesn't know any better. Very likely he will jump all over the pup for the pup's lack of manners. Normally, if the pup had gone to try to get the thing back himself, he would have got a warning not to approach too close, and certainly not without all kinds of signals that he wasn't considering theft. The pup would have been able to avoid a whacking. As it is, his owner returned the item to him, so he is back in possession and thinks this is okay. He is very surprised when the adult dog suddenly jumps all over him. His brain is not complex enough to understand the human behaviour that led up to this, nor what the adult dog is thinking. He doesn't know the chance to be warned about theft was taken away — skipped — due to his owner's actions. As a result, he learns that other dogs jump all over him without warning when he has something.

Step three is that this same owner is concerned about her image in the eyes of other humans at the park. When her puppy gains possession of another dog's object fair and square, she marches over and takes it away from him. She gives it back to the other dog. After all, this is the only way not to look like she's favouring her puppy above others by insisting on her own £2 ball — and to keep from looking like a molly-coddler total cheapskate. Again, with their non-complex brains, dogs don't understand this. The pup just sees that now the other dog suddenly has the item without any kind of social interchange having taken place, again a skipped step. His owner took something away from him and now it's suddenly over there. He misses the experience of being allowed to keep what he has. He has no way of knowing this isn't the other dog's doing somehow.

By the time this pup is grown up, he expects other dogs to jump all over him any moment when he has an object. He also thinks the object can disappear suddenly, materialising in the other's mouth. He doesn't know how to get it back. He has no idea he's supposed to let the other dog keep an object. Touchy already while he has the object, frustrated when the other gets it, unaware of the rules, this is the dog who seeks conflict when another dog takes his object fair and square.

Puppies

Adult dogs do sometimes take things away from a puppy by growling and staring at the pup, making her move away and relinquish the object. Sometimes an adult dog will make a puppy move away from her food bowl. Not all adult dogs do this. The objects they do it with vary. They won't do it all the time, just occasionally. This seems to be a kind of bullying, but it also seems to be part of the parenting process (production of functioning, non-aggressive system parts). I have seen many adult dogs bully a puppy this way several times, then leave the pup alone after that — as if the adult is satisfied the pup will avoid conflict, so now she can keep what she has.

There seems to be a moment in a pup's life when the pup decides the grown up rules apply to her too, and she doesn't have to take it anymore. As far as I can tell, this is a fairly reliable behavioural indication of the onset of adolescence. The pup (who is now five or six months) starts to growl when an adult dog approaches while she chews on her ball or while she eats. She may suddenly lash out if the adult dog grabs the ball they were both chasing right out from under her nose for the millionth time (which she never got annoyed about before). She air-snaps, or she symbolically jumps all over the other dog (whose size she now nearly equals or even surpasses). Many people are taken aback when this happens. They worry that their always-sweet puppy is undergoing some mysterious change and becoming a fighter. The adult dog can sometimes be amazed too, because the script has suddenly changed. But the adult dog will understand what's going on and will leave this young dog (who has announced that she's no longer a pup) alone in the future, allowing her the respect of the adult dog rules.

Watch out for observing only your own dogs

Some people live with a group of dogs in which one is always taking things away from the others. They conclude that this is normal behaviour. Because their other dogs tolerate it, they think the Grabber must be the dominant dog and the leader. They then think that all dog groups will have a Grabber — that all groups will tolerate having a bully around.

When the Grabber gets out into the wider world, he is suddenly having arguments with lots of other dogs in the park. His behaviour upsets them. It might scare them. If he's small, he gets jumped on or even chased off the playing field. If the Grabber is a big and pushy dog, other dogs might try to stay as far as they can from him, or even flee the field when he arrives. Big or small, others start to avoid the Grabber or make him avoid them, refusing one way or another to interact with him.

You can't generalise about normal domestic canine social organisation just by watching your own group of dogs, nor in fact by watching any single group that has no choice but to live together, or who pretty much interact only with each other. An isolated group of dogs may arrive at some comfortable or uncomfortable equilibrium, but this doesn't necessarily mean they've done it by universally normal canine means. It doesn't tell you how theirs fits into general canine behaviour. The rules they follow may not be universal rules, nor will those rules necessarily work with strangers. Some of them may be human-generated rules. Other dogs in the world may not know these rules. Before you can draw conclusions about the behaviour of dogs in general, you have to watch many, many dogs interacting. Dogs who do and dogs who don't know each other, who were raised by other people in other situations, and who are free to leave the space if they want or need to.

The best way to know whether a dog's behaviour is normal is to watch how other, well-socialised dogs react to it.

Myth 26: A puppy's personality is inborn. In other words, such things as fearfulness, 'dominance' and 'submissiveness' are genetically determined qualities in a dog.

There is one specific quality that is inborn in a dog — namely, the coherence between mind and body. If a breed had been specifically selected and bred to perform some specific task we want them to perform, this human selection leads to changes in both the brains and the bodies of the dogs. We have, for example, formed the skeleton and the muscles of the Border Collie, so they are slightly different from the skeletons and muscles of other dogs. They are adapted so that they move comfortably in the stalking stance, and easily alternate from lying down to standing up and running, in the wink of an eye. A Border Collie can lie down, stand up, lie down, stand up, all day long, day in, day out, whereas this would exhaust another dog and give him early arthritis. But that's just her body. Her brain (which is the seat of her mind) will inevitably make neural connections to her special skeleton and muscles as it grows, and this brain will develop the structures necessary to deal with her special body. A Border Collie will naturally go into the stalking stance and lie down occasionally while she does it, whether you teach her to do this or not. The Border Collie has also been bred to work with great concentration for long periods of time. The specific structures involved haven't been researched, but the Border Collie's behaviour justifies the suspicion that the parts of the brain that govern concentration and learning ability are different from other dogs'. It may well be that the Border Collie's brain chemistry (the balance of neurotransmitters) is also a bit different. It's not enough to tire a Border Collie our physically. If you want her to be a bearable pet, you also have to tire her out mentally each day. This is, to a large extent, genetically determined.

However, although physically determined primary characteristics can be important, a dog's total personality is something else, and more complicated. Only part of the brain's structures and properties are determined by the genes and by the body the brain grows in. Most of the brain's physical growth (the development of neural connections) takes place in an exchange with the animal's external environment. This is called learning. Personality is the entire collection of characteristics that the dog will develop or acquire in the course of her life, according to the learning experiences she has.

If you keep an eye on what kind of learning experiences your pup has, you can play a huge role in determining how her personality turns out. You can help her brain develop a rich network of neural connections by providing her with an interesting, enriched environment (and by not leaving her home alone all day in a silent, empty house while you go to work). In this enriched and stimulating environment, she'll develop a brain that is easily capable of processing stimuli, thus avoiding both an apathetic and an ADHD personality. You can make sure that connections are not made between certain stimuli and the fear areas of the brain (by getting your pup used to new things gradually and avoiding traumatic experiences). She'll develop a brain that doesn't immediately lead all incoming stimuli along the fear network, thus avoiding a fearful personality. If you don't make her share the food bowl, and don't constantly take food and objects away from her, she won't develop an aggressively competitive attitude in life, thus avoiding an anti-social, uncompromising personality. If you train her with treats instead of with punishment and pain, you create dog who is not afraid to experiment, nor mistrustful of humans — thus shaping a trusting and intelligent personality, ending up with a dog who learns fast and is not quick to get defensive. By keeping an eye on your own behaviour and watching out not to intermittently reward unwanted behaviour, you raise a dog who knows what to expect — thus avoiding a nagger's personality.

Fact: Such qualities as 'dominance' and 'submissiveness' have nothing to do with dog reality. These 'properties' don't exist. They are nothing more than our verbalisation and projection of how *we* feel when our dog does some things, but they don't describe anything that is really going on in the dog. The behaviour in a dog that makes us feel this way isn't genetically determined. It is mostly determined by learning, and the wise dog owner will take advantage of this fact to shape an enjoyable personality in her dog as she grows.

Myth 27: It's better to get a puppy than an adult dog or a shelter dog, because you can raise the puppy to be the dog you want her to be.

It's true that eighty percent of the brain's growth takes place in the first four months of a dog's life. It also true that the experiences a dog has in these first four months will greatly influence how her brain develops. This means that, indeed, the owner of a pup will be able to play a role in forming the brain the dog will be using for the rest of her life.

However, this doesn't mean our own pup will necessarily grow up to be any better than someone else's adult dog. The person who buys a puppy has just as much potential to make big a mess of things as the owners of all those adult dogs whose behaviour you don't like. If you leave your puppy alone all day in an empty, silent house while you are at work, you will be shaping a brain that is not able to handle lots of stimulation from the outside world. You might end up with an ADHD dog, who is unable to concentrate on anything, and who reacts wildly to every stimulus she meets as an adult. You need to take an honest look at your kids. Ask yourself whether they are old enough and have enough self-control to interact kindly with an animal, otherwise they might (without necessarily meaning to) teach your puppy that children are unpleasant or even scary. If you don't know how to housetrain a puppy, or if you believe that you do this by punishing her, you may create one of those dogs who does it quick behind the sofa when no one is looking. People who believe in dominating or punishing dogs all too often create either frightened dogs or aggressive dogs. The list of mistakes we make is long.

Raising a puppy well takes a huge investment of knowledge, patience, and kindness, in addition to loads of time and energy. Don't assume too quickly that you'll do better than anyone else ever did unless you are genuinely prepared to cough up this investment. Our power to mould a puppy doesn't always mean we will mould a pleasant dog. And even if we do succeed in raising a good dog, this doesn't necessarily mean we'll enjoy the two whole years of work it always takes.

There's another fact we need to know before we decide to buy a malleable puppy, namely that a mammal's brain continues to grow and change for the whole of the animal's life. This growth is more limited and goes more slowly in an adult dog than in a puppy, but that's not of crucial importance. A beaten — and therefore aggressive — dog can learn to trust humans again. A fearful dog can conquer her fear with our help. A hyperactive dog can learn to concentrate, to control her impulses, and to react more calmly to things. An adult dog is already housetrained, has already been through her adolescence, and is perhaps old enough that she doesn't absolutely have to get hours of exercise every day. She's been abandoned to a shelter, feels lonely and scared, and is in the mood to be grateful for a new tie with a human. If you teach her your own routine by using rewards and kindness, she will quickly start to adore you. It's an old wives' tale that you can't teach an old dog new tricks. The vast majority of old dogs are perfectly capable of learning, of developing strong new emotional ties, and of becoming just the dog you want. Of course, a lot depends on whether you are willing to learn about how dogs learn, and about the rules they follow as they organise their relations and social groups (see Myth 11).

Finally, it's a myth that shelters are full of dogs with behaviour problems. Quite the contrary. Most dogs are abandoned because their human's situation changed, and not because the dog had a problem. The human has to move, and the new landlord won't allow pets, or the human doesn't want dog hairs in his new house. People get divorced, lose their jobs, or just get tired of having to walk the dog even when it's raining out. Sometimes they decide they just want a new flavour, depending on which breed has recently starred in a hit movie. The large majority of shelter dogs are good dogs, who will quickly adapt to your household routine.

Fact: A puppy isn't always the best choice. It's often much more sensible to get an adult dog.

Myth 28: Commands are the most important thing my puppy will ever learn.

The truth is, the most important things your puppy will ever learn are impulse control and bite inhibition.

We've invented all these myths about dogs being wolves and wolves (thus dogs) living in a kind of fascist system, in which everyone has to do what the higher-up says, and in particular what the creature at the apex of the pyramid says. Others have drawn whirls and swirls and criss-cross lines, still basically drawing a system of bullying (see Myth 15). Having read this far, you now know that dogs are not wolves but dogs, and that they live in complex, highly flexible, self-organising systems, without a central authority, and that their systems are based on building predictability and trust. These dog social systems preserve peace by finding mutually acceptable balances for all participants (see Myth 11). It's not a dictatorship or a bully system, but a complex web of mutually chosen compromises, arrived at one-on-one between all present.

In order to participate in this dog system, a puppy has to learn a number of things. He has to learn to be reticent about using aggression. He has to learn that social peace and companionship are resources to be valued, which he can lose if he impulsively goes for the purely material stuff in life. He has to learn the rules dogs live by (no real aggression, don't approach without permission, and respect each other's preferences where possible). In Myth 12, we saw that dogs' body language is all about expressing and exchanging information about dogs' inner states, so they can take each other's feelings into account as they interact. In Myth 13, we explained how even 'fights' are (normally) actually about trust-building between dogs.

Impulse control is the first, main cornerstone of how the whole thing works. This means that a dog learns not to just follow any old impulse he has, but that he first runs it past the parts of his brain that dampen the impulse and conceive a socially appropriate and acceptable plan of action. This means taking that nanosecond to consider the consequences of an action, and to adjust it accordingly before your muscles even have time to move.

Without impulse control, there is no bite inhibition. And a dog that doesn't (or can't) inhibit his bite can't take part in any canine social system. He's just too dangerous for the others present, too likely to destroy the system by destroying its participants. A dog also needs impulse control to take part in the back-and-forth of signals by which dogs arrive at trust, compromise and social stability. A back-and-forth can only take place, after all, if you're willing to stop and listen to what the other says before doing anything. He needs impulse control as he moves on a field (or any space) where other dogs are, keeping an eye on the individual personal zone each other dog needs to feel okay. You can whizz by within three inches of Patch, but Prince needs three feet, and when Rover has a ball the whizzing dog had better give him three times as much space as when he doesn't. If the whizzer does bump Rover when Rover has a ball, both of them need bite inhibition (thus impulse control) to work out the argument without hurting each other or their relationship. It's impulse control that is behind wanting the ball Rover has, but trying to wheedle it out of him rather than just take it, and behind deciding the friendship is worth more than the ball after all.

You don't have to worry about how to teach your puppy these things, because they are part of learning how to be a dog. Only dogs can teach a pup how to be a dog. So it is of essential importance that you allow your puppy not only to play with other puppies, but also with socially skilled adult dogs. It's essential that you allow the adult dogs to do parenting behaviour with your puppy, which means sometimes giving him a symbolic whacking (see Myth 6).

Now, don't go thinking, 'That's all well and good, but those are things he'll need with other dogs. For life with *me*, the commands are the most important.' Because impulse control and bite inhibition are essential doggy characteristics that make it possible for a dog to live with us. No matter what other obnoxious things you won't mind your dog doing, if he doesn't learn to control his impulses and inhibit his bite, your life with him won't be safe, either. Not all of his behaviour will be dangerous. He'll bounce around the room, reacting to whatever stimuli come in and the impulses they arouse in him. Much of this will be harmless, though annoying. The trouble is, if a conflict arises, he may well impulsively lash out — unable to consider the consequences, unable to wait and watch your own signals first. When he lashes out (even if you just step on his toe on accident), he'll bite too hard — not because he necessarily wants to, but just because he never learned to control it. Even giving him a treat can be dangerous to your fingers and hands.

The third most important thing your puppy will ever learn is trust in human beings. This is something only humans can teach him.

When dogs threaten, they are telling the other party that they feel unsure of his or her intentions. If your pup learns to trust humans — and that means that you and everyone else you allow near him have to behave in a trustworthy way — he won't feel the need to threaten when a person approaches him. Behaving in a trustworthy way means respecting the dog rules. It means not approaching without signalling somehow that you have good intentions, and stopping in your tracks to reassure him if you see your approach is worrying him. It means not taking things away from him and not using violence with him. In a nutshell, it means allowing your pup to feel safe with you and other humans.

A dog who has learned the things I name in this myth will not bite you too hard because you step on his toe by accident. He won't grab your food off your plate and then bite you for objecting. He will incline to be tolerant of various mistakes you make or things you do that bother him. This dog will be looking to preserve the relationship with you and the social peace, keeping the little social system the two of you occupy together stable and safe, and he will be willing to compromise (i.e. sacrifice much) to do so. If for some reason a human does make him very worried about what's coming next, he will use all the warnings he knows to give the human a chance to avoid a direct confrontation. If he lashes out, he will do it reticently, controlled, dosing it exactly according to his estimation of the danger the human presents.

Though it's important to his safety that he eventually learn to come when you call him, and though it's convenient if you can ask him to sit or lie down somewhere and even to stay that way for a while, these things are trivial by comparison.

Fact: What it comes down to is that the most important thing your pup will ever learn is to be a dog according to the rules dogs follow, and that humans will follow these reasonable and peaceful rules, too. The cornerstones are impulse control, bite inhibition and trust in us. Aside from making sure he learns these essential things, you can also teach him a command or two.

How do I know an adult dog is mentally healthy and can safely parent my pup?

It's not always a good idea to just let your round-bellied, lumbering, naïve pup of seven or eight weeks dash up to an unknown dog in a park. He knows nothing about dog politeness yet, and he's not yet physically able to make a quick escape if need be. Some adult dogs are psycho and some owners are in denial about this. If the owner of a dog says it's okay to let the pup approach, do still watch the adult dog's body language yourself. If the owner of a dog does warn you that her dog isn't very good with pups, always take this seriously. Avoid the dog. The best way to find socially skilled dogs is to watch a group of dogs playing. If you see them doing all the things we've talked about so far, playing without more than the occasional carefully resolved argument, then you know you are dealing with dogs who have learned impulse control, bite inhibition and dog rules.

See also: Myths 38-40.

Part 3

Aggression

Myth 29: The domestic dog is a naturally aggressive species.

One reason people believe this myth is because of the romantic idea that the domestic dog descended from the great grey wolf (see Myth 1), which he didn't. We now also know that the domestic dog isn't a hunter, but that he became what he is precisely because he gave up hunting to scavenge our leftovers (see Myth 4). But all these romantic ideas don't die easily. It is now fashionable among biologists to talk about the domestic dog as a 'predator'. What they forget to say when they tell us this is that sheep, tapeworms and mistletoe are also predators. A predator is anything that has to eat from another living being, maybe or maybe not killing it in the process. A predator is not necessarily a hunter. Dogs have to have a certain amount of animal protein, but so does a tapeworm. The dog gets his protein by eating our leftovers, while the tapeworm actually steals stuff we still need right from under our nose. This biological wordgame has brought us right back to the old, false picture of the dog as a killer whose desire to kill is always right there under the surface just dying to get out. This need to feel we have a barely contained killer walking obediently next to us tells us something about ourselves, but it remains a false perception of the dog.

Then there is a second thing that contributes to this myth, namely confusion about what we mean by the word 'aggressive'. Strictly speaking, aggression is some act that is intended to cause harm or pain. In everyday speech, we also use the word for acts that are intended to dominate or intimidate another. We use the word not only for acts that cause physical pain or damage, but we also include behaviour that is intended to cause psychological pain or damage. When we're talking about humans, this broad definition isn't entirely wrong. We are such an aggressive species that when we so much as raise our voices, this is often a real indication that danger is at hand — that we may attack the person we're shouting at. We often fight to the death about things. Our social intercourse is strongly based on competition and domination, so we are often on the offensive and a lot of what we do is indeed aimed at dominating someone. We have complex minds, and are able to damage each other psychologically and emotionally. In the end, we may rightly call much human behaviour aggressive. However, dogs are not human, and it's not fair to project human qualities onto them.

So what is going on with dogs? Dogs are non-human animals. Biologists know and acknowledge that fights to the death between members of the same species are very rare in Nature (as long as you leave us out of the equation). This is because a non-human animal recognises others of his species as a kind of social partners. Dogs are special, because they are able to include us and many other kinds of animals on this list. When they are dealing with social partners, non-human animals usually use only what biologists call 'ritual aggression'. This is a kind of social discourse. The animals simulate a fight, but they aren't actually trying to damage each other. The thing is, if it's social discourse (which it is), it can't simultaneously be aggression. It's one or the other — either an animal is trying to damage his opponent, or he's not, and if he's not, well, it's not aggression. Among dogs, aggression means delivering an uninhibited bite to the other in question, using the full and uninhibited strength of the jaws. Normal dogs rarely do this. In fact, the basic rule of dogs' social interaction is that they will *not* revert to uninhibited biting, even in a very heated argument (see Myth

11). A dog who does use aggression is frightening to other dogs. They think he's insane, and will do their best to avoid him. A dog who reverts to aggression can't be part of any canine social system. Aside from the fact that other dogs avoid him, he will destroy any social system he joins by destroying the other participants.

Let's take a look at what normal dogs really do. If you observe without projecting, and if you understand their language, you see that dogs generally do everything in their power to avoid aggressive encounters. Dogs have an extended warning system they use to tell the other that they are feeling worried and to ask the other to please keep a little distance. We've seen (in Myth 12) that it's not aggression but anxiety that makes a dog use his warning signals (threat signals). We know that the use of anxiety inhibiting medicines greatly decreases threat behaviour in most dogs. Knowing this, we know that biologists make a mistake when they call threat behaviour 'aggressive'. They miss the point that these signals express worry about what the other is going to do. They miss the point that these signals function specifically to give the other lots of time and opportunity to avoid a confrontation. We know that even when the other ignores the signals, and it does come to a confrontation, both dogs use their teeth with great reserve. In fact, they don't use them at all except symbolically. They wave their teeth around, maybe pinch the other dog a little — even a toothless dog is not the least bit at a disadvantage in one of these symbolic 'fights'. It remains easy during the whole affair for one of the dogs to stop the symbolic show of teeth by giving off a subtle signal that he's seen enough and is satisfied that the other dog will follow the non-aggression rule. This signal can be so subtle that we don't see it. To us, it looks like the 'fight' — which wasn't a fight but an exchange of signals in a social discourse — suddenly ended, for no visible reason. We examine our dogs and find not a wound anywhere, or at the worst a small puncture caused by a fang — which is a kind of wound dogs get just as often in rough play, analogous to the child who comes home with a skinned knee after an afternoon of roller skating. We have to conclude the dogs were not being aggressive to each other, no matter how scared the whole thing made us feel.

Before a normal dog 'bites' a human, he also, very reliably, uses his entire warning system to give us the time and plenty of chance to avoid a confrontation. Just because we didn't see it, doesn't mean he didn't do it.

Mistakes start with the fact that we often have no idea how a situation looks or feels to the dog. A dog might be lying in an armchair with a high back and arm rests. It looks comfy to us, and we forget that the dog is — in his own perceptions — lying in a corner without a quick exit. He might be lying on the rug in the middle of the room, and we want to get a book from the shelves behind him. We head for the bookcase, not even thinking about the dog as we focus on the spot we expect the book to be. We don't realise that we are — in the dog's perceptions — suddenly walking straight at him with quite a decisive step, starting to enter his personal zone while he's in a supine position and can't shoot out of our way very quickly. His language isn't our native language, so we often don't see the signals he's sending us (that he's worried about why we're approaching, and to please give him time to stand up and move away). We don't see how long and how hard the dog has tried to avoid a confrontation. It seems to us like he suddenly lashed out. We think he 'bit' without a reason, and that this means he's aggressive 'by nature'. We're so shocked by his lashing out that we don't notice we aren't damaged, and that his 'bite' was only symbolic. Again we fail to understand his native language. All we have is some spit on our sleeve, perhaps the imprint of a tooth on our unbroken skin, or (if the dog was very scared) a small puncture with a bruise developing around it. Our bones and tendons and muscles are all intact. Among dogs, this is all a very clear sign that no damage was intended, and that the bite wasn't in any way meant to be real. To another dog, this *inhibited* bite is a clear sign that the 'biting' dog is, despite his anxiety, trying hard to preserve the peaceful social relationship. We humans totally miss this message. We forget what a dog can do with his teeth if he wants to, we ignore the role our own behaviour plays, and we foolishly call this symbolic, highly controlled gesture 'aggression'.

Strong selection against aggression is woven throughout the domestic dog's origin and entire evolution as a species. If you look at things fairly, you'll see that normal dogs do everything in their power to avoid the use of aggression. Real aggression among domestic dogs is an anomaly. When it does occur, it is not because the dog is a naturally aggressive species. Aggression in dogs is usually a result of human tampering with a breed's genes, or of traumatic experiences a dog has had in his life up to that moment. Many of these traumatic experiences are due to the Nazi myth that we have to be dominating our dogs all the time. This myth leads us to behave in ways that are confusing and frightening to dogs, often leaving them no alternative but to lash out. Bad science has burdened us with a self-fulfilling prophecy that has nothing to do with what dogs actually are.

Fact: The domestic dog is, by nature, anything but an aggressive species.

Please also read: Myth 30, however, because we don't want you drawing the wrong conclusions from the facts about natural, normal dogs.

Coppinger, R, Coppinger, L, *Dogs: a startling new understanding of canine origin, behaviour, and evolution,* Scribner, New York, 2001.

Dunbar, I, Bohnenkamp, G, *Preventing Aggression,* Center for Applied Animal Behaviour, Berkeley CA, 1985 (3rd ed June 1986).

Lockwood, R, The ethology and epidemiology of canine aggression, in Serpell J (ed), *The Domestic Dog: Its Evolution, Behaviour & Interactions with People,* Cambridge University Press, 1994.

Miczek, KA, Weerts, E, Haney, M, Tidey, J, Neurobiological mechanisms controlling aggression: Preclinical developments for pharmacotherapeutic interventions, *Neruosci Biobehav Rev* 18: 97–100, 1994.

Semyonova, A, The social organisation of the domestic dog; a longitudinal study of domestic canine behaviour and the ontogeny of domestic canine social systems, Carriage House Foundation, The Hague, The Netherlands, 2003. www.nonlineardogs.com.

Sidman, M, *Coercion and its Fallout,* Authors Cooperative, Inc, Publishers, Boston, 1989.

Myth 30: There is no such thing as a truly aggressive dog.

It's true that the domestic dog evolved as a species in an environment in which there was strong selection pressure against aggression. Living near humans and their livestock meant that aggression was very bad for a dog's chances of survival. The present day dog is, in general, a non-aggressive creature who does everything she can to avoid aggressive encounters. However, this doesn't mean that no dogs are aggressive by nature. There are definitely dogs who are, and there are a number of reasons for this.

1) In Myth 18, we saw that humans arrived at a point of luxury and boredom in their history, at which point they decided to start fooling around with the dog's genes to make her into a consumer item fit for conspicuous consumption. Now it's also a fact that humans are different from most other animals — but not for the reasons our vanity often leads us to think. The real major difference between us and other animals is that we are especially aggressive. There's no need to go into a long scientific story here, since a week of watching the nine o'clock news is a much easier way for you to check this fact. Some of us actually enjoy a blood bath, but are too cowardly to engage in one ourselves. Some of these cowards believe they can prove their manliness by *watching* a blood bath without batting an eye. Because of our own aggressive nature, we are often frightened of each other. Many of us decided we wanted a legal weapon we could have with us at all times, without having to apply for a permit or getting in trouble with the police. But where do you find a blood bath in the middle of a civilised country, and what kind of weapon can you carry without being prosecuted? The answer was (some 200 years ago already) the fighting dog. Humans began to breed the long lost killing bite back into dogs. They wanted dogs who would tirelessly tear apart a tied-up, de-clawed bear or a bull (who was often de-horned). These humans gave us the English Bull terrier. They wanted dogs who would tear each other apart in an inescapable pit, dogs who wouldn't stop even after the other dog was long dead. These humans gave us the English Staffordshire terrier, and later the pit bull (also known as the American Staffordshire terrier, see Myth 40).

We reached a point when all the activities these dogs were bred for (tearing apart other living animals or each other) were prohibited by law. In England this was in 1911; in the United States it was in the 1920s, though dogfighting remained legal in states whose legislatures were controlled by the Ku Klux Klan. For a long time after that, these dogs became and remained a rarity, kept only by a few men who were very worried about their masculinity. Then, at the end of the twentieth century, we saw the rise of various violent subcultures in our cities, which found their expression in music, certain brand names of clothing, and other consumer items — one of which was the killer dog. These subcultures were popularised by (for example) MTV and TMF. Killer dogs became a fashion item, and are now more widespread than ever before. In our culture of one-upmanship, the more deadly incidents there were with pit bull type dogs, the more people who wanted one. And of course, in our consumer culture, bigger is always better, so it didn't stop at the medium-sized pit bull type dog the rappers sported. In fact, there's a sort of arms race going on, who can breed and possess the biggest, most aggressive breed of dog. We now have the Presa Canaria, the Dogo Argentino, the Fila Brasiliero, the Boerboel, and various other breeds in which the killing bite has been revived, in combination with an ever-larger body and greater mass. The kennel clubs have large commercial interests involved, and pretend that these are dogs like any others. Breeders advertise in covert terms. They praise their dogs as guardians of home and hearth, wary of strangers, courageous, powerful — all of it secret language that indicates that the breed that has been specifically bred for unbridled aggression.

And it's a fact — these dogs are, by nature, always prepared to be highly aggressive. They don't want to avoid aggressive encounters at all, and often look for an excuse to start attacking. These dogs will approach and present a stick or other object as if they are inviting play, and they then begin an all-out attack on the first animal in the area that so much as moves (which animal is all too often a human one). They are renowned for suddenly killing another dog or cat with whom they have lived peacefully for years. Incidents with humans and children show that these dogs have an unpredictable hair trigger (which, if you are lucky, you may never accidentally touch, in which case you might think you have a 'nice' pit bull, American Staffordshire terrier, Presa Canaria, etc.). Once triggered, the attack all too often can't be stopped except by killing the dog.

These dogs were the first ones we created to be aggressive by nature. But there is now a second group of problematic dogs starting to arise: the breeds that are most commonly used as guard dogs and police dogs. These dogs are not only used and trained by police, but also by hobbyists who engage in competitions for points. In their anxiousness to gain points at contests, these hobbyists started to mess around with the breeds they work with. The German Shepherd and the rotweiler are the most common victims of this trend. In some countries, more local breeds have suffered the same fate. Some kennels breed these dogs to be both nervous (the hair trigger) and capable of real aggression.

When we breed dogs for these qualities, we are in fact breeding changes in their brains. Recent research (Peremans 2002) has shown that this artificial selection results in abnormalities in the parts of the brain that govern aggression and impulse control, and in the brain's chemical housekeeping (the neurotransmitters). The breeders make no secret of the fact that they do this. If you buy a dog at a kennel that advertises its dogs for guard and police work, you know you will get a dog that bites soon and doesn't stop until a lot later. Unfortunately, we don't live in a laboratory where our experiments are securely contained. The German Shepherd and the rotweiler are also popular as household pets. Owners don't always know what kind of kennel they are visiting, and kennels don't always care who they sell to. The genetic selection for aggression has ended up leaking into the general population of these breeds, and they are now becoming more generally problematic than one would expect from pet breeds.

The fact that these police dog breeds are so strongly represented in the dog bite statistics is sometimes used to prove that the truly aggressive breeds are no more dangerous than any normal dog. After all, the German Shepherd and the rotweiler are old breeds with a long history as household companions. Serious bite incidents with these dogs are cited in attempts to prove that the all-out aggression of the triggered pit bull (or American Staffordshire terrier, or Presa Canaria, etc.) is perfectly normal canine behaviour. People conveniently forget (or omit to mention) that for at least several decades these breeds have been subject to the same slanted artificial selection that produced the pit bull (etc) in the first place. The increasingly aggressive behaviour of these police dog breeds constitutes, in fact, proof that breeding for aggression most certainly does get you a genetically aggressive, abnormally dangerous dog. These breeds account, together, for almost one hundred percent of serious to fatal dog bite incidents. Eighty percent of serious to fatal attacks (on humans or other dogs) are committed by pit bulls/American Staffordshire terriers and other fighting breeds. The remaining twenty percent is claimed mostly by the breeds that are used for police work.

So the first group of naturally aggressive dogs is the group whose genes we have tampered with, making them less like real dogs and more like ourselves.

2) The domestic dog has been living with us for at least 14,000 years. Our tie with him is so close that we often forget that each of us has to learn, separately and anew, how to raise a dog so that his natural gifts will blossom. We grow up with dogs all around us, and think anyone can raise a dog. Our well-intended ignorance leads us to make some common mistakes. Some of us overprotect our puppy; others use a lot of harsh punishment in raising him. In such cases, one of the following things can happen:

a) The puppy doesn't get to play freely and sufficiently with adult dogs before he loses his milk teeth. He never learns to control and inhibit his bite. He grows up unconscious of how much damage he can inflict with his teeth. These dogs don't bite hard on purpose — they just have no idea. They can also be too quick to bite, because they have missed the education adult dogs would have given them about impulse control and seeking compromises.

b) The harshly punished pup, or the pup whose human is preoccupied with 'dominating' him, grows up learning that humans torture him, and that we display all kinds of other unpredictable and scary behaviour. The dog learns that he has to defend himself against us because we are dangerous and insane. These dogs are aggressive out of self-preservation.

Fact: The domestic dog is a highly non-aggressive species, but this doesn't mean there's no such thing as a truly aggressive dog. Plenty of dogs exist who are, by nature, aggressive, and there are plenty of others who have learned to be aggressive.

Clifton, M, Dog attack deaths and maimings U.S. & Canada September 1982 to November 13, 2006. www.dogbitelaw.com. Accessed May, 2008.

Clifton, M. Cultural differences, Best Friends Animal Society, No More Homeless Pets Forum, March 21, 2005: http://www.bestfriends.org/archives/forums/032105cultures.html#two. Accessed February 2009.

Lockwood, R, The ethology and epidemiology of canine aggression, in Serpell, J, (ed), *The Domestic Dog: Its Evolution, Behaviour & Interactions with People,* Cambridge University Press, 1994.

Peremans, K, *Functional brain imaging of the dog; single photon emission tomography as a research and clinical tool for the investigation of canine brain physiology and pathophysiology,* Universiteit Gent, Faculty of Veterinary Medicine, Gent, 2002.

http://www.uznuclear.ugent.be/research/phd_dissertations/Functional_Brain_LowRes.pdf (Accessed April 2006).

Phillips, K, Esq, www.dogbitelaw.com.

Twining, H, Arluke, A, Patronek, G, Managing stigma of outlaw breeds: A case study of pit bull owners, *Society & Animals,* Vol. 8, No. 1, 1–28, 2001. http://www.psyeta.org/sa/sa8.1/arluke.shtml.

Myth 31: A dog will become aggressive once he's tasted blood.

This myth is the popular attempt to explain a phenomenon that can occur in reality. It does sometimes happen that a dog who bites once ends up biting increasingly often. The trouble with this myth is the cause it points to for this biting behaviour. In fact, the increasing biting has nothing at all to do with the smell or taste of blood. A dog is not a hunter. The smell or taste of blood doesn't arouse her appetite. The truth is that most dogs even refuse to eat raw meat. Rather, the smell of blood tends to arouse a lick reflex, so the dog will clean up and take care of wounds. You often see them do this even if the wound is on another dog (or your hand). So what is really going on?

Animals can't talk. They can't think in abstractions the way we do. An animal looks for successful ways of dealing with her environment by trying things out. It's a process of trial and error. A dog usually tries out some behaviour in response to some stimulus in her environment. If the behaviour she tries gets her some kind of satisfying response from that environment, she'll try it out again next time. The more often it gets her a satisfying response, the more often she'll engage in the behaviour. In the end, she might always show a particular behaviour in the presence of a particular stimulus.

There are various situations in which this process of trial and error can lead to a dog biting more and more often.

1) Anxiety and fear: A dog's first experiment with biting is usually motivated by fear or anxiety. We see this especially in dogs who are raised with a lot of punishment. The human is getting ready to punish his dog again. He doesn't see the dog's calming signals, or doesn't understand them, and doesn't understand that he mustn't continue the punishment for too long. This owner goes on punishing the dog despite all the dog's attempts to calm him, and despite the dog's signals that she is starting to feel real fear. Because the dog's signals don't stop the punishment, the dog starts to feel increasingly frightened of her owner. Now, a dog has to be able to find a way out of an argument, and she has to be able to trust her calming signals to work, otherwise she starts to despair. Comes the day when she sees this angry human coming at her again, knows her signals won't work, and knows there is no way out of the argument. A painful punishment is inevitable. The dog's fear is so great that she lashes out for the first time ever, in a desperate attempt to defend herself from this thing she doesn't understand. Her angry owner is shocked by her reaction, stopped dead in his tracks as he realises the dog could well defend herself against his unfair behaviour, and goes off to the kitchen to put iodine on the scratches on his arm.

The reward the dog gets out of this is anxiety reduction. Anxiety reduction is a powerful reward, and it is one that a dog usually gets by seeing the other relax when she uses her calming signals. Here, however, she is placed in a situation where those calming signals will not get her this reward, since those signals have no influence on the human's punishing behaviour, so she tries something else. It works. This dog will start to bite more and more often when she is scared of someone. Whether she limits herself to inhibited bites will depend on the human's reaction to her fear biting. If we love dogs, and if we don't want the behaviour to worsen, we must recognise that punishment is not the right reaction to this dog. And with this, we come to the second situation in which a dog will start to bite.

2) Fear of death, i.e. self-preservation: If a dog bites because she is cornered and scared, and the human responds by continuing — or worse yet, increasing — the punishment, the dog will start to fear for her life. She may try to flee (and this *is* generally a dog's first reaction), but inside the house or the fenced-in yard she'll eventually end up in a corner with no escape route. Confronted with a punishing owner, and without a way of escaping his wrath, the dog will lash out again — but this time she'll do it much more fiercely. Her physical safety is directly threatened, and she feels that she now has to defend her very life. Once a dog starts to fight in earnest for her life, you are doomed to lose. Never mind the tall tales told by insecure (and lying) men, about how they had that one last life-and-death fight with the dog in the back yard, and never had another problem with her since. One look at them is enough to know they are inventing the whole story. But even if they weren't, the only thing a battle like that would teach the dog is that we have an oppressor's mentality, and that she really and truly does have to fear we will try to kill her.

In a situation like this, where the owner tries to beat down a panicking dog, the dog learns that ordinary biting isn't enough. She learns that she has to aim at inflicting as much serious damage as she can, as fast as she can. Her reward isn't mere anxiety reduction, but the feeling that she is saving her own life. It's not that she likes the smell of blood, it's not wanting her own blood to be spilled and her own life lost. Dogs who have been forced to learn this lesson about human behaviour are very difficult, often impossible, to keep in our communities.

But before we leave this subject, we have to point out that it isn't only beaten dogs who end up as frequent biters. There is a third situation in which a dog can learn to bite more and more often.

3) The spoiled little yappy dog: This is one we've all seen, the small dog who yaps all day long and who bites anytime she is displeased with something. The reason these are so often small dogs is probably because their biting doesn't seem so scary to us. It is easier to ignore (or even to think it's cute for a while), so it may take a while to realise there is a problem. By then, the dog's behaviour may be quite firmly anchored.

These dogs are, as pups, extremely small. They are, therefore, often overly protected against other dogs. The pup ends up missing all the essential lessons other dogs would have taught her. The puppy never learns to control and inhibit her bite, and she never learns about compromising. Comes the moment when the small-dog puppy feels anxiety about what her owner is going to do: 'Is she going to take away my toy?' The puppy tries out what happens if she bites at the extended hand. Her owner thinks this is cute. 'Ha, ha, look at that tiny thing trying to act just like a big dog.' Either the owner takes the toy away anyway, since that biting isn't scary at all. Or she thinks it's so cute that she just lets the dog keep the toy.

In the first case, the puppy learns that humans can't be trusted. They rudely remove things from your personal zone, whether you like it or not. Within a few short months her teeth and jaws have grown, and the owner does start to back off the toy when the dog lashes out. In the end, we get the same result as the second owner who immediately backed off her biting puppy in the first place. Either way, the dog ends up learning that biting is a successful tactic in life. She isn't offered any other learning experience. Eventually she elevates biting to Life

Tactic Number One, to be used in all doubtful situations, and sees biting as the solution in any and every kind of social traffic. These dogs are often difficult to retrain because anxiety doesn't play a role anymore in their biting behaviour. They are perfectly confident that biting is the way to go and are different from fearful dogs, who do have good reason to be glad if we offer them some other solution to use in social traffic.

Even here, punishment is not the answer. If we don't want a dog to learn to bite, the best thing is to make sure she never has to try it out in the first place. Make sure your puppy plays with lots of grown-up dogs, no matter how small she is. Don't protect her from their lessons about controlling her teeth and seeking social compromise. Build your own relationship with your puppy on trust, not dominance. Be sensitive to her signals, no matter how small she is. If you see she feels insecure about what you are going to do, give her time and space to get over her anxiety. Don't take things away from your dog. Do not use physical punishment of any kind in raising her. Make sure you are predictable, and make sure she doesn't have to fear your anger. Again: watch her signals. If you are angry, stop when she uses calming signals, so she will learn that that is the way to go.

Fact: Increasingly aggressive behaviour has nothing to do with the taste of blood.

Myth 32: Eating raw meat makes a dog aggressive.

This myth is related to the previous one, that a dog bites increasingly frequently because 'he's tasted blood'. We've seen that this is a load of nonsense. But what about eating raw meat? Many people believe that this will make a dog more aggressive. Is this true? No. Let's suppose that your dog likes raw meat (which most dogs don't) and that he learns to like the taste of blood. Even so, all he learns is that sometimes there's blood in his food bowl, yummy. He still doesn't suspect that other mammals are, in fact, walking bags of blood.

So let's suppose that one day he bites someone or something and discovers that blood comes out of the creature he's just bitten. Will he now think this is a great way to get yummy blood? No. Biting in a social situation is a very different thing from biting in a food situation. Even if the dog does bite a human or another dog at some point, he still won't confuse us with food. His tendency to bite again next time might increase, but this isn't because he's tasted blood, nor because he eats raw meat. If he bites again, it'll be because he's finding out that biting is an effective way to keep the other out of his personal zone when the normal signals don't work. As we saw in Myth 31, this gets him the powerful reward of anxiety reduction. And we know that rewarded behaviour will tend to increase in probability.

Now let's suppose that one day he catches a rabbit during his walk in the woods. Look back at Myth 5 — your dog doesn't eat the rabbit. He drops it where he caught it once it no longer moves, or he brings it back to you, whole, in his mouth. He might start getting into the habit of chasing (and sometimes catching) rabbits, but this still has nothing to do with the raw meat in his food bowl. To him, the various parts of this behavioural sequence are a game (he no longer knows, as his ancestors did, that the aim of the chain as a whole is food acquisition), and games are just fun to play.

An important fact to consider here is the fact that animals have to *learn* what to see as food. Even wolves can't just switch from hunting deer to hunting moose, for example. In their normal habitat, wolves generally don't suddenly get confronted with a totally different prey species. This only happens when humans have to move the wolves for some reason. When wolves are moved from a deer area to a moose area, they have to *learn* to see the moose as prey (i.e. food). Their human caretakers have to cut moose carcasses open and lay them out for the wolves to find. Eventually, the wolves will associate the shape and smell of a moose with the same kind of innards that they always found (as food) in deer. After that, the wolves have to figure out new hunting techniques to catch the much more dangerous moose. It can take twenty-five years for a group of wolves to become completely adapted to eating a new kind of prey.

Finding a lump of raw meat in his food bowl will not make your dog confuse other mammals with food. If you cut open a rabbit's gut and offer it to your dog many times over, and he turns out to like raw meat, he might start to associate the shape and smell of a rabbit with edibility. Possibly, but only possibly, and only if he hasn't eaten for several days, he might then be willing to expend the energy to catch a rabbit with the real intention of eating it.

Then there's another issue that sometimes comes up. The story goes that eating raw meat means a dog gets too much protein, and that too much protein makes a dog aggressive. It's true that some of the proteins in meat are more easily digestible when the meat is raw. But other proteins are more easily digested when cooked. In fact, this isn't so important anyway. Proteins are chiefly used as building blocks inside the body. Proteins can be used as an energy source, but that only happens when not enough fat and carbohydrates are ingested. The reason for this is that proteins are huge molecules and very difficult for the body to cut up into small enough pieces to use as fuel. They are a rather inefficient source of energy. On the other hand, a dog that eats too much protein (raw or cooked) can become nervous and edgy. This isn't so much a result of the protein as of an imbalanced diet, and is more likely due to the lack of certain vitamins and minerals than to an abundance of proteins. If an edgy dog then bites, this isn't because of raw meat, too much protein, too few vitamins, or anything else along those lines. When my dogs get edgy, they bring me the tennis ball again and again until I get edgy myself — but they'd never dream of biting anyone, because they haven't learned there would ever be any reason to do so. If a dog bites when he's edgy, this is a result of learning experiences in his life, and nothing to do with what he has or hasn't eaten.

Fact: Eating raw meat won't make a dog aggressive. Eating raw meat can, however, be dangerous for other reasons. See Myth 90 to find out what these are.

Myth 33: It's pure luck when a biting dog doesn't inflict serious wounds.

In a park, or in our house, two dogs somehow get into an argument and, when all else fails, they end up 'fighting'. Or a pup is 'attacked' when he 'didn't do anything at all to deserve it.' We jumped heroically into the fray, and we end up thinking we saved one dog from the other. Whether it's the adult dog or the pup, we examine him for wounds and... we don't find any. There are just wet patches on his coat, maybe a scratch somewhere, or in the worst case a tiny puncture wound (usually on the muzzle, where the dogs have been waving their teeth at each other, or on the back of the neck where they pinched a loose fold of skin). Oh, thank heavens, we're so lucky it isn't any worse!

People get 'bitten' by dogs, too. This is because a lot of dogs have very good reason to be worried about what humans will do. We don't speak their language, don't bother to learn it, and we don't see him telling us he needs some distance until he decides we're trustworthy. Or we do something that causes him pain. The dog lashes out, and we see his teeth flashing as they meet our body somewhere, or at least come close. We are shocked and scream out, 'He bit me!' In our upset and hurt feelings, we forget to look at what the dog really did. Either he bit a piece of air close to our body, or he touched our body and refrained from using the full strength of his jaws. He grabs our arm for a sec, maybe he clamps down just a tiny, very controlled little bit, and then immediately lets go again. Then he waits and watches to see what we'll do next — when he could perfectly well just go into full attack if he wanted to. Usually, all we end up with is a wet patch on our clothes. Sometimes there's a tooth-print on our unbroken skin. If we are talking about a tortured dog, there may be a fang hole or two, with a bruise developing around the wound. This is a traumatic experience for us. We think, 'Oh, my heavens, I'm so lucky it isn't any worse!'

The truth is, luck has absolutely nothing to do with it. It's not that you got there in time to save your dog, or that you pulled your arm away quick enough, not at all. What is going on is that *the dog purposely refrained from using his weapons for real.* Normal dogs do not want to have to use aggression. They have a huge aversion to aggression. It scares them to do so, it upsets every single relationship and social system they take part in, and they run the risk of ending up wounded themselves because they are escalating the conflict. If a dog is socialised in a normal way he learns in his youth, before he loses his milk teeth, to exercise precision control over how hard he bites. A dog can aim his teeth with the same precision, and he can move them five times quicker than we can move our hands, without losing accuracy in his aim. Now *that* is a lucky fact of Nature. Your dog bit an eighth of an inch away from your hand or face *on purpose.* Or it was, despite all the growling noises he made while doing so, *on purpose* that he only grabbed your arm for a fraction of a second, and only softly to boot, and then let go. It isn't luck that he didn't wound the other dog or the pup, it's because he was being very careful not to do so. Unless there are huge, multi-coloured bruises, deep wounds in skin, muscle and tendons, that show the dog clamped down hard and/or made a grasping and tearing movement as he bit, we have only a dog who was refraining from using his weapons *on purpose*, because he didn't want to use them.

A dog who refrains from using his weapons for real thinks he is giving off a social signal. He has no idea that we don't understand this signal, and that we will call this a 'bite'. The truth is that even as he lashes out, he is trying to preserve the relationship with the other. He wants go on being friends, which you can't do if you've damaged each other for real. He thinks, as he lashes out symbolically even in an escalating situation, that he is delivering proof that he's trustworthy. It's truly sad that we miss the meaning of it all, and draw the opposite conclusion.

Fact: When a dog bites the air near you or your dog, or when he delivers only an inhibited and symbolic bite, you are dealing with a trustworthy dog who purposely refrains from using his weapons. Luck has nothing to do with it.

Semyonova, A, The social organisation of the domestic dog; a longitudinal study of domestic canine behaviour and the ontogeny of domestic canine social systems, Carriage House Foundation, The Hague, The Netherlands, 2003. www.nonlineardogs.com.

Myth 34: Myth 33 means you can always trust dogs not to inflict serious wounds when they bite.

Before you believe this, please have a look at Myths 30 and 31, and 38–40. There are definitely dogs who do use their weapons without restraint, and who do inflict serious to deadly damage. These dogs are, by definition, abnormal. The proof of this lies a) in the dog's evolutionary origin as a species, and b) in the fact that the great majority of dogs never do use their weapons with the intention of hurting anyone. Dogs who do inflict serious to deadly damage can be divided into four categories:

1) The fighting dog breeds (the pit bull/American Staffordshire terrier, the English Staffordshire terrier, the English Bull terrier, the American Bulldog etc.), who have all been bred to tear apart one or another kind of animal. These dogs have been bred either to fight to the death in the pit, or to tear apart a bear or a bull that was tied to a tree so it couldn't escape, and often whose own weapons had been removed to keep it from defending itself. Since most dogs won't bite unless severely provoked, breeders selected for dogs who would attack unprovoked — and not only that, they wanted dogs who would go on attacking once they started, even though they met no defence, and even after the other dog, the bear or the bull was dead on the ground. These breeds are still used for these purposes all around the world. Don't let anyone tell you that this is past tense, or that these are now household breeds, or worse yet that they have always been household breeds. They are working breeds that are still bred and used for killing purposes.

2) Other breeds (the Presa Canaria, the Dogo Argentino, the Fila Brasiliero, the Boerboel etc), who have been bred to have a sort of general, unbridled aggression not only toward animals, but also toward humans. Some of these breeds (the Dogo Argentino and the Fila Brasiliero) were, in fact, specifically intended to direct this aggression toward humans. According to the breeding tales, they were meant not to catch and return escaped slaves, but to rip these slaves apart on the spot as a lesson to other slaves. In order to make them able to do this, they were bred with a body mass so large as to make resistance futile. This body mass also means that by the age of about four months, they are too large for other dogs to teach them to shun aggression. By the time they are adolescents, it can be lethal for another dog to try to discipline them or teach them anything at all

When you are dealing with a dog from one of these two categories, you are dealing with dogs who have genetic defects. They have been bred to have different brains and different body structures than other, normal dogs. They are also not at all like our romantic wolf, who does hunt and use his weapons for real, but wouldn't think for a second of wasting scarce energy on pointless aggression. These dogs have, in fact, been created in Man's image, ready to destroy just for the joy of destroying, and to enjoy aggression for its own sake, whether it serves any real goal or not. So don't kid yourself, nor let the owner of the pit bull (or Presa, or Dogo) next door kid you either. These dogs may not be triggered for quite a while (or if you're very lucky, all their lives), but if they are, they will inflict maximum damage, if possible killing whatever they happen to be aiming at, and continuing to attack after the target is long dead on the floor. This is the one way in which these dogs are very trustworthy. Now I know that a certain kind of man (and, increasingly, woman) likes to have these dogs in the house, proud to show all the world that s/he's capable of keeping one of these dogs under control, and smiling condescendingly at visitors who are frightened of the 'sweet' pit bull/ Presa/Dogo/etc. However, this sweet dog, who you think is so nice because he smiles the brachiocephalic smile at you all the time, will — once triggered — kill your child without losing that sweet brachiocephalic smile on his face, which you probably won't think looks so sweet anymore.

These two categories are dogs we have genetically designed so that they will not just bite but attack. Because of this, they will quite reliably inflict serious to deadly damage when they are triggered.

3) Then there's the poorly socialised dog. If you don't allow your dog to socialise enough with adult dogs before he loses his milk teeth, or if you protect him too much while he does socialise as a pup, he never learns the lessons about controlling his impulses and inhibiting his bite. These dogs don't always mean to damage anyone. They just have no idea how hard they are biting, nor what they are capable of doing with their teeth. They can, therefore, inflict real damage if they are driven to biting. They can also become casual biters, because they were never taught about preferring compromise, nor how to peacefully negotiate this, nor that you can lose relationships if you don't

4) Finally, we have the tortured dog. Some dogs have had such terrible experiences with other dogs or, more often, with humans that they don't at all feel like keeping the door open for friendship. They've lost all hope that this is possible. The dog feels endangered by the very presence of another dog or a human. All this dog wants is to be left alone. He wants you to leave. Because they are concerned about their own survival, and because they don't care about being able to continue the relationship later, these dogs can inflict serious damage when they bite.

So don't let Myth 33 make you careless, nor make you believe in a Fairytale World of Dogs.

Fact: Some dogs most certainly will inflict great damage when they bite.

Myth 35: When a dog is wagging her tail, it means she's in a friendly mood.

This is a dangerous misunderstanding. This misunderstanding has caused many an unpleasant surprise for some well meaning child or adult who approached a dog who was wagging her tail. As we have seen, dogs use their body language to transmit information about their inner state — their moods, feelings, wishes and intentions. We've also seen that dog language isn't our native language, and that we often don't understand what the dog is saying (or don't even see that she's saying something). Even if we do know a little about their language, we sometimes miss small nuances of meaning.

Tail wagging is a case in point. When a dog wags her tail, it means two things for sure:

1) The dog is excited.
2) The dog is prepared to enter into contact of some kind with the other.

However, neither of these two certainties means that the dog's excitement is a positive or pleasurable excitement, nor that the contact the dog is prepared to enter into will be friendly contact. All our certainties mean is that the dog is excited and will interact with you rather than fleeing.

A dangerously tense dog will wag with her tail lifted up high, above the level of her back and hips. This dog feels unsure about what you're planning to do, and wants you to keep your distance from her. However, her uncertainty about your intentions doesn't mean she's unsure of her ability to force you to back off if you don't voluntarily honour her request. This certainty is what the high wagging tail shows. The tail wags short and sharp, with a tight, quick movement. The dog is standing high on her legs, showing her muscles are tense from adrenaline. She stares you straight in the eye and shows her front teeth to you — although she may just have her lips pushed a little forward, as if she's about to say something. Her ears are directed at you, alert to any sound you might make. She might freeze up (except for that wagging, high tail), and she might lift one of her front feet just a bit off the ground. This dog is ready to enter an interaction with you, with the single intention of making you back off and leave her alone. If you don't freeze up yourself (instantly!) and avert your gaze (thus breaking eye contact), this dog will use her teeth against you. Whether this will be a symbolic bite or true aggression will depend on her experiences in life up to that moment. In other words, it will depend on her estimation of how dangerous humans (including you) are.

Then we have the fearful dog. This dog is tense and insecure, but not at all sure about her ability to make you back off. The fearful dog presses her tail against her buttocks, or she puts it between her legs up against her belly. With the tail in this position, you may still see the point wagging. Again the wag is short, sharp and quick. The dog is crouching somewhat, as if she expects a blow. She turns her head away from you and averts her gaze, but she still watches you tensely from the corner of her eye. She shows the typical 'fear grin' — the corners of her mouth are pulled backward, so she may seem to be smiling. A dog can also do the fear grin with open lips, in which case you see all the teeth, right on back to the molars. Her ears are folded tensely back on her skull. They don't point back and downward as a dog's ears will do in a calming signal, rather they point directly backward to the space behind her head. This dog feels she is cornered without an escape route (being leashed, is, to a dog, the same as being cornered, never forget that). This is why she wags that tail — she is going to have no choice but to enter into contact with you, and is ready to make you pay a price for hurting her. So don't be fooled by the wagging tail. What this dog desperately needs you to do is to stop looking her in the eye, because that scares the heck out of her, and to give her space by backing off.

Then there's the dog who approaches you with a low and relaxed wagging tail, which wags in big, lazy sweeps. Now, this is a socially secure dog who is feeling pleasurable excitement at the idea of interacting with you. This is a dog whose wagging tail shows a willingness to enter into an interaction because she expects people to be friendly and fun. Her ears may be folded back in her neck, telling you she has no evil intentions. They may be up and alert, but she will turn the openings outward as she gets closer to you, indicating her friendliness. She might pant a little (from excitement), thus opening her mouth a tad — but her relaxed lips will naturally drape themselves so that she is not showing her weapons to you. She might look you straight in the eye, but it isn't a stare. Her face is relaxed, her forehead is smooth. When she gets close to you, she might sit down (a calming signal), and you might see only the point of her tail still wagging. But that's okay, since all her other signals are telling you she would just love to get a pet from you.

Fact: If you want to know what a wagging tail means, you have to look at the whole combination of signals the dog is giving off. If you are feeling any doubt at all, don't approach the dog. Don't let your children try to pet her, either. Do not be fooled by a wagging tail alone.

Myth 36: If a dog approaches me and growls, it means he's trying to dominate me.

First review Myths 11, 12 and 13 if you have forgotten them, because to understand what's going on, we have to leave the Nazi Party — and the human mind set in general — behind and keep in mind which function dog signals actually serve.

If a dog wants nothing to do with you (or another dog), he can always use the very simple and easy method of passing you by without seeking contact or even seeming to notice you. If a dog approaches you (or the other dog), this means either that he wants social contact, or that for some reason he feels he has no choice but to deal with you. In Myth 11, we saw that dogs can't share a physical space with another creature until they feel sure they are safe in the company of that other creature. When a dog approaches you and growls as he does so, you know you are dealing with a dog who feels unsure of your intentions and trustworthiness, and unsure whether he's safe with you around. This is usually a dog who has had too few good experiences with humans in his life. He isn't dominant, it's just that his life experience has taught him that he needs to worry about what humans might do. He feels the need to try out your reactions, in the hope that he will find out you obey all the dog social rules (at this point mostly the ones that say 'no aggression' and that you must signal your peaceful intentions with reassuring calming signals).

When he's outdoors, the insecure or worried dog can usually just avoid a stranger. So it's no wonder that approaching and growling happen most often indoors or in a fenced-in yard. A stranger enters the place where all the dog's life necessities are kept. The dog is dependent on this place to stay alive. His home is the one place he absolutely must be able to feel safe. There is also no escape route. He has no choice but to engage and ask for signs that the stranger is not dangerous. He can't relax (that is, his inner state can't return to a comfortable equilibrium) until he's seen such signs.

The dog's threat signals mean that he is worried. When a dog is worried and he can't leave, he will attempt to get the other to give off signals that allow his own inner state to return to equilibrium (e.g. allow adrenaline levels to return to normal). If a person interprets these signals as 'dominance' and threatens back, believing the old myth that you always have to be dominating dogs, the dog will get even more worried. Depending on his experiences with humans so far, the dog might decide to lash out symbolically. But this 'dominate the dog' stuff is dangerous, because the dog who has already had very bad experiences with humans might just go into full attack. After all, you've entered his last bastion against the outside world, and you have him pretty much with his back up against the wall. This dog isn't dominant, he's close to despair.

We don't have to prove our power and authority over this insecure, threatening dog. We can kill dogs whenever we want to, we do it all the time (about 6,000,000 a year in the United States alone). So don't be petty and vain. Give the dog the signals that you aren't dangerous. Ignore him. Avoid eye contact. Freeze up and sit (or stand) still. Ask his human not to punish him or talk angrily to him. This will give the dog the time to realise that you've been in his house for an hour already, and all this time neither you nor the dog's human have done anything unpleasant, scary or cruel.

It's important not to do anything but ignore the dog. Don't get into an interaction with him, not even a nice one. Do not try to offer this dog a treat (see Myth 86). It's not that you risk rewarding growling behaviour, because this dog is too tense to learn anything at all by food rewards. The problem here is that if a dog is this insecure, there's a risk that he has learned to see even a squeaking, food-offering human as dangerous. If he has ever been lured with a nice voice and a treat so his human could get hold of him to punish him, then he might attack you as soon as you put on a nice voice or offer a treat. So ignore him, and avoid eye contact. If you need to use the bathroom, ask his human to please put the dog in another room for a minute (without getting angry at the dog) until you've returned and sat down again. If it's time to go, ask him to do the same until you're out the door and off the property.

Fact: A threatening dog feels unsure about what the other is going to do. You can't solve this problem for him, because his insecurity is the result of a long history and perhaps of the way his own human treats him. But do refrain from getting into petty power contests with the poor dog, while at the same time taking care of your own safety. Don't be angry at the dog, but at the human or humans who taught him we aren't to be trusted.

Myth 37: A watchdog has to be big and scary, and you have to make him aggressive.

The truth is that most of the watchdogs in this world spend their lives either chained up in the area they're supposed to guard, or else in an enclosure, or otherwise behind some kind of fence. How can a confined dog guard our possessions?

The reason they are effective anyway is because most burglars, rapists and other scum are concerned, above all, about their own safety. They would rather not have to steal, rape, or commit their other crime by the use of brute force in a direct confrontation. The burglar wants to get in, gather your valuables, and get out without being noticed. The rapist wants to get the woman to an isolated place where no one will hear her screams. The rapist tries to choose a woman who will be too frightened or passive to put up a fight in the first place, because this is the least risky situation for himself. Most criminals look for ways to commit a crime so that the crime won't even be noticed until it's too late — the thing is done and he is gone, before we've even seen him.

A watchdog doesn't have to be big and scary. In countries where lots of people carry guns (that is, most of the countries in the world), the burglar won't be afraid of a physical confrontation with the dog, anyway. What he *is* afraid of is being noticed by other humans. All a dog needs to do is make a lot of noise, so that everyone's attention is attracted and the intruder has to worry about getting caught. The same goes for the shepherd dogs who live with the herds in developing and/or agrarian countries. The dog doesn't get rid of the leopard, the wolf, the bear or the poacher by hand-to-hand combat, but by making noise. The intruder is interrupted in what he was doing, is worried about all the attention focused on him, and he takes off to look for easier prey.

You don't have to teach your dog to be aggressive for her to react this way. Although it has been proven that dogs don't guard a large territory, they do guard a core resting area, such as a vestibule or a clump of bushes, where they sleep, play and bear young. Your dog might actually try to guard your home (see Myth 9). But even if she doesn't, even if she's used to having visitors and welcoming them, she'll still tell you there's a stranger in your house. You don't have to teach her to do this.

This is because a dog is a creature of habit. A dog likes things to be predictable. She gets used to the fact that visitors come in through the front door, and that you do certain things as you welcome them — greeting them with a smile and maybe a hug, hanging up their coats — and then accompany them to the living room, where everyone sits down and settles in for a visit. If something happens that is different from the usual routine, like a 'visitor' suddenly coming in through a window, or coming in when you're not around, this worries the dog. She'll feel like she can't predict what's going to happen next. And (as we now know) a worried dog barks and growls and gives off all kinds of other threat signals. There's a good chance the burglar will decide to go visit some other address, where the 'alarm' doesn't go off. If you do happen to be at home, and the burglar decides to get into a physical struggle with you, your dog will probably help you without you having to teach her this in advance. Dogs don't like impolite behaviour. They often break up arguments among their own kind or join in on collectively reprimanding an impolite group member. At least, she'll help you if she feels like she's allowed to behave like a dog, and if you haven't raised her with so much punishment that she has learned not to butt her nose into your business no matter what. That your dog comes to your aid is a result of what we call social facilitation; the fact that dogs who know each other tend to join each other in certain behaviour, such as barking, playing, sniffing a certain smell, running — and jumping all over a stranger or group member who disobeys the social rules. Don't forget that even a small dog can bite, thus providing (at the very least) distraction, so that your assailant can't give you his undivided attention.

The same will happen out on the street, if a stranger approaches you. Your dog is extremely sensitive to body language. She'll notice that the situation is unusual, that the stranger's body language is weird (due to his inner adrenal state), that you're tense, that you don't appreciate the stranger's approach. If you're scared she'll see it, and if you get angry, she'll join in. She'll start to bark, attracting the attention of passers-by. If it comes to a fight, she'll be inclined to fight with you.

Fact: Criminals generally look for easy prey. They are concerned about their own safety, and about not getting caught. A dog doesn't have to be big and scary, nor aggressive, to be an excellent watchdog. A little yappy dog is just as effective.

Beck, AM, The ecology of 'feral' and free-roving dogs in Baltimore, Ch 26, in Fox MW (ed), *The Wild Canids,* Van Nostrand Reinhold Co, MY, 1975.

Beck, AM, *The Ecology of Stray Dogs: A Study of Free-ranging Urban Animals,* York Press, Baltimore, 1973.

Brownmiller, S, *Against our will: Men, women and rape,* Bantam Books, NY, 1976.

Coppinger, R, Coppinger, L, *Dogs: a startling new understanding of canine origin, behaviour, and evolution,* Scribner, New York, 2001.

Smith, S, *Fear or Freedom; a woman's options in social survival & physical defence,* Mother Courage Press, WI, 1986.

Myth 38: You can make a pit bull, American Staffordshire terrier, or any other breed that has been specifically bred for aggression, into a sweet dog if only you raise him right.

Despite everything you have read here so far, there are some breeds of dogs who will likely, at some point, get into uncontrolled aggression no matter how you raise them. It's a myth that there's no such thing as a fighting dog, and a myth that aggression is not genetically determined in the aggressive breeds.

There are huge economic interests involved when we talk about these breeds of dogs. The breeders and the various kennel clubs are not inclined to be honest about the kind of dog they have created. They tell us that despite at least two hundred years of careful selection for the willingness to fight to the death, there is no such thing as a fighting dog. On the other hand, where it's to their advantage to do so, they cheerfully claim that all kinds of other breeds most certainly do have genetically determined characteristics that you can rely on if only you buy their puppy. At the moment, there is great social pressure not to speak or write the facts about the breeds of dogs that have been specifically selected for aggressive qualities. Economics, human vanity, male worries about masculinity — they all conspire to make it extremely difficult to get accurate information, and the whole discussion can be confusing to the layman.

Because of this, our present myth is sometimes spoken by people who just don't know any better. They have had good experiences with dogs in general, and they can hardly believe that a dog could be an unpredictable and dangerous creature. In other cases, this myth is spoken by the person who bought a pit bull (or American Staffordshire terrierf, or Presa Canaria, etc.) *because* they are known to be dangerous, and whose vanity is served by belittling those who do fear these dogs. And of course, there are the breeders and the kennel clubs, who are protecting mostly their own financial interests.

So, what are the facts?

Much of a dog's behaviour is, indeed, learned. Not all of a dog's behaviour is inherited or genetically determined. However, there are most definitely specific parts of a working breed's behaviour that are most certainly, incontrovertibly and inevitably determined by the breed's genes. This is a phenomenon that biologists call behavioural conformation. Behavioural conformation is a term used to indicate that there is a hereditary, genetic basis for certain specific elements of a working breed's behaviour. This is how it works. By artificial selection, humans can get a whole breed (that is, a population) of dogs, all of whose members will perform a specific task better than any other dog ever will. This is why they are called working breeds: breeders select dogs who are especially good at some task, never mind what Cruft's thinks of the dogs' appearance. As they select for performance, the dog's body changes — although breeders often have no idea exactly which physical characteristics they're changing as they go along. They often don't realise that they are, by selecting for best performance of a specific task, also selecting for changes in the dogs' brains — again without knowing exactly which changes they're selecting for. In the end, the entire breed ends up with the specialised physical and behavioural characteristics necessary for their task. The entire population is different from other dogs, both in body and in brain. In addition, the breed's brain and body posses a highly specific unity, which unity is dedicated to the equally highly specific task we've thought up for the breed. As the working breed puppy grows, his brain and body will inevitably connect up, so the slightly different brain will be able to steer the slightly different body efficiently in doing the task humans have thought up for the dog. As he does what he's been bred for, it feels comfortable and good and right to the dog. It fits his brain, it fits his body. Breed-specific behavior is internally rewarding — the mere doing of it feels good to the dog. In fact, it's so internally rewarding that external rewards (or punishment) have little power over it.

Let's look at some examples.

The Border Collie has a slightly different body than other dogs, which enables him to easily go into the stalking posture. As he stalks, he 'gives eye' — executing a genetically anchored behaviour pattern of orienting toward a moving object and staring at it while in the stalk stance. The Border Collie will 'clap', moving or swinging his whole body around his head (which stays stationary) to keep 'eye' on the sheep. This is a variation of orienting behaviour that you won't see in other dogs — people have manipulated this breed's genes to get this highly specific behaviour. It is *breed* behaviour, not just individual dog behaviour. The Border Collie also easily switches between standing up and lying down, because his skeleton and muscles are just that bit different from other dogs'. But it's not just his body. The Border Collie's brain is also structured for stalking, giving eye, lying down, standing up — partly due to genetic selection for showing these behaviours, partly because our brains always grow in coordination with the bodies they were born in.

You don't have to teach a Border Collie these special behaviours and attitudes. He just arrives at an age when he spontaneously begins to stalk, give eye, lie down, stand up. You can't keep a Border Collie from executing these behaviours (unless you confine him in a cage where he can hardly move). You can teach him to do these behaviours on command, so that he does them exactly when you want him to. But even so, he will, in his free time, look for or create opportunities to show these behaviours. He might do it with a ball in your living room (which he bumps away himself so he can stalk it, eye it, grab it, lie down, stand up again), or he might do it with the children at the school playground down the street, or with the cat, or with the geese in the park. But he will do it. It is his nature. It feels good because he is exercising his unity of body and mind: he is using his special brain to seek the postures that feel good to his special body. This is self-rewarding behaviour — doing the behaviour is a reward in itself because doing it feels so good. No external reward or training is necessary. If you don't want a dog who does this, then you shouldn't get a Border Collie. They aren't fit to live as household pets, because their minds and bodies have been so strongly bred for a certain kind of work. Most breeders and kennel clubs admit this fact.

The same is true of the Husky. These dogs have a slightly different gait than other dogs, having been bred to pull a sled with great energy efficiency, and at the same time without constantly kicking either the harness or the dog who is harnessed next to them. Huskies have brains and bodies that are oriented to running — they love to run and get great pleasure from the doing itself, without needing any other reason or motivation. You don't have to teach a Husky the special gait, because his brain is oriented to using his special body for the purpose it was meant for. As his brain, skeleton and muscles mature, the Husky starts to use the special gait without any help from us. He'll look for or create opportunities and excuses to run simply because doing so feels so good. You can't teach him not to do it. You *can* teach him to also do it in the harness. The Husky is sometimes difficult to keep as a household pet, because he has been bred to run, and to run long distances. Most breeders and kennel clubs admit this fact.

The dog who has been selected for aggression — the pit bull, the so-called American Staffordshire terrier, the Presa Canaria, etc. — also has this unity of mind and body. But it's not a special gait or the ability to stalk, lie down, stand up. These dogs have been bred to execute the killing bite and for impulsive, uncontrolled aggression. Their bodies have been bred for exaggerated jaw and neck muscles and often for huge body mass (e.g. the Boerboel). Their brains have also ended up structured slightly differently from all other dogs, oriented to using the exaggerated jaw and neck muscles for the special purpose they were meant for. The chemical housekeeping in the brain is slightly different, so that impulse control has been diminished in these dogs. The human intention was to have a dog who doesn't hesitate and warn, who doesn't then use just enough controlled aggression to open up an escape route or get the other to increase distance a little, but who surprises his opponent with a sudden all-out, sustained attack in the pit (or out on the field where he found the escaped slave). And this is what we got. When he reaches a certain age, this dog will, without our help or teaching, start to execute the full-fledged attack and the killing bite. The first attack comes suddenly and without warning, surprising the dog's human and everyone else — just as the dog has been bred to do. Once he starts attacking, the specific chemical housekeeping in his brain (and the fact that attacking just feels so natural and good) makes sure he doesn't stop. He won't (and probably can't) honour calming signals or surrender signals, because his impulse control has been bred out of him. Since the behaviour the breed was bred for feels good to the dog, the dog will look for opportunities or create excuses to be able to do this enjoyable thing. You can't teach him not to do it. And teaching him also do it on command? Now why would any mentally healthy person want to do that?

Fact: The killing bite and uncontrolled aggression are most certainly genetically determined in a number of dog breeds. The brain abnormality behind this behaviour is strongly heritable. Just like the Border Collie and the Husky, these breeds have been developed to perform a specific task. You can't take the behaviour out of their genes — i.e. make them 'sweet' — by raising them a certain way, anymore than you can take the stalk out of the Border Collie or the sled gait out of the Husky just by raising him differently. The main difference is that it's generally not a tragedy when the Border Collie or the Husky does his thing.

PROBLEMS WITH THE DISCUSSION ABOUT THESE BREEDS

Dog-to-dog tragedies

Most of the discussion about these breeds is about whether they are dangerous to humans. To me, an equally important tragedy is what these breeds are doing to other dogs since they have become so popular. Many, many more dogs than humans have been maimed or killed since the fashion started, and I have never understood why people who claim to love dogs seem unconcerned about this.

The myth that you can raise a killing breed dog to be 'sweet' is mostly aimed at preserving these breeds by claiming they aren't always dangerous to humans. This myth has contributed to an ongoing slaughter of ordinary household dogs by encouraging the owners of these breeds to take them to dog places and insist that they be allowed to interact with other dogs. It has also led to a revival of the dogfighting culture in many countries, including the theft of ordinary household dogs from back gardens, who are then kept leashed as they are ripped apart as practice material for groups of fighting dogs. Shame on the humane societies and 'scientists' who have contributed to this.

Comparing apples and oranges

Breed specific laws have always been aimed at decreasing maiming and killing attacks on humans. However, scientists and other self-appointed experts consistently switch variables when they evaluate such laws. Instead of looking at whether killing and maiming attacks on humans have decreased, i.e. evaluating the variable such laws were aimed at, they insist on evaluating whether any and all dog bites have decreased. This fact invalidates all such studies, since they don't answer the question that was actually posed. Sometimes even the statistics on killings are padded — e.g. including a dog that choked someone by pulling playfully on a scarf as a directed dog attack on a human. It's clear that an 'expert' who doesn't understand the difference — and the difference in significance — between an inhibited bite and an uninhibited all-out, sustained attack isn't qualified to be evaluating anything to do with dogs at all. It's also clear that someone who includes such things as the scarf incident in an evaluation of maiming and/or fatal attacks, without emphatically telling us he is doing so, is looking for ways to come up with the answer commercial interests have asked for in such a study.

In addition, there has not yet been a study of a decrease in dog-dog maimings and fatalities where certain breeds were banned. On the basis of anecdotal evidence (the situation in the country I live in), it's clear that dog-dog maimings and deaths drop dramatically where breed specific legislation is introduced and enforced.

Psychological maiming

It's not only humans who are psychologically damaged for life after experiencing an attack by a dog whose aim was to kill them, and in particular by a dog big enough to reach this goal. Normal dogs are also highly traumatised by such an experience. Normal dogs depend on the non-aggression rule in order to move in their world. They need to trust the ability of their signals to control interactions if they are to feel safe interacting with other dogs. When a dog has experienced an attack by another dog whose aim was to kill him, all firm ground is swept out from under the attacked dog's feet. His universe is literally shaken, as ours would be if the sun suddenly didn't come up tomorrow. If he can't trust his signals to control interactions, he has to live in fear all the time — because the world becomes an uncontrollable place where an attack can come at any time, and upon which his own actions have no influence.

Attributing the attacks to dominance

Some tell us that a dog attacking another dog is normal dog behaviour, to do with 'dominance'. However, 'dominance' has nothing to do with it. Even biologists who still believe in the idea of social dominance define 'dominance' as a social and controlled behaviour, which is specifically aimed at avoiding or minimising the need for real aggression and the risk of injury. Being bred with a body specialised for fighting with and killing other dogs has nothing to do with 'dominance', nor does an all-out, unbridled attack aimed at killing the other. The behaviour is not normal dog behaviour. It is, in fact, highly abnormal and is generally confined to a very few breeds.

The size of a breed matters

One of the cutesy favourites is to point out that Chihuahuas bite, too. Aside from the fact that this ignores the difference between a bite and an all-out attack, the issue here is the ability of a breed really to kill a human or another dog by directed attack. I've never understood why people who bring Chihuahuas (or dachshunds) into the discussion expect to be taken seriously ever again.

But besides the ability to really kill a human or another dog, there is second problem size and body mass brings with them: the ability of other dogs to teach the extremely large and/or heavy young dog impulse control and compromise seeking. Most of these breeds are so heavy by the time they are four or five months old that it becomes dangerous for an ordinary adult dog to try to improve their manners and teach them the rules. The more so because of the inbred predisposition to fight and the genetically determined diminished impulse control. I have seen Fila Brasilieros, Bull Mastiffs, and Boerboels of four months try to kill the adult dog who told them to watch out with the bumping or not to try to steal the stick. Where another dog isn't able to parry such an attack just sheerly due to the body mass of the attacker, the young dog ends up (on top of his genes) learning that aggression is the way to go.

Clifton, M, Dog attack deaths and maimings U.S. & Canada September 1982 to November 13, 2006. http://www.dogbitelaw.com/Dog%20Attacks%201982%20to%202006%20Clifton.pdf. Accessed May, 2008.

Coppinger, R, Coppinger, L, Biological bases of behaviour of domestic dog breeds, in Voith, VL, Borchelt, PL, eds, *Readings in Companion Animal Behaviour,* Veterinary Learning systems, Co., Inc., Trenton, NJ, 1996.

Coppinger, R, Coppinger, L, *Dogs: a startling new understanding of canine origin, behaviour, and evolution,* Scribner, New York, 2001.

Cronly-Dillon, J, The experience that shapes our brains, *New Scientist*, November, 366–369, 1982.

Lockwood, R, Rindy K, Are 'pit bulls' different? An analysis of the pit bull terrier controversy, *Anthrozoos* 1:2–8, 1987.

Moyer, KE, Kinds of aggression and their physiological basis, *Comm Behav Biol* 2[A]: 65–87, 1968.

Peremans, K, *Functional brain imaging of the dog; single photon emission tomography as a research and clinical tool for the investigation of canine brain physiology and pathophysiology,* Universiteit Gent, Faculty of Veterinary Medicine, Gent, 2002. http://www.uznuclear.ugent.be/research/phd_dissertations/Functional_Brain_LowRes.pdf.

Phillips, K, Esq www.dogbitelaw.com.

http://www.pitbullsontheweb.com/petbull/articles/crecenteart2.html, sourced 16 April 2009.

http://www.drpolsky.com/Vet%20News1.pdf, sourced 16 April 2009.

Myth 39: The serious to fatal damage the aggressive breeds inflict when they attack isn't due to their genes, but rather due to having the wrong kind of owners.

We've seen that the killing bite and unpredictable, uncontrolled aggression are genetically anchored in these dogs, and that they can't be taught not to execute killing behaviour. They inevitably reach a certain age when they start to do it, looking for opportunities and excuses to do what we have bred them to do (see Myth 38). If you're lucky, the first attack will be on your cat or another dog, and not on your child. This killing behaviour is not caused by the owner in individual cases; it's just part of what the dog is. However, the killing behaviour *is* caused by certain people's consumer behaviour. By buying these dogs, these people are responsible for making it economically profitable to breed for the killing bite and the hair trigger. Are these people all 'the wrong kind of owners'?

The answer to this question lies in the kind of person who wants a dog with the killing bite in the first place. So who are they?

Well, in fact, they are the wrong kind of owners. Take a look around you. It's mostly a group of people who — for some reason related to their personal psychology — specifically want a dog whose breed standard explicitly states that the breed has been selected for extreme aggression. Often these are people with an inferiority complex of some kind. They want something that will finally enable them to intimidate other people. They have an ego problem, and need to prove something to the world. Many are men who are (perhaps unconsciously) worried about their masculinity, that maybe the world won't see it. Others are adolescents who watch too much MTV and learn that an aggressive dog is an essential consumer item, just like the Nikes, if he wants to keep up his macho hip-hop or skater's image. Sometimes they are naïve people, who think all dogs are cuddly plush toys. None of these people have any idea of behavioural conformation (see Myth 38), of the unity of mind and body Nature gives to all creatures, and they are all, in their own way, consumed by vanity.

Experience (of which this author has a lot, alas) teaches that the owners of aggressive breeds can be divided broadly into three categories.

1) We all know there are people who try to conceal their inner feelings of inadequacy by acting extra tough outwardly. Many of them nowadays go buy a 'tough' dog. These people, who are struggling with an inferiority complex or an ego problem, then try to force their pit bull/American Staffordshire terrier (or Presa, or Dogo, etc.) on you because they feel the world owes them recognition. Many of us have experienced this. You try to avoid these people (and their dog) on the street or in a park, but they follow you, determined to inflict the dog upon you. (After all, what's the use of having this proof of Manliness around if no one will look at it?) They cross the street to follow you so you can't avoid a confrontation. Their dog runs up to yours in a park, and they refuse to call it when you ask them to. Usually, the dog wouldn't obey anyway, and they don't want this embarrassing fact revealed to you. But above all, they enjoy your worry about what their aggressive dog will do. They shout at you to stop acting so weird about their dog. They get angry, and they often get verbally aggressive. It is of extreme importance to these people to force their dog on you, because their need is so

great to show the world they know better than everyone else. The dog is the way they can seek arguments and win for a change, since they never succeed in doing this on their own strength. When their dog does attack another dog and try to kill him, they are dumbfounded, because they really are too stupid to understand what these dogs are all about. Their cowardice surfaces — they don't dare interfere with their attacking dog, and once it's over, they disappear as quick as they can. Often you never see them in the park again, which is great, except for the fact that someone's normal, peace seeking dog had to pay with his life first. But some of them don't disappear for good. Some of them actually enjoy watching their dog's aggression, and just make sure they're gone before the police arrive. Tomorrow they're back again, and blaming you for having called the police. There have been cases in which the owner of the attacked dog was terrorized as punishment for reporting the attack to the police, to the extent that the owner of the horribly wounded dog had to move to a different neighbourhood. Finally, many of the people in this category of aggressive dog lovers enter their dogs in illegal pit fights, a phenomenon which has resurfaced in many of our cities since these dogs became so widespread. Some of these specifically go to places where other dogs come, in the hope that if their aggressive-breed dog practices on your cocker spaniel, he'll do better in the pit.

2) These are young adolescent male humans, who have reached the brink of adulthood but aren't there yet. The adolescent male is searching for his identity and trying to get himself a satisfying spot in his peer group. The adolescent doesn't always have bad intentions, but his brain isn't ripe yet, and he isn't yet capable of understanding the consequences of his actions (which is also the reason he has to pay so much more for car insurance than the rest of us). He sees the macho rapper on television, accompanied by the aggressive dog, and he wants one, too. After he's finished saving up for Nikes, he saves up for a dog. He has no idea what he's bought once he has the dog, thinking it's just another consumer item. To him the dog isn't any different than his other fashion accessories, to him the dog is a thing that will — just like his Portable Play Station — turn on and off if you press the button. The adolescent is, by virtue of his age, a bit rebellious. He is exploring various boundaries, sometimes pushing the envelope in his search for an identity. He just loves to show adults that he won't do what they ask him to do, but that he makes his own decisions. Of course he won't leash his dog just because some grown-up makes the request, are you kidding, what a loss of face! He isn't prepared for it when his dog attacks a person or another dog, and he doesn't know what to do. His toy is suddenly acting up. So he does nothing, offers no help, doesn't dare interfere with his dog, and most probably just leaves the scene as quick as his little adolescent legs will carry him. Adolescence is an age of natural egotism, and a time when even sympathetic boys often lose their ability to empathise with others for a while. So this kid isn't capable of imagining the suffering the attacked dog goes through, nor the grief of the dog's owner. He's just glad his parents didn't find out about what happened, otherwise they might take his dog away. 'Tomorrow's another day, hey, don't be so serious about life, and besides, what could I do about it? The dog did it, not me.'

3) These are the Egotistical Innocents. They are members of animal protection clubs and humane societies. They read lots of sentimental stories about animals,

and they watch lots of programs on Discovery Channel. They believe that all animals are sweet-natured cuddly toys. These people's egocentricity is different from the adolescent's. These people think they are the measure of all things, and they therefore believe that if a dog is nice to them, well, it means he's nice, period. How the dog behaves towards others isn't so important. The Egotistical Innocent lives in a fairy tale, failing to see that a dog is a living being with a will and personality of his own, and that the dog hasn't been informed of the fairy tale. The Innocent is reinforced in the fairy tale by breeders who agree that the stories about these dogs are all lies, after all, look how sweet he is to the prospective buyer. The Innocent doesn't understand what 'fierce protector of home and hearth, averse to strangers' means, doesn't know a secret language has been developed since these breeds started causing so much tragedy. She likes the idea of proving to all the world that even these dogs fit her fairy tale, and that they are the poor victims of vicious anti-animal propaganda. The Egotistical Innocent is delighted with her puppy and sees him as a sort of four-legged human baby. She doesn't see that the pup is playing in an abnormally aggressive way at the age of eight weeks already. She is dumbfounded on the day when her 'puppy,' who meantime is actually a young dog, suddenly, out of the blue (because the warning phase has been bred out of these dogs), launches an unbridled attack on another dog and seriously wounds or kills the other dog. She is stricken and disillusioned — not only about the suffering of the attacked dog, but also because her fairy tale has caved in. But not to worry. It only takes her a few days to restore her view of the world. She decides her dog is as sweet as she'd thought after all. After thinking a while, she realises the whole thing was the other dog's fault. After all, the other dog growled at her sweetie, so what else could her sweetie do but defend himself? Sometimes the Egotistical Innocent will cry out that German Shepherds bite too, or that even a dachshund can be dangerous under the right circumstances. Unfortunately, there is always a way for people who don't want to face realities. The great tragedy is that the Egotistical Innocent's dog will harm or kill many other dogs, because she continues to take him to dog parks, in the belief that it's up to the other dogs to make sure they don't get killed.

Fact: This myth is true in the sense that these dogs always have the wrong owners, people who shouldn't have a dog in the first place. However, this myth is false because it's the genetics of the dog that make him a killer, regardless of what kind of owner he has. In other words, these dogs aren't killers because they have the wrong owners, rather they attract the wrong owners because they are killers.

Brown, S-E, The human-animal bond and self-psychology: Toward a new understanding, *Society & Animals*, electronic version, Vol. 12, No. 1, 2003.

Burrows, TJ, Fielding, WJ, Views of college students on pit bull 'ownership': New Providend, The Bahamas, *Society & Animals*, Vol. 13, No. 2, 139–152, 2005.

Frommer, SS, Arluke, A, Loving them to death: blame-displacing strategies of animal shelter workers and surrenderers, *Society & Animals,* Volume 7, Number 1, 1999.

Peremans, K, *Functional brain imaging of the dog; single photon emission tomography as a research and clinical tool for the investigation of canine brain physiology and pathophysiology,* Universiteit Gent, Faculty of Veterinary Medicine, Gent, 2002. http://www.uznuclear.ugent.be/research/phd_dissertations/Functional_Brain_LowRes.pdf.

Oral history collected from dog owners in The Hague, 1994–2009.

Myth 40: The pit bull and the American Staffordshire terrier are two distinct breeds; a.k.a. 'an Am Staff isn't a pit bull.'

In the Netherlands, after about seven children were killed by pit bulls in the space of about two years; and in a third year three toddlers died from attacks by pit bulls, people had had enough. Parliament initiated a law to ban the pit bull and possibly other aggressive breeds. The breeders and owners of these dogs felt that their economic and consumer interests were being threatened, so they tried to salvage what they could. First they tried to convince everyone that the aggressive behaviour of the pit bull was not genetically determined. No one fell for that one. After all, ten children had died a sudden and horrible death, and people weren't much in the mood to go with the propaganda. So the breeders and owners decided to abandon attempts to salvage the pit bull as such and just to concentrate on keeping as many commercial options open as they could. To achieve this aim, they began to assert that the American Staffordshire terrier isn't a pit bull. The National Kennel Association threw its weight into the battle, because there were huge financial interests at risk. The Kennel Association affirmed that the pit bull and the Am Staff had nothing to do with each other, not now and not in the past. Genetically totally different dogs. This disinformation campaign was, in the end, successful. People did fall for it. This means that the pit bull ban ended up removing only about half of the pit bulls from the streets.

Because if the truth be told, the pit bull and the American Staffordshire terrier are one and the same dog. This fact was freely advertised on the Internet up until about 2001. A Google search with the terms 'American Staffordshire terrier' inevitably led to sites that told all about the pit bull. These sites proudly told that the pit bull and the Am Staff are the same dog, and that the different names are just a result of the way kennel clubs offer pedigrees. The sites proudly described these dogs' aggressive nature, their propensity for seeking a fight any time, any place, including the admirable way in which they attacked without warning, surprising their opponent, what a big advantage in the pit! There were proud tales of how these dogs will always fight to the death, continuing even after the other dog is long dead. There were also warnings. The owner of a pit bull/Am Staff must never leave the dog home alone with another animal, not even one he'd lived with peacefully for years, because the dog might suddenly kill the other dog or the cat. The pit bull/Am Staff must never be allowed off-leash in the presence of another dog, because a fight to the death would probably result. There it was, in writing, the American Staffordshire terrier is a pit bull with another name, always dangerous for other animals, be proud of this, but be conscious of what you are buying.

In the meantime, various towns and cities in the United States have started to consider banning the pit bull. And now, all of a sudden, the websites have been revised along the lines of the European trick that worked so well. The same sites that proudly sung the praise of the Am Staff as a pit bull by any other name are now asserting that the two breeds have nothing to do with each other, not now and not in the past. The suspicion arises that the American clubs hope, just as the European clubs did, to be able to keep at least half the pit bulls on our streets — to keep this specialised and lucrative market bringing money in. In the United States it isn't only the kennel clubs' financial interests that are at stake, but also the financial interests involved in the organised dogfights these dogs are used for.

So what's the truth about these 'two' breeds? The truth is what the breeders and owners published on the Internet up to 2001. There is no distinction between a pit bull and an American Staffordshire terrier, at least not as far as their genes go. In 1935, the American Kennel Club decided to register what had, until then, loosely been called the pit bull as an official breed. Anyone with a dog who met the standards of physical and behavioural conformation could apply to have the dog registered as a Staffordshire terrier. The name was intended to avoid associations with the breed's pit fighting past (see Myth 30). Some people did register their dogs, some didn't. In 1972 the name of the breed was changed to American Staffordshire terrier. The reasons for this are unclear, unless it was because the American dog had meanwhile become so much bigger and heavier than the English one. As the trade in pedigreed dogs became more and more lucrative, many owners of pit bulls regretted not having registered their dogs. To accommodate this group of customers, the registers were re-opened for a time in 1978. Pit bull owners in the United States were given a new chance to register their fighting dogs with the American Kennel Club as American Staffordshire terriers. So the American Kennel Club's Am Staffs are not as 'pure' as they would like us to think they are. They have always been pit bulls by any other name. Besides, you can, right up to this day, take the same dog and get two different pedigrees for it. You can register the dog as an American Pit Bull terrier at the National Kennel Club, and you can simultaneously register him as an Am Staff at the American Kennel Club. You can enter your dog in a pit fight regardless of which (or both) pedigree he has. If he survives the fight, you've got bingo. You can sell his pups for double the price of a dog that hasn't been in the pit (or who lost, or who didn't try hard enough to kill the other dog). Because of the double registration, your pit bull can sire Am Staff pups and vice versa. The pups will be entered in the registry of your choice — or in both, no problem. The pit bull's genes and the Am Staff's genes are not at all kept separate, not in the past and not in the present, and there is still selection going on for extreme aggression. Huge amounts of money are involved in the dog trade, and the motivation to deny the truth is strong.

And breeders who do try to keep the genes separate? They are kidding themselves if they think they can, in ten short years or so, breed out behaviour that took more than two hundred years to breed in. Besides, behavioural conformation (see Myth 38) means that you can't preserve the appearance of these dogs without preserving their abnormal aggression — pedigree or no.

<u>**Fact:**</u> Don't let anyone kid you. The pit bull and the American Staffordshire terrier are genetically identical. They are the same dog, regardless of the name.

http://www.pitbullsontheweb.com/petbull/articles/crecenteart2.html, sourced 16 April 2009.
http://www.drpolsky.com/Vet%20News1.pdf (version December 1998 versus version 2005).
www.kennelclub.nl (version March 2006).
Phillips, K, Esq, www.dogbitelaw.com.
www.dogsbite.org.

Myth 41: 'What? How dare you growl at me!' A.k.a. If your dog snaps or growls at you, you should punish this severely.

If you have read this far, you now know that a threat signal is just the way a dog tells you she is feeling very worried and insecure about what you are planning to do. Her inner state is out of balance (too much adrenaline, too much fear or worry), and she wants to restore the balance. She is also worried about the equilibrium in the social landscape, because she doesn't know whether you are planning to disturb this equilibrium by breaking the peace. A threat signal is, in essence, nothing more than a request to give the dog some space until she feels more secure that the other can be trusted. This means that a threat signal is, in fact, a request that you give off a calming signal, so the dog can feel reassured about your intentions. We have seen that it is the insecure dog who threatens the most. It is the socially secure dog, the one who is confident that social intercourse will follow the rules and thus be safe, and confident that her own calming signals will always work, who threatens the least. She is confident enough to be the first to use her calming signals. She is the one who, by her calming signals, takes control of the situation and leads it to safe equilibrium. She takes the other dog by the hand, as it were, and helps him past his anxiety.

See also Myths 12, 13 and 28.

When a dog growls at you or even snaps at the air very near you, she is doubting whether you are trustworthy. She is worried that you might be violent or dangerous. She isn't 'dominating' you, but asking you to stay out of her personal zone for the moment. If you make the mistake of punishing her for her insecurity, all you do is affirm that you (and perhaps humans in general) aren't to be trusted.

Unfortunately, a lot of dog owners do punish their dogs for growling at them. What this leads to depends on how far the owner goes in punishing his dog's insecurity. Some owners end up teaching the dog not to growl or indicate her worry. The dog ends up waiting until she is so scared that she feels she must deliver an inhibited bite, learning, in other words, to bite without warning first how she's feeling. Some owners punish this, too, and get themselves into a cycle of violence with their dogs. As this escalates, the dog ends up feeling she has to defend her very life and the owner ends up (eventually) severely bitten. Sometimes the dog's owner accidentally gives her some other way out. For example, the owner stops when he's beaten the dog so badly that she pees herself. These owners ascribe the fact that they haven't been bitten to the punishment. They end up with a dog who is terrified of them, but who — by pure chance — hasn't had to fight for her very survival... yet. Research has shown that these owners are not good at understanding the dog's body language. They confuse her fear with 'submissiveness' and think they've arranged the dominance hierarchy just fine. They have no idea how miserable the dog is. The pattern is similar to the cycle of violence we find in the wife-beater in a domestic violence situation.

So what is the right thing to do if your dog growls or snaps at you? The behavioural therapy for a growling (or even snapping) dog always, but always, consists of a series of exercises that will gradually build trust with the dog. We gradually habituate the dog to various things the owner does, teaching the dog that the owner's actions will have a pleasant ending for the dog. The dog is allowed to take her own time, while getting lots of rewards for relaxed behaviour, in learning to trust her owner's approach and touch. In other words, the *dog* gets to decide how fast the therapy progresses. Sometimes the dog has been tortured so long and so often that we have to use safety measures during the exercises — anxiety-inhibiting medicine, a muzzle, a trailing leash during the sessions. This trust building therapy is usually successful, if only the owner can follow the instructions, stop punishing the dog altogether, and learn to see and respect her as a living being.

Fact: Dogs run their relationships on the basis of trust, not dominance, violence and punishment. A threatening dog is a worried dog, who is asking for some space. Don't blame the dog — rather, learn to be trustworthy. A dog who feels sure your behaviour is predictable, and who is confident that she can influence your behaviour with her calming signals, will start to feel at ease with you. After a while, after you have been willing to give enough proof that you are to be trusted, she will stop needing to ask you to stay out of her personal zone.

Fact: Trust is the key with dogs, and it has to be arrived at on their own terms.

Finding a good dog therapist

This is not a how-to book. If you are interested in trust building exercises with a growling, snapping dog, the best thing to do is find a good behaviour therapist in your area. Even if this were a how-to book, dealing with a dog who is so worried that s/he growls and snaps can be very distressing and even dangerous. It's all too easy to make beginner's mistakes that aggravate the problem. So it's important to get the help of someone who can guide you as you work on it

How do you know whether a behaviour therapist is competent? You can ask about membership in the Association of Pet Dog Trainers (the APDT) or the International Association of Animal Behaviour Consultants (the IAABC), or some other organisation that does some kind of training and quality control before admitting members. Not all good therapists are members of a club, though -- I am not. You can ask about the therapist's education, whether the person has a college or higher degree in animal behaviour. But not all good therapists have degrees, either (I do). You can call your local Society for the prevention of cruelty to animals and ask for names. You can ask friends. You can ask at a dog school that rejects the choke chain for training dogs and uses treats and/or the clicker instead.

When you contact a therapist, you can present your case briefly and let the therapist start talking. Then...

One thing to watch out for is that the therapist doesn't just have a standard, ready-made answer. A good therapist will ask you lots of questions about your dog and his/her history, how you brought the dog up, when the problem first started, when and where it occurs, and so on. The therapist will want to make a house visit and watch you with the dog. S/he might ask you to do various things with the dog, perhaps even asking you to do something that will make the dog show the growling or snapping behaviour. (A good therapist will not ask you to do this in a way that puts you or your dog or another dog at risk -- neither physical risk, nor emotional and psychological risk.) A good therapist will take a thorough look at you and your dog as individuals and at your particular relationship. If the therapist already knows the answer before you even tell your story, it's better to look for someone else.

Another very important thing to watch out for is that the therapist doesn't start talking about dominating your dog by any technique that sounds the least bit like intimidation or punishment. Some good therapists still talk about dominance and ranks and leadership -- but when they start explaining how to change these things, they will not be telling you to intimidate your dog, hit your dog, kick your dog, jerk on the choke chain, nor do anything else that is scary, painful, or intimidating for your dog. They will start talking instead about things like asking the dog to sit or lie down very frequently for a treat, not letting the dog get on the couch or other high places anymore, eating first before the dog does, never approaching the dog but letting the dog approach you, and such like. A good therapist will know exercises for you that make the dog feel less intimidated and worried rather than more.

The instant a trainer or therapist starts talking about punishing your dog or doing anything that is intimidating, scary, or painful for your dog, it's time to say, 'Thanks, but no thanks', and call someone else.

For an explanation of why even a therapist who talks about ranks and leadership can still be a good therapist (as long as this does not include punishing, hurting, scaring or intimidating your dog), take a look at Myth 97.

Part 4

Myths about dogs' thoughts and feelings

Myth 42: We're just projecting when we think dogs have feelings similar to ours.

When we project human characteristics onto non-human things, this is called 'anthropomorphism.' It's one of the worst things a scientist can be accused of, so they avoid it like the plague — and that is what's behind this myth. It's not a bad thing to recognise that an animal's feelings and emotions won't be exactly the same as ours. Our emotions are always affected by our very complex thought processes, which animals don't have. It's a good thing to say, 'the animal is clearly feeling something, let's be careful until we find out what it's feeling.' It's quite another thing to say, 'We'll assume they don't feel anything at all until someone can prove to us that they do.' This myth is one of the most tragic wrong turns we've ever taken.

This myth has a long history. In the Middle Ages, when the animal kingdom was divided up in our minds into noble and not noble animals, people also assigned noble and not noble emotions and feelings to animals, according to the animals' social standing (see Myth 10). Animals were thought to feel just as deeply as we do. They also supposedly felt along the same lines people do: noble animals had noble feelings, ignoble animals had ignoble feelings. A few centuries later, at the beginning of the Renaissance, the Church doctrine arose that there is a definite split between body and soul, and that animals don't have a soul. But most people still saw feeling beings when they looked at animals, and the Church still afforded animals some protection. As the Renaissance progressed, a small movement arose that wanted 'knowledge' (as opposed to mere 'belief'), and we saw the early beginnings of what we now call 'science.' This meant a struggle with the Church, among other things about what scientists were allowed to kill and cut up. We have all heard the stories about how Michelangelo had to steal corpses in the night, hoping to improve his art by finding out what was actually inside us. Frustrated by the limitations that were being imposed, scientists finally came up with a way around the Church in the seventeenth century. They didn't dare challenge the Church about cutting up humans (even dead ones), but they hit on this great argument for at least being allowed to cut up animals (even living ones). The argument was: animals don't have a soul, so we must assume that they also don't have feelings. And if they don't have feelings, we can cut them up, right?

The Church agreed, but the public did not. So science set out to prove that animals were different and that there was no reason not to cut them up. This was the beginning of a process in which science has claimed to find ever more proof that an animal is essentially different from, and lower than, a human. By the nineteenth century, science had gotten the powers that be to believe that animals don't even feel pain. At universities, hundreds of dogs and cats were tied up and muzzled, then dissected alive for the anatomy lessons. The dissection was done in such a way that the fully conscious, struggling, screaming animal was kept alive as long as possible, so the students could see the organs working. Anyone who suggested that the animal did seem to be feeling pain was ridiculed and flunked the course. After all, since you couldn't prove what exactly all that struggling and screaming meant, you had to assume it meant nothing at all. This was the only 'scientific' attitude.

We are still stuck with this. It is only in the past two or three decades, and only with reluctance, that science has been willing to acknowledge that animals feel even pain, and this acknowledgement has been limited to mammals. Many scientists still think even this is nonsense. They continue to bitterly resist having ethics committees approve animal experiments, and continue to resist the requirement that animals be anaesthetised during painful procedures. But this is only pain. As far as other emotions go, we are still told it is utterly ridiculous and totally projection to think that animals might have emotions that are in any way similar to what we feel. They just have conditioned, mechanical reactions, that's all, don't kid yourself there's feeling behind it.

There are a number of big problems with this standpoint.

To keep it up, scientists have to deny an awful lot of what we do now know. We know now that emotions originate in our brains. We also know which parts of the brain they come from and how these parts are connected. We know that animals have the same structures in their brains, too, and that these structures are connected in the same way ours are. We know that these parts of the brain work pretty much the same way in the dog as they do in us. They often respond in the same way to various psychoactive drugs. We know that certain behaviour in an animals correlates with electrical activity and chemical changes in specific areas of the brain (and in the body), same as in ours. Not only an animal's behaviour, but also its brain and body react in the same way to pain, boredom or an unexpected reward as ours do. On the other hand, we know that animals don't have the large frontal lobes in their brains that we have, where our (relatively) complex cognitive abilities are situated.

Scientists do use this last fact as proof that animals can't think complex thoughts, and that they are inferior to us — but this is wanting to have it both ways. You can't say that the lack of a structure (the large frontal cortex) proves the lack of a capacity, and at the same time that the presence of a structure (e.g. the amygdala) is meaningless. It is more logical and, it must be said, more scientific, to conclude that an animal most certainly must share our capacity to have emotions and feelings, and that these must be very like our own. In the end, it is already very clear that animals have measurable responses that we call joy, anxiety, pain, etc., in pretty much the same kinds of situations that trigger these feeling in us (see the rest of this section). It is also very clear that the reasons scientists continue to deny this are rather suspect.

A second problem with the 'scientific' position is that it ignores what human emotions truly are. Scientists forget that our emotions are also nothing more than changing electrical patterns in certain parts of our brains and changing chemical balances in our bodies. They forget that our own emotions are also nothing more than conditioned reactions to our surroundings, no more and no less than in any other animal. What we call boredom is nothing more than any animal's reaction to an impoverished environment. Our 'delight' is our physical, measurable reaction to the introduction of a pleasant stimulus in this impoverished environment. Our anxiety is a physical change that takes place in our brains and bodies when we expect something unpleasant or painful. 'Joy' or 'relief' are the names we give to the response of our brains and bodies when something pleasant that was taken away from us is returned, or when the unpleasant or painful thing we anticipated doesn't happen after all. The fact that we can think all kinds of complicated things as we are feeling these feelings is irrelevant. That an animal can't think while it feels or emotes doesn't mean it doesn't have the feelings and emotions themselves.

So here's the truth. We now have to assume not only that animals *can* have exactly the same primitive emotions we do, but also that they *must* have them. Your dog does feel joy, anxiety, pain, uncertainty, something you could call a 'depression,' anger, a longing, sadness, bafflement, and all the other basic things you feel. It's just that the dog does all this feeling differently — in a less complicated way — than a human does. A dog can't but honestly and directly express what he's feeling, because he (indeed) doesn't have the big brain parts he'd need to think up all the strange side roads we come up with. In other words, a dog isn't, and can't be, calculating. And his feeling are gone as soon as the thing that caused them is gone — unlike us, who tend to hang onto old feelings for a long, long time in the form of resentment. But it's a mistake to say that just because a dog can't be calculating or vengeful, he also can't feel something like joy or sadness. Those who say this are either not up on the facts, or else they are just not thinking clearly.

Fact: Don't let anyone tell you you're projecting when you see that your dog has feelings. It is not 'anthropomorphism' to acknowledge that a dog is a living, feeling being, and that he shares all our *primary* emotions. It's a good thing to be kind and merciful, and to take his feelings into account. Be wise as you do this, keeping in mind that his feelings are less complicated than ours are, and that he can't do all kinds of abstract or nasty or vengeful thinking.

Aiello, S, (ed) *The Merck Veterinary Manual Eighth Edition* Merck & Co Whitehouse Station NJ 1998.

Bentham, J, *An Introduction to the Principles of Morals and Legislation* (1789) in Burns, JH, and Hart, HLA, (eds) Athlone Press, University of London, London (1970).

Carson, G, *Men Beasts and Gods: A History of Cruelty and Kindness to Animals,* Charles Scribner, NY 1972.

Descartes, R, Animals are machines, in Armstrong, SJ, and Botzler, RG, eds. *Environmental ethics: Divergence and Convergence,* McGraw-Hill, NY, pp 281–285 1993.

Griffin, D, *Animal minds,* University of Chicago Press, Chicago and London, 1992.

Griffin, DR, *Animal Thinking,* Harvard University Press, Cambridge MA, 1984.

Herek, GM, The instrumentality of attitudes: Toward a neofunctional theory, *Journal of Social Issues* 42: 99–114, 1986.

Hills, AM ,The motivational bases of attitudes toward animals, *Animals & Society,* Volume 1 Number 2, 1993.

Katz, D, The functional approach to the study of attitudes, *Public Opinion Quarterly,* 24: 163–204, 1960.

Kennedy, JS, *The new anthropomorphism,* Cambridge University Press, NY, 1992.

Lattal, KA, A century of effect: Legacies of EL Thorndike's *Animal Intelligence,* Monograph, *JEAB* 70: 325–336, 1998.

Nibert, DA, Animal rights and human social issues, *Society & Animals,* Volume 2, Number 2 1994.

Pernick, MS, *A Calculus of Suffering: Pain Professionalism and Anesthesia in Nineteenth Century America,* Columbia University Press, NY, 1985.

Phillips, MT, Savages, drunks and lab animals: The researcher's perception of pain, *Society & Animals,* Volume 1 Number 1, 1993.

Phillips, MT, Sechzer, JA, *Animal Research and Ethical Conflict,* Springer-Verlag, MY, 1989.

Regan, R, Singer, P, (eds) *Animal Rights and Human Obligations,* Prentice-Hall, Englewood Cliffs NJ, 1976.

Ritvo, H, *The Animal Estate: The English and Other Creatures in the Victorian Age,* Harvard University Press, Cambridge MA, 1987..

Rollin, B, Animals in experimentation: Utilitarian objects pets or moral objects, *Anthrozoos* 3: 88–90, 1989.

Seligman, MEP, Hager, JL, *Biological Boundaries of Learning,* Appleton-Century-Crofts, NY, 1972.

Seligman, MEP, On the generality of laws of learning, *Psych Rev* 77: 406–418, 1970.

Sidman, M, *Coercion and its Fallout,* Authors' Cooperative Inc Publishers, Boston, 1989.

Skinner, BF, *The Behaviour of Organisms: An Experimental Analysis,* Appleton-Century-Crofts Inc, NY, 1938.

Skinner, BF, *Science and Human Behaviour,* The Free Press (a division of Macmillan Publishing Co.) NY, 1953.

Skinner, BF, *Contingencies of Reinforcement,* Prentice-Hall Inc, Englewood Cliffs, NJ, 1969.

Thomas, K, *Man and the natural world: A history of modern sensibility,* Pantheon Books, NY, 1983.

Varela, FJ, Thompson, E, and Rosch, E, *The Embodied Mind: Cognitive Science and Human Experience,* MIT Press, Cambridge MA, 1991.

Myth 43: My dog can't feel love for me the way humans do.

'He doesn't love you', says the trainer and the shelter personnel with a smug smile, 'it's just that you give him dinner every day.' They think they are being scientific by saying this. What they don't know is that they are greatly overestimating what human love is.

You see, dogs don't just love any old body anymore than we do. Our love grows as we spend time with someone and find that this is a pleasant experience. This person fulfils all kinds of needs and longings we have, much better than anyone else does. S/he listens better and understands us better than anyone else. S/he brings us small presents, gives us the feeling that our company is wonderful, is a great lover, is there for us when we have a problem, and so on. Just seeing our beloved awakens a feeling of happiness in us, because of all the pleasant and joyful things his or her presence means. The other becomes our 'home' because we feel so safe with him or her. In the end, we call this love.

As you can see from the previous paragraph, human love is, in essence, and with all the Hollywood trappings taken off for a sec, nothing more than a conditioned reaction to a conditioned reinforcer, a result of associating him or her with the many primary reinforcers we've received in his/her presence. Or to say it ordinary language, our own love is a learned reaction to something (our beloved) that we now experience as a signal that many of our needs are about to be met.

Novels, Hollywood and the advertising industry have adorned our 'love' with all kinds of romantic fantasies. We fell for it. Most of us believe that human 'love' strikes suddenly, and that it is magical, uplifting and eternal, selfless, unselfish, and without any expectation of personal gain. But this is just a belief. The statistics show a different picture. Most of the time, we love the other as long as s/he brings the wage packet home, cooks for us, gives us sexual satisfaction, and as long as s/he doesn't nag too much or ask too much of us. The statistics show that we often (secretly) cheat, that others of us have a pattern of being serially and only shortly 'in love' and monogamous, and that yet others walk out the door the instant something younger or prettier or richer comes along. When we do stay together, it's often hard work. The heavenly image of our love isn't truly justified, because it turns out that we don't really behave all that differently from a dog.

Which brings us back to the dog. You understand his needs with a glance. Wonderful things happen for him whenever you're around, making his life interesting and fun. He feels safe and sheltered as long as you're at his side. He enjoys your company. When he sees you he is filled with real joy and happiness, he misses you when you're gone, and he is willing to give up other things to stay with you. He is much more willing than your human partner to make compromises with you and to try and meet your wishes. He doesn't get bored with you because someone else pets him better. He immediately forgives every mistake the instant you stop making it. If he is re-homed, and he seems happy in his new place, this isn't because he's forgotten you. He does miss you at first, terribly — but he resigns himself to his fate because we give him no other choice. If he runs into you a couple years down the road, he'll jump for joy at the very sight of you, without feeling the least bit of resentment because you left him.

Fact: If you ask me, this is love. Don't let anyone take this away from you just because they think they're being 'scientific.'

Myth 44: A dog can/can't be jealous.

If we want to know whether a dog can be jealous, we first have to take a good look at what we mean by 'jealous.' If jealousy means being afraid something will be taken away from her when someone else is around, or if it means anxiety that the other's presence is going to mean an unpleasant experience (like less attention or being sent away), or if jealousy means worry that the other will get a treat instead of herself, then a dog can be jealous. Biologists will call this projection and anthropomorphism, but that's because biologists aren't psychologists and don't truly understand what *human* jealousy is.

Here are some examples:

1) Your dog is normally allowed to sit next to you on the couch, but now you have a new boyfriend or girlfriend. Every time the two of you sit on the couch, the dog tries to join you to share in the cosiness, just like she always does when you settle down alone to watch TV after work. After you've sent her away six times in the presence of your new friend, the dog starts to act withdrawn whenever this friend shows up. The dog has learned, just as a human can, that this person's presence means something she values will be withheld from her. We could call this jealousy, just as we would if we were talking about a three-year-old child who rejected your new friend for the same reason.

2) You've just brought a new puppy into the house. You're worried about what your adult dog will do. In your worry, you tend to be a bit grouchy toward your adult dog when the pup is in the room, you prevent her from parenting the pup and teaching him the social rules (e.g. you demand that she 'share the bone fairly' with the pup), or you send her away when she tries to teach the pup by growling at him. The pup gets lots of special treats and extra attention, which the adult dog doesn't get to share. The adult dog learns, just like the jealous human, that the other — in this case, the pup — is a signal that unpleasant things will happen. She begins to act as if she doesn't like the pup, refusing to let him get near her or even chasing him out of the room. Wanting the other to go away because bad things happen in his presence and because you aren't allowed to be yourself when the other is around is an emotion we can call jealousy.

3) If you live alone with a single dog, your dog doesn't know what will happen when you hand out treats with other dogs around. If you get out a treat in a park, she may be defensive toward other dogs who are attracted by the sight of a treat, snarling at them and trying to get them to go away. She'll stop doing this once she learns that she will still get her treat, even if other dogs are crowding around, too. The fear that someone else will get a valued thing instead of you is another emotion that dogs can share with humans, and that we can call jealousy in both.

What it comes down to is that another person or dog can become a signal that the satisfaction of a need is in danger. The truth is that 'jealousy' is a kind of extinction aggression, both in humans and in the dog (see Myth 58, paragraph 6).

It's a good thing to acknowledge that a dog can have feelings of impending loss and can learn not to like the thing that signals this loss. But it's important not to take this too far, because then we do get into mythical thinking. Jealous humans can sit around brooding for days about what someone else has that they don't have themselves, coming up with all kinds of sneaky or complicated plans to get back at the other person, cut them down a notch, show them a thing or two. This is a kind of jealousy dogs can't have. They don't have the large frontal lobes where this kind of brooding and planning takes place in our brains. They don't worry obsessively about the other if the other isn't present, and they can't think up complicated plans about what they'll do tomorrow or next week. This kind of jealousy is a strictly human capacity.

So why does a dog sometimes stay withdrawn even after the new friend or the pup has gone home again? She refuses to get on the sofa with you now that you are inviting her, she doesn't want the bone you offer her now. Is she jealously pouting? Is she trying to punish and reject you back out of jealousy? The answer is no. She is hesitant because you just sent her away ten times, or you just took the bone away from her ten times. She isn't sure why you did that. She thinks maybe the rules have changed, so she is holding back until she figures out what the new rules in your relationship are. She's not 'jealous', she's just confused.

Fact: 'Jealousy' is, both in dogs and in humans, a reaction to a signal that predicts loss or exclusion. Extinction aggression can play a role in the emotions and reactions that arise. But a dog isn't jealous in the brooding way a human can be, holding onto her jealousy long after the object is out of sight, or trying to punish you emotionally afterward. As soon as the threat of loss or exclusion is clearly over, her feelings of uncertainty will be gone and, with them, her jealousy.

Appearances can be deceiving

My white German Shepherd, Weasel, was severely beaten and radically underfed in her first home. After some four years in my home, Weasel looks like a happy and confident dog most of the time, but some of her behaviour betrays that her past — her learning history — is still with her. She still responds to a new human visitor in the house by slinking away. Once she decides to trust the new person (i.e. that the person is not a threat to her integrity as a functioning system, nor to the stability of the social landscape she's in, nor even to her well-being position within the array of available options), her reaction is equally exaggerated the other way. She is then more welcoming than my other dogs, to whom it's just normal routine that humans are to be trusted. For Weasel, each trustworthy human is a huge new resource added to her fitness hill (her well-being position), whereas for the others it's just another one on a big pile. The same goes for food. Weasel never tries to take the other dogs' food, but she will sometimes suddenly stop eating to do a round of growling at the others as they eat, as if she's worried they might try to take her food away. Then, once she's done that and been completely ignored by the happily eating others, she goes back and cheerfully eats her own bowl empty.

Learning is a crucial production process in the self-organising system we call a dog. A dog's past doesn't go away. It's there, time and events solidified in the brain in the physical structures that hold memory. Weasel knows that life can be different. To avoid complicated behaviourist language here, let's just say she knows the new happiness she has can be lost. She is more unsure of herself than the dogs who have never known violence or neglect. Put in terms of self-organising systems theory, her feeling of equilibrium, predictability, and safety is easily threatened — her internal state is easily perturbed.

Wolfie is a visitor dog, also female, who has been spending two days a week with my group since her eighth week. Wolfie is a socially skilled black-and-tan German Shepherd, who has never been mistreated or traumatised in her life. She's always had enough to eat. Parented from infancy by my two males, used to sharing my home with other visitor dogs, Wolfie has no insecurity about belonging in the group. It's just how life is. Her equilibrium is not easy to disturb. She has never experienced perturbations she couldn't compensate or solve, some other satisfying well-being position was always available. She has never been beaten, has full confidence in the power of her non-threat signals. These facts are expressed by her tolerant social behaviour. Big as she is, she's perfectly happy to reassure (i.e. to give off non-threat signals) when some other dog expresses uncertainty (i.e. gives off threat signals).

These two female dogs get along wonderfully well as long as they are together. They play with each other, do wild, beautiful, full-speed chase games with each other outdoors, are always near each other. You could say they love each other (see Myth 43).

All the same, there are moments when Weasel makes threat gestures toward Wolfie. The most intense moment is when Wolfie returns to us after an absence. Weasel threatens her at the door, follows her into the room, growls, circles, barks, runs to me, then repeats the whole routine. (Remember, threat gestures are an indication that a dog feels unsure of how the other will behave, or unsure of the effect the other will have on her well-being position; see Myth 12). All the while Weasel is doing this, Wolfie stands there giving off non-threat signals (which serve to reassure the worried other), looking with all her seventy-five pounds like a puppy who is saying, 'but I'm just very small, and I really intend to behave politely here.' Within five minutes, the two of them are playing together, clearly delighted to be together again. The other moment that sets Weasel off is when Wolfie approaches me for a pet. Weasel dashes in between us, stares at Wolfie, grumbles, then bats me with her behind. Wolfie ignores it except for laying her ears back and letting Weasel glide along her body without an answer. As soon as I've petted Weasel too, she stops the threats and makes play gestures toward Wolfie, and there they go again being happy sisters.

People observing according to the old dominance hierarchy model would, if let into my living room, observe without knowing (or caring about) any history and conclude that Weasel is a 'dominant' bitch and that Wolfie is the more 'submissive' of the two, lower down on the ladder in the group. Some might say, 'Well, even if dominance hierarchies don't exist, Weasel is still showing social dominance right now. She's controlling space and access to the human.'

None of this really tells you anything about the two dogs or their relationship. In fact, Wolfie is by far the more confident of the two dogs. She has known stability all her life and just feels less easily threatened in her happiness and safety. Weasel isn't 'dominant,' rather, she's insecure, quick to fear loss and exclusion, and is looking for reassurance. Once she's got that, she returns to being her cheerful, playful self.

In other words, Weasel is just jealous, and it only lasts a moment.

Myth 45: My dog is sneaky, because he always poops in a corner behind the couch, even though we were just out for a walk.

The dog who does this isn't sneaky. This is a dog who was housetrained by punishment, resulting in a fearful dog. In other words, someone *tried* to housetrain him by punishment, but now he secretly poops in a corner, quick, while no one is looking.

It could be that his (previous) owner shoved his nose in it when he had a puppy accident (see Myth 23). It could be that the (previous) owner just shouted at the pup when s/he saw the pup starting to squat in the living room. It doesn't matter which of these the human did, because either way, the dog has learned that humans get angry when they see him relieve himself.

Now, your puppy and your adult dog are generally trying with all their might to figure out what we want and do things that way. Someone has indicated that we find it offensive when the pup or dog poops in our human presence, and he has absorbed the lesson. So when you take this pup or dog out for a walk on the leash, he'll try as hard as he can not to do so while you are just a leash-length away and will see him do it. Obviously, this can't go on forever. Comes a moment when he just *has* to go, and then — because he doesn't want to make you angry — he finds a corner where he can go without you having to behold the act.

The solution for this problem is to take away the anxiety humans have taught him to have. Whoever has the dog now needs to stop punishing him in any way, shape or form, immediately. Make sure the dog is always within sight indoors, putting him in his crate when you can't keep an eye on him, so he just can't have any 'accidents'. Wait until you think he'll be needing to go, then take him outside for a walk. Walk however long it takes, until he just can't hold it anymore and, despite his fear for your reaction, poops while you're just a leash length away. When he does that, show him you are very happy with him. Squeak at him what a good dog he is, give him a special yummy treat, make him feel you are very proud of him.

Fact: As long as you consistently prevent indoor accidents and consistently reward him for doing it outside while you watch, it will take him no longer than two weeks to stop pooping in a corner.

See also: Myth 46.

Myth 46: My dog is trying to get revenge on me, because when she urgently has to go, she always does it on the carpet, never on the lino in the kitchen or somewhere else that's easy to clean.

The dog who does this isn't trying to get revenge for something. It's just that someone taught her in her puppy days to pee and poop on a newspaper. Her owner didn't feel like taking the pup out every two hours, or for some reason s/he just couldn't. So the pup was taught to do it on a newspaper as long as her sphincter muscles were so undeveloped. This pup didn't learn to do it outside until later on, when she could hold it longer and the newspaper was removed.

The thing is, housetraining doesn't only happen in the sphincters, and the decision to relax these holding muscles isn't entirely a conscious decision. The sphincters are controlled by both voluntary and involuntary parts of the brain. During an animal's early growth, the involuntary part of the brain that controls these muscles learns a signal for 'it's safe to do it here.' When an animals needs to go and the 'safe' signal appears, the muscles will start to relax in and of themselves, without an animal's conscious will being involved. It works the same way with us. We learn at an early age to go on the toilet, and that it's more polite to go in a private place. This is the reason why, when we urgently need to pee, it gets harder and harder to hold it the closer we get to a bathroom. This is the reason why some people can't pee while someone else is watching, no matter how great their need to go. The involuntary parts of our brains are playing us tricks and taking things out of our conscious hands. In addition, an irritated bowel will sometimes start to empty itself no matter where we are. When we feel that starting to happen, we look for a place that we've learned is acceptable, or at the very least for a place where no one will see it happen.

This is no different with a dog. The newspaper is anchored early on as a 'safe' signal in the dog's brain. When she's in dire need, the sight of this signal will make the dog's sphincters start to relax involuntarily. Whether the dog was also punished during housetraining makes no difference here. If it's diarrhoea, she'll perceive a newspaper as 'acceptable.'

So why the carpet? A dog has no grasp of logic or money or paper pulp vs. woven textiles. She has learned to relieve herself on a flat, absorbent thing that is lying on the floor, and never on the bare floor itself. When she's in urgent need, as she is when she has diarrhoea, she will look for a way not to relieve herself on the bare floor. She looks for a newspaper, but there isn't one. She has no idea that your expensive Persian carpet is a worse choice than the bare floor. To her, it's rather like a newspaper: it's flat, it's absorbent, and it's lying on the floor.

These signals are physically anchored in the brain and can't be made to go away anymore. She can't learn now that the bare floor is the place for emergencies, because the bare floor is anchored as a signal for 'unsafe.'

The only solution here is to help a dog who's in dire need. You can learn the signals a dog gives when s/he is desperately holding diarrhoea or an overly full bladder. She'll go lie down somewhere and start to pant. She might walk restlessly back and forth, as if she's looking for something. She might go sit at the door and whine. For heaven's sake, take her outside! If your dog is sick and you know it, and you are worried she might be in need in the middle of the night, you can help her by putting down some newspaper, just as you did in her puppy days. Then she won't have to use the carpet.

Fact: A dog who relieves herself on a carpet when her need is dire thinks she's accommodating you. As badly as she needs to go, she's still trying to do what someone taught her in her early puppy days, looking for a place other than the bare floor. Once she sights the carpet, she loses power over what happens next. The whole thing is, in the end, involuntary behaviour, and not at all lust for revenge.

Myth 47: My dog knows when he's been naughty.

Many authors have already tried to debunk this myth, but for some reason it remains a stubborn belief in many human minds. So we are going to do it over here one more time.

A dog is not a little human. He does have all the simple and primary emotions we have — stuff like joy, happiness, anxiety, fear, anger, feeling unsure of himself, and love (see Myths 42–44). But it remains a fact that a dog most definitely does not have our ability to think complicated thoughts or make complicated connections between things. Dogs don't think way ahead. A dog doesn't sit around worrying about the past. Rather, they react to realities at the moment these realities present themselves. Even a dog who has a fear or phobia as a result of some past experience doesn't think about this unless the thing he's afraid of suddenly appears right here, right now; or unless for some reason he's afraid it will. Dogs live by a number of simple rules that you could call a sort of moral code: we don't use real aggression in our social interactions, we respect each other's personal preferences and personal zone, and we look for compromises rather than absolute power over each other. A well socialised dog won't be quick to break these rules, and dogs have no idea why we do.

Our society is very different from dog society, with very different rules. Our moral code is also different. I'm not talking about what we say, but about what we do. We have no qualms about committing mass slaughter among our own kind (just watch the news tonight if you doubt this). We are constantly ignoring each other's preferences and invading each other's personal zone (just look at the statistics on sexual harassment and sexual abuse, domestic violence, and violent crime on the streets). We admire people who refuse to compromise and who go for absolute power, calling this person a winner (just look at the political leaders we have re-elected because they took us to war, and how quickly we then rejected them when it turned out they couldn't get us absolute power fast enough for our taste). These are all things a dog would find very, very 'naughty' — if he could think about it at all. Which he can't, because he doesn't have the brain parts for it.

A dog doesn't understand that he doesn't live at the local dump anymore, where the pre-dog found us and evolved with us in the first place. He doesn't understand why we would object to the garbage being spread around the kitchen floor. He doesn't know what a microscope is, or that such a thing as bacteria exists. He has no idea why the kitchen should stay clean, or even what clean is. To him, it's a lot more inviting with leftovers spread all over the floor so it's easier for everyone to find some snacks. A dog has no idea about the division of labour, or that you go out the door every day to work for money. He has no idea that the sofa cost you an awful lot of this hard earned cash. He doesn't know that your claim to the sofa still holds even after you've left the house, and the sofa is thus no longer inside your personal zone. A dog doesn't think his own body is dirty or disgusting, not one single part of it. He prefers to deposit his faeces outdoors, but he doesn't think they are disgusting. It's no earth-shaking big deal if he's in dire need and has no choice but to deposit them indoors just this once. And a dog truly doesn't understand why we would get angry when he tries to calm us down by letting go of a little bit of pee for us.

So if you come home and you see your dog slinking up to you, seeming anxious to appease you or frightened of you, this does not mean he 'knows' he'd been 'naughty.' This just means he's learned that you are often angry when you walk in the door. Being the peace seekers that they are, the dog will try to calm you every time you come in the door, using all kinds of non-threat (that is, calming) signals to greet you. He will do this without needing to know why you always come in angry, because dogs are very forgiving and just want to get relations back on track as quick as they can.

If he starts to slink and look (to you) 'guilty' when you call him into the kitchen full of rubbish, or to the corner where he just pooped, or over to the sofa he tore up while you were gone, this is not because he knows he did something wrong. This is because he hears the anger in your voice, yes, even if you try to hide it. He will try to calm you whenever he hears this tone, it's just how dogs are. It doesn't mean he understands your reasons and motives. A dog can even learn that you only get angry when the rubbish is spread around the kitchen. But he won't connect this with his own act of having spread it around. That's too far in the past for him to make the connection. He also won't be thinking of your anger as he plunders the rubbish next time, because that is too far in the future for him to anticipate. All he knows is that rubbish spread around plus your presence equals anger. This fact has led many a person to punish the wrong dog, since a dog makes this equation whether or not it was him or the other dog who spread the rubbish around a couple hours ago.

Fact: A dog will usually start to give off non-threat signals when he knows you're angry. This doesn't mean he knows why you're angry, or knows that he was 'naughty' or 'bad'. It doesn't even mean that he was the one who did the 'bad' thing. A dog lives by simple rules. Our complicated reasoning about cleanliness, bacteria and the value of money are way over his head.

Myth 48: A well bred dog has an instinctive need to fulfill our wishes whenever she can, the so-called 'will to please'.

Neither evolution nor history have, in all of time, ever produced a creature that lives only to fulfill someone else's wishes, putting aside its own wishes at all times in order to do this. Not even humans do this. When we want to please someone else, there is always — be it secretly, be it unconsciously — some kind of profit in it for ourselves that we are aiming at. We never do something for nothing. We always expect something back, be it secretly, be it unconsciously. This is a psychological fact. But despite the fact that we always want something back ourselves, many of us would (be it consciously, be it unconsciously) just love to go back to our toddler days, when Mum served our every need without seeming to want anything back from us. Take but not have to give, delicious. The painful fact is that this wish is only normal until you're about three, upon which it becomes time to grow up and start learning to give as well as to take.

But we keep dreaming. This infantile wish stays with many of us (consciously or unconsciously) long after we've reached adulthood. Some of us satisfy it by dreaming over a drink at a summer pavement café, 'Here's what I'd do if I won the lottery…' Others reserve a room in an expensive hotel for a weekend so they can have this fantasy fulfilled for a moment (the beds made when you get back from shopping, lots of room service). Others are less realistic. Some people marry in the hope their (emotional) needs will be taken care of by someone else, hoping a marriage will free them from their adult responsibilities (just turn on Dr Phil if you don't believe this). Some people suddenly turn into three-year-olds as soon as they step onto a plane, throwing a temper tantrum if they aren't catered to fast enough (this is a growing problem for airlines).

The whole thing remains a fantasy. We don't win the lottery, the hotel room has to be paid for. Marriage turns out to be give and take if you don't want to end up divorced. The man in the plane has paid for his ticket, but he still ends up being carted off in handcuffs if his demands and behaviour get all too unreasonable. We just aren't willing to serve a grown up human as if s/he were still three years old.

So the 'will to please' is not a projection of any human characteristic onto a dog, because letting others act like a three-year-old isn't a human characteristic. The idea that a dog should have a 'will to please' is, rather, the projection of a human *wish* onto the dog.

This wish gets in the way of being able to train a dog. The owner who has this wish will, just like the egocentric toddler, want the dog to do things for him/her 'just purely because it loves me' or 'just purely because I'm the leader.' These owners resist the idea of training with treats. They say feel like they are bribing the dog. What is actually going on is that they don't like it that their whims and wishes aren't enough motivation for the dog. They don't like it that they have to give something back in return for the dog's interest, efforts, and willingness to work for them. Told by their surroundings that the dog was the one place where the infantile dream of 'take and never have to give' would apply, they are disappointed to find out that even here the dream has to be abandoned. That hurts.

The world is full of trainers who will try to cater to this wish. They will tell you all about 'the will to please.' They will tell you that your dog has to behave like your mother did when you were three. Just as Mum knew without being told when it was time to change your nappy or bring you a bottle, the dog should know without being told what it is that you need now and how to satisfy this need for you. These owners feel they have a right to punish a dog when the dog can't accomplish this task, just like the toddler who throws a temper tantrum at Mum.

And voila, after much deprivation, bullying, and/or pain, the dog starts to fear this owner, to anxiously watch him/her, and to desperately search for what this person wants now. In other words, the dog starts to seek behaviour that will avert an unpleasant or painful experience. The dog thinks her owner is scary, but — unlike the spouse who can seek a divorce, or airline personnel who can get out the handcuffs — the dog has nowhere else to go and nothing else she can do.

'See, see,' says the owner, 'my dog does what I want without treats, purely out of love for me.'

I think most of us will agree that being bored, restricted, deprived, worried, and/or frightened, and therefore being abject, alert, and servile is a rather strange definition of love (or leadership). In fact, this is a revealing example of human self-deception, of how far we are willing to go to preserve the dream that we can only take and still be loved. Or that only we set the conditions, only have to give when the whim arises, not at all when the other needs us to give. And that in the one relationship we have in our lives — the one between animals and us — in which the power is distributed all on one side.

Fact: We need to give up this myth. Those of us who don't want to give it up need to take a good look at ourselves, because we are probably doing this in other relationships, too. The 'will to please' doesn't exist, not in us and not in dogs. The owner who uses the word 'love' or 'leader' when a dog is watching him or her with worry or even utter fear is stuck at an infantile stage of development. In fact, dogs need us to take the role of grown-up, to meet their needs, and to help them figure out what we want them to do in a way they can understand.

Myth 49: My dog tore up the newspaper today because I slapped him with it yesterday.

This sounds like a completely logical idea to us. In fact, there are various reasons why a dog might tear up a newspaper, but logic has nothing to do with any of them.

A dog is simply not capable of logical thinking. Even a human child of six can't master logical thinking yet, though the child is already at a cognitive level a dog will never achieve. This means a dog can't have the following thought process:

> 'Look, there's the newspaper s/he hit me with yesterday. If I tear it up, s/he won't be able to hit me with it anymore.'

The dog can't think this because it would mean he is capable of thinking:

> 'Yesterday A was the cause of B. Today A can be the cause of B again, unless I make sure A no longer equals A. I will now make sure A equals C, because C is never the cause of B.'

Where: A = the newspaper, B = a slap and C = tiny shreds of paper.

This is much too complicated for a dog.

If you often hit the dog with the newspaper, the dog learns to associate the newspaper with an unpleasant and scary experience. When the dog sees the newspaper lying somewhere, he feels a jolt of the unpleasant feelings that are always connected to physical punishment. He is more likely to want to avoid the newspaper than to do anything with it. And he will definitely want to avoid us when we start waving it around.

If your dog tears up a newspaper, this is probably because many dogs just enjoy shredding paper. It's a fun distraction to them. It may be that you slept late today, or that you stayed out longer than the dog is used to, and that the dog looked for something to do when he got bored. It may be that your dog is slightly anxious if he's alone too long, so he looks for something to do to distract himself. Same reason we sometimes bite our nails. It has nothing to do with what you did or didn't do with the newspaper yesterday.

The same thing goes for the dog who tears up the sofa if you leave him alone. He's not following the complicated logic, 'The sofa was very expensive, Boss has to work hard for his money, if I tear up the sofa whenever he goes out, he'll stop leaving me alone because he doesn't want to work hard for a new sofa all over again.' Nor is he following the logic, 'Boss made me get off the sofa when that new girlfriend was here yesterday, I'll tear up the sofa today, that will teach him not to make me get off the sofa anymore.' A dog who tears up the sofa is usually just very anxious when he's left alone. He starts to bite his nails, as it were.

Dogs can't conceive of long, logical, causal chains. The only living creature that can do this is the adult human. Dogs are always reacting in a direct way to signals and feelings, without any complicated thoughts behind what they're doing. This means that dogs don't do things to get revenge on us, not for what we did yesterday and not for what we did today.

Fact: The destructive dog is either bored or (more often) scared.

Myth 50: Besides being able to read our minds, the dog also has a sense of duty, a sense of honour, logical abilities, the ability to scheme for revenge and the ability to think up sneaky plans.

We certainly do a lot of projecting onto the dog! Of course, it's human nature that we don't like to see our own failings, so when things don't go the way we want them to, we have the natural inclination to seek the cause of this in someone else. We also sometimes have trouble putting ourselves in someone else's shoes, so we tend to think their motives for being so difficult must be the same as our own would be. Nature has determined that living creatures will be thrifty with their energy, so we tend naturally toward laziness. It's just too much exertion to inform ourselves about what a dog truly is. And, by the way, there's no need to do that anyway, since the dog has been living with us for millennia already and must be totally adapted to us by now. Or our parents had dogs when we lived at home, so we already know how to deal with dogs. All we have to do is do what Mum and Dad did (we don't realise they also just did what their Mum and Dad did). Or we do go to the trouble to try to find out what a dog is all about, and we end up with books that tell us all the fables and myths this book is trying to debunk.

In the end, the dog becomes a mirror in which the only thing we see is ourselves. Looking in this mirror and seeing our own image, we then think that if the dog doesn't do what we want her to do it's because:

1) She knows what we want but she's just too stubborn. This is one an awful lot of trainers just love to lean on; this is the moment when the whole dominance myth starts spouting out of their mouths.
2) She is ungrateful and lacks a sense of duty.
3) She feels it's beneath her dignity.
4) She is angry about something we did yesterday and wants to get back at us.
5) She knows she's frustrating us, but she just wants to taunt or tease us.

And maybe the cruellest of all:

6) When she is so frightened of us that she only dares to try to meet her own needs and fulfill her longings when we aren't around, we call her sneaky.

She doesn't bring the ball back when we throw it, so we say she is dominant and refusing to give the prey to the leader — because we think she should magically understand our logic that she's supposed to go get a non-edible thrown object and bring it to us (and not to that other lady standing over there, either). But of course, she's also supposed to know *not* to go get us that greasy, disgusting McDonald's wrapper some passing teenager just littered on the pavement, even though it does smell like food.

What this all comes down to is that we often don't know how to get the dog to understand what we want or how to motivate her to do it. In our frustration and ignorance, we end up attributing all the qualities to her that are named in this chapter.

In fact, a dog lives by a number of very simple rules: no real aggression in social traffic, respect each other's personal zone, and always try to solve a conflict by a mutually acceptable compromise. It is these three rules that make the dog so wonderfully able to live among us. But a dog still has no idea what other, more complicated wishes and desires we have, and there will always be wishes a dog just can't fulfill for us. This is caused precisely by that fact that a dog is just a dog, with a brain too small and simple to encompass duty, honour, logic, revenge, taunting, teasing and sneaking.

Fact: When you look at a dog, try to see an honest and simple creature who places high value on social contact and harmonious relationships, but who is just too limited to know what we want without our help.

Part 5

The meaning of dogs' behaviour

Myth 51: My dog pulls on the leash because he wants to be the leader of the pack.

This is a romantic idea that sprung from a number of the Myths we've already covered (Myths 1, 2, 3 and 10). These Myths have caused many people to believe that dogs naturally live in a pack, that the pack always has a leader, and that the leader always walks at the head of any procession. He does this just to show off his status, but also because — as the leader — he gets to determine the route the procession will follow. So now many people believe that their dog pulls on the leash in an attempt to commit revolution. He does this to show he's the leader and that he will determine which route you follow on the walk.

Aside from all the other silliness this involves, the people who have written this stuff about dogs clearly haven't thought much about what they mean by 'leader'. They seem to take it for granted that the concept needs no explanation in spite of the ongoing philosophical, psychological and political discussions that still rage about this question. So we aren't even sure what leadership among humans means, let alone animals (who lack our huge frontal lobes in their brains). Sure, we tend to put our leaders at the head of our processions. But this doesn't in any way justify the assumption that non-human animals do the same. It's rather questionable whether walking up front when the group moves — even if you could observe this, which scientists have only rarely been able to do — means that a non-human animal is some kind of general 'leader' in the group, or assumptions about what being the 'leader' would mean to a group of non-human animals.

So we are dealing with just plain unclear conceptual thinking. But it's also a fact that this myth — which transfers ideas about wolves straight onto dogs — is not based on much real observation of wolves. The wolves people watch live in enclosures and don't go anywhere, so you can't see who would head the procession if they did. So let's look at wild wolves. These are generally observed from planes. You can't see from a plane whether it's always the same wolf who is walking up front. Therefore, we don't know that it's always one animal who always walks up front and determines the route the whole pack will take. Wolves at rest have been observed occasionally from the ground. It turns out that they all decide for themselves whether to move around and where. As the group rests, a single wolf or a pair of wolves might go off on a little excursion, returning to the group later. It's a fiction that the whole group lies around breathlessly watching some 'leader', and otherwise not budging. When such a group departs for the hunt, it isn't always the parent pair that trots up front; nor is it always the up-front animal who determines the route the group takes. Now, we are talking about just a few observations here. You can't base general conclusions on just a few observations. On the other hand, just a few observations can debunk a myth. Glad to oblige.

Aside from the fact that this story about wolves isn't based on real observations, it's also rather silly to go looking at wolves if you want to know about dogs. After all, the two have developed into separate species under entirely different circumstances.

So why does your dog pull on the leash? Observations of *dogs* show that they do this for several reasons:

1) The first reason is that a dog has four legs. This means that his gait is, by definition and by anatomy, different from ours. A dog moves with the greatest

energy efficiency and the least effort if he trots. So he has the natural tendency to break into a trot while leashed. If he's not leashed, he'll trot out ahead of you and then stop to wait, turning around to make sure you're still there. Once he's assured himself that you are, he'll trot ahead another little way. This doesn't mean he's trying to be the leader. He trots ahead because this is the most comfortable gait for him, and he looks back once in a while because he doesn't want to lose you. He likes a walk with your company better than one without. If you turn left when he has trotted ahead and turned right, he'll hasten himself back to you as soon as he sees this, not at all minding following the route you choose.

2) Even if he falls back from the trot to a walk, he still has four legs. His walk will still be just that little bit faster than yours. This isn't because he thinks he's the leader, but because he is stuck with his anatomy. In fact, the natural speed of a dog's walking gait is one of the things we pay attention to when we pair up blind people with guide dogs. We try to choose a dog whose natural walk fits a particular person's pace without too much discomfort for the dog. I.e., we aren't matching leadership qualities, but trying to match a particular guide dog's anatomy to a particular blind person's anatomy, so the two of them can have a happy life together.

3) Motivation can play a role in how fast a dog walks. He knows we're heading for the park, and he can't wait to get there. The younger and livelier the dog is, the more difficulty he'll have containing himself with the prospect of so much pleasure just a small ways ahead. This has nothing to do with wanting to be the 'leader' and everything to do with joy and a healthy lust for life.

4) In particular, the puppy or the adolescent dog will be anxious to get to the park. Both of them are in a phase of their development, in which it's of critical importance to interact as much as possible with other dogs. They are immature, can hardly wait, and are not yet developmentally equipped to control their natural impulse to get there as fast as they can. Their brains just haven't grown to that point yet.

5) A dog is a living being, not a machine you can programme. Maybe he does want to go somewhere different from where you want to go. As a living being, he has a right to his wishes and desires. And he has a right to express them. You want to turn right, he tries out whether you won't be willing to follow him around the corner to the left instead. You shouldn't interpret this as a revolution, but as a request. You don't have to say yes, but it's a bit unfriendly to get angry about the very asking.

Fact: It's not easy to spend your whole life leashed, always and eternally walking at someone else's pace, struggling with your own anatomy because the pace is so uncomfortable, suppressing your heart's desires, not allowing a sudden wish to bubble up. Pulling on the leash as a form of palace revolution? The whole idea is pitiful. In fact, a dog pulls on the leash because he is a living being with his own anatomy and longings, and he has just as much of a right to that anatomy and those longings as we have to ours.

Myth 52: The leader always goes first through a door.

This myth is a corollary of number 51 (the leader always walks up front). Now comes the myth that the Alpha leader among wolves would always be the first to go through a narrow passageway or a small opening. When they tell this fantasy story, many writers also add a heaped tablespoon of human projection. By being the first to go through, the Alpha leader supposedly shows off to his pack mates how courageous he is, in order to increase their awe and respect for him (after all, you never know what's at the end of the tunnel or behind that cave door). To top the whole thing off, the leader is also thus showing off his willingness to offer up his own life for the sake of the group if the thing at the end of the tunnel or behind that cave door turns out to be something awful.

By now my reader knows what kind of observations this is based on (i.e. none). My reader also knows that a dog is not a wolf anyway. And s/he knows the dog doesn't have the big frontal lobes that allow us to conceive of 'the other' and imagine his or her thoughts. A dog can't grasp such an abstract concept as 'courage'. A dog also cannot conceive of the other's thoughts in an abstract way, let alone imagine what the other will now be thinking, let alone that the other will be thinking something like 'aren't you brave.' Besides which, not even humans behave this way. When there's danger, the first thing we do is remove our leaders, since they are supposedly less expendable than the rest of us.

Now for the results of a longitudinal study of domestic canine behaviour, in which a group of dogs was continuously observed for many years. It turns out it's not always the same dog who is first through a door. It turns out that one of the following factors decides which dog will go through the door ahead of all the others:

1) Who happens to be standing closest to the door when the door opens.
2) Who is most anxious at that moment to get outside (be it due to diarrhoea, be it due to smelling a female in heat out there, be it due to any one of millions of momentary personal reasons).
3) Who is hungriest when the group gets home from the long walk in the woods.
4) Who is least tired after the long walk.
5) Who is the youngest and thus the least able to control her excitement.

There is, in other words, not a single reason why always being the first out the door would in any way make you into something like the dog's leader.

On the other hand, there are a number of good reasons — certainly in the cities — to teach your dog to wait until you've gone out the front door before her. If she dashes out the door as soon as it opens, she might find herself eye to eye with a passing pit bull who just happens to be in the mood for a fight. She could get run over by one of the many mopeds or cyclists who, for some reason, persist in using our pavements to ride on. She could cause someone to fall as she storms out the door, leading to broken bones or spilled groceries, and probably to irritation with your neighbours.

Fact: Who goes first through a door has utterly no meaning to a dog. Safety is the only reason to pay attention to this at all.

Myth 53: I should always eat before I feed my dog, so he will understand that I am leader of the pack.

This myth is part of the same series (and has the same roots) as Myths 51 and 52. Many a dog psychologist will tell you that besides heading the procession and being first through a door, the leader of the pack always eats first. If need be, you're to make sure your dog sees you eat a dry cracker at the kitchen counter before you give him his food. This is accompanied by a long story about evolution and about wolves, and how it's logical that the strongest and fittest takes all the best food for himself by claiming first rights to eat.

The whole thing is, however, just another romantic dream. We've already decided not to accept conclusions drawn about natural behaviour from watching captive wolves (the ones who live in refugee camps — see Myth 3). When free-living wolves catch a large prey, they all eat together and simultaneously. There may be some tension, but that's likely because they as they eat, they have to be inside each other's personal zones — unless one or more manages to take a chunk off and shove up a few metres. And when a wolf catches a small prey (for example, a rabbit), he just eats it all by himself.

But that's wolves. Our domestic dogs aren't hunters, they don't live in packs, don't even live in stable groups, and whatever they find at the rubbish dump they find alone. They eat it without worrying about what anyone else is doing. That anyone else is probably also eating whatever he found two (or twenty) yards further up.

Your dog thinks everyone eating at the same time is perfectly natural, as long as it's at a polite distance from each other (which distance can vary according to how much they like and trust each other). You over there, me over here, and simultaneously eating whatever we've found. If you decide you are always going to eat first, your dog will probably mostly feel indifferent about this fact. After all, dog rules say you have a right to keep whatever you have near your front feet and your mouth, and that you don't steal food from each other unless you're desperate. Don't expect him to draw any conclusions about who's the leader around here, though he may think it's strange that you eat a dry cracker, since you usually put something yummy on your sandwiches. And don't expect him watching you eat first to cure whatever behaviour problem he has. This is magical thinking, and it can — depending on what the problem is — end up being dangerous.

Fact: A dog doesn't give a hoot who eats first.

See also: Myth 56.

Myth 54: I should be able to take my dog's food away at all times, because a dog is naturally willing to surrender his food to the Alpha leader.

Domestic dogs are scavengers and don't have any idea of prey (see Myths 1, 4, and 5). Dogs are also semi-solitary travellers (see Myths 7 and 8). They don't live in stable groups. They have no idea about leaders (see Myths 10 and 11).

What dogs do have is a personal zone, which has a radius of anywhere from two to six feet. When food is involved, the centre of this zone is their mouth and front feet. The polite rule is that you get to keep whatever you have in this zone, regardless of your age, size, etc. Free-living dogs generally don't take food away from each other. Why should they, when they can shove on down a few yards at the dump, go look behind some other hut in the village, or tip over their own waste bin?

The exception to this rule is when there's a famine going on, in which case this social rule goes into abeyance because everyone is concerned about their own bare survival. However, it wouldn't be wise to base general statements on a famine situation. Famine only occurs among free-living dogs when the humans they live near are also suffering famine. Until a few decades ago, famine among humans was a relatively rare occurrence. If you want to know about normal behaviour, you do better to observe normal situations. Besides, when there is a famine, both the human and the canine social systems start to fall apart. Examining social systems that are in decay and heading for chaos won't tell you much about how the members normally behave when the system is functioning as it is supposed to.

There is another exception, which sometimes takes place in a normal situation. Dogs will, indeed, sometimes ignore the rules and get into an argument if a particularly delicious or rare piece of food is in question. It's quite possible that the largest and most aggressive dog will end up taking the rare titbit from the other dog, and that the other dog will resign himself to the loss. But being big and aggressive is not the same as being a leader. A dog who bullies another dog out of what he's got will end up being somewhat feared and very much avoided. Rather than becoming the leader, he or she becomes the pariah and ends up doomed to live pretty much alone.

Our well-fed household dogs don't understand why we would want to take their food away from them. To them, this is perplexing, anti-social behaviour. They end up losing their trust in us. They might start to growl, warning us to stay out of their personal zone while they eat, since we persist in showing such terrible social manners. The owner who believes in this myth is in danger of getting into the cycle of violence with his dog. The end result will be destruction of all trust, thus total deterioration of the relationship.

<u>Fact</u>: It's completely normal that your dog doesn't want to surrender his food to you. He thinks it's completely abnormal that you want him to. It totally baffles him. It teaches him that you are a bully, and we all know bullies are unfit for leadership — even if a dog did have such a thing as a leader, which he doesn't.

Myth 55: My dog doesn't bring the ball back because she is uppity and doesn't want to surrender the prey to her leader.

Dogs eat either from their food bowl or from the rubbish dump. They have no idea about prey. Many dogs won't even run after a stick or ball if you throw it. The whole business has utterly no meaning for them. To them, throwing inanimate objects through the air is just one of the many harmless but inexplicable things humans do. Some dogs do tend to run after an inanimate object you throw through the air. They do it in a reflex, and just for the fun of having an excuse to run. But even so, this doesn't mean they are seeing the thing as prey, or that they are stupid enough to confuse a piece of plastic or wood with food.

So you're out in a park and want to play with your dog. You throw something through the air. Suppose your dog does chase it. Then the inanimate, non-food object you just threw comes to rest on the ground. The tennis ball or the stick immediately stops being interesting once it's hit the ground and stopped moving, and thus stopped serving as an excuse to get a good stretch of the legs. So the dog sniffs it and walks away bored. Or she might sit down next to the thing and wait for something to happen. Your dog would be perfectly happy to see something fly through the air again. She's sitting there thinking, 'People sometimes throw inanimate objects through the air. If I wait long enough, maybe he'll do it again.' She has no idea what we want or what criteria we've invented for that to happen. She has to be *taught* that you will throw the thing again if only she brings it back to you first. There is just no way she can guess all by herself, because her brain just isn't big enough — and contrary to myth, she can't read our minds.

In other cases, the dog will pick the thing up and come back to you, then refuse to let go of whatever it was you threw. This has nothing to do with keeping prey, nor with power. Very often, the dog is trying to tempt you to play a game of tag with her, a game dogs love and often play with each other without any evil or revolutionary intentions. It might be that your dog loves to play tug-of-war, another game dogs play without uppity intentions.

Which brings us to another myth, namely that you always have to win a tug of war with your dog. In fact, if a dog starts to display threat signals during a tug of war, this tells you someone has, in the past, either always insisted on winning, or else has done the thing of being the 'leader' by constantly taking things away from the dog. The dog ends up feeling unsure whether tug of war with a human is an innocent game, or whether humans will always break the rules and use the game as an excuse to bully her. It still has nothing to do with 'keeping the prey'.

In all cases, all you need to do is teach the dog that if she brings the thing back to you and lays it at your feet, you'll throw it again. You can start by rewarding her with a small food treat every time she drops something anywhere near you — at home, in the park, wherever, and be it a sock, a ball, a toy, whatever. After a while, the dog will start bringing all kinds of things to you and dropping them at your feet. You reward, pick the thing up, throw it a couple feet. The dog thinks, 'Great! Now I can go and bring it again for a yummy treat!' — and does so. You can then gradually increase the distance you throw things. If your dog turns out to like this running game, you can soon dispense with the treats. The game itself becomes the reward.

Fact: The dog who doesn't return a ball or a stick is not refusing to surrender prey. She has just never learned the punch line our game is supposed to lead up to.

See also: Myths 57 and 58.

Myth 56: If my dog begs at the table, this means he's dominant, because he's trying to make the leader of the pack surrender the prey.

If your dog is begging at the table, a number of things could be going on.

1) Your dog is a young puppy. He hasn't had time yet to learn all the grown-up rules about possession and the personal zone. He is also too young to be able to control both his curiosity ('it sure smells good, wonder what it is') and his impulses. So he comes over completely innocently to see what you're eating. Despite the innocence of this behaviour, I'd advise humans not to share food with their puppy from the table. Your puppy has enough of his own food to eat, and you don't want to train behaviour now that will irritate you later...

2) ...Because the second reason a dog begs at the table is that someone trained him to. Most of us don't do this on purpose. It's just that we forget that training doesn't only take place when we're standing at attention at our dog school, but that training takes place every second of every day, in everything we do with our dogs. Dogs are *always* learning. At dog school, we give him a treat when he does a perfect 'sit' next to our knee. We know we are training him to sit. In the end, he will always do a perfect sit next to our knee out on the training field. We are pleased about this. The trouble is, it works the same way at home, except we aren't always conscious that we are still training the dog. You, or your guests, or your children, give the dog a little bite of food as he sits next to someone at the table. In the end, he will always come and sit next to someone at the table. We are not pleased about this. We forget that the dog doesn't know the difference between the training field and our dining room, and that all he's doing is repeating behaviour we reward. It's not fair to get angry at behaviour we have trained him to do ourselves, and which the dog is thus doing in all innocence and having no idea we don't like it. And don't be fooled. A dog's behaviour always tells a tale about his past learning experiences. His behaviour always tells the truth, because dogs don't have the large frontal lobes you need to think up lies. So when your children claim they never sneak a bite to the dog, someone is lying, and it's not the dog.

3) If your dog gets very insistent when he begs at the table, it means someone has been using the technique of intermittent reward. Intermittent reward means sometimes you do reward a behaviour and sometimes you don't. This technique will cause behaviour to intensify and become persistent. For a complete explanation of this technique, see Myth 68.

4) If your dog sometimes gets a titbit from the table, but on other occasions he doesn't, and your dog starts to growl as he sits there next to you, you are still not dealing with 'dominant' behaviour. You are dealing with what we call extinction aggression (see Myth 58, paragraph 6), aggression that can take place when an expected reward is not forthcoming. This is a general animal reflex (which humans also have), and it has nothing to do with social status and such like. It can, on the other hand, be related to learning experiences. If your dog shows extinction

aggression, then it's possible he has learned in some other situation that growling works, that is, it will yield a reward of some kind (see Myth 31, the spoiled little yappy dog).

Fact: If you don't want your dog to beg at the table, don't give him anything in the first place. Begging at the table is learned behaviour that has nothing to do with social status.

Myth 57: You should remove the dog's food bowl and any leftovers when he's finished eating, because only the Alpha leader is allowed to eat whenever he pleases.

Because a free-living dog spends his time scavenging on his own, there is no such thing as 'the leader gets to eat first.' If you're alone, then you are simultaneously both the first and the last to eat. At the rubbish dump where the dog came into being (and where the dog still lives in many countries in the world), there's food scattered around all over the place. All the resident dogs eat whenever they feel hungry. If some 'Alpha leader' wanted to be the only one to eat when he pleased, he'd have to spend all his time trying to defend the entire dump and all the scattered food. He would soon die of either starvation or exhaustion. Animals don't waste energy this way.

The best rule is to leave your dog's food bowl and his leftovers for him to return to later if he feels like a snack.

There are two exceptions to this rule. The first one is if someone has tried to be the leader by constantly taking a dog's food (and/or non-edible objects) away from him. (See Myth 58.) In this case, it's likely the dog has learned he has to defend his food against humans, because we are insane and anti-social. Try to remember that this has nothing to do with some human projection like a 'dominance hierarchy', because pasting this kind of sloppily conceived label on a dog's behaviour blinds us to what is truly going on. Threat behaviour around food is a sign of damaged trust between the dog and humans. Further attempts to set up a 'dominance hierarchy' about food will only make matters worse. If your of your the relative dog has learned he has to defend food from humans, the best thing to do is leave him in peace while he eats. Wait until he's finished eating and has left the kitchen, then remove the food bowl and the leftovers. The reason for this is not to prove you are the leader of the pack, but because a dog who has learned to defend food might get touchy about his leftovers if you need to go into the kitchen for some reason while he happens to be there.

A second reason to quietly remove his leftovers can be that you are planning to do some training with him later in the day. Since a good trainer usually works with food rewards, it's a good idea not to start the lesson with the dog feeling stuffed. If he's slightly hungry, the rewards will look more attractive to him, and he'll be willing to work harder for them. However, be careful not to exaggerate this. In the laboratory, it has turned out that animals don't need to be starved first to get them to work for food rewards. Most animals will work for the pleasure of solving a puzzle — i.e. for the pleasure of feeling less bored and for the pleasure of experiencing behaviour being successful. Animals achieve better when they are not overly hungry. The reason for this is that extreme hunger creates distress, and distress of any kind will always slow down a learning process.

Fact: Let your dog keep his leftovers — unless you have a trust issue with him, or unless you want to train later in the day. In both of these cases, you should wait until he's finished eating and left the kitchen before removing his bowl. This will prevent making the trust issue even worse, or creating a trust issue with him if you don't already have one.

Myth 58: I should practise taking things away from my dog (balls, sticks, and other toys) because a dog must surrender the prey to the leader of the pack at all times.

See also Myth 54. Aside from the fact that dogs have no idea of prey, and that they generally don't take food away from each other, it's a bit far-fetched to think your dog would confuse an inedible object with prey even if he *were* a hunter, which he is not. As far as inedible objects go, the realities are as follows:

1) Dogs generally respect each other's personal zone, a.k.a. the possession zone. You're usually allowed to keep whatever you have in that zone. This has nothing to do with social status.

2) Whether or not you want to keep or take a thing depends entirely on your subjective valuation of that thing at that particular moment. Even food has no value if you're not hungry at the moment you happen to see it.

3) A dog will only value an inedible object if he has learned in the past that the inedible object has some kind of value. A dog who has never learned to play with a tennis ball won't show the least bit of interest in the tennis balls lying around the house.

4) If a dog has learned to play with a certain object, then he will perceive that thing as a source of satisfaction in life.

5) If you consistently take sources of satisfaction and pleasure away from a dog, you are teaching him you can't be trusted. You are teaching him that you are anti-social, and that you don't value social peace above the possession of objects. The dog will start to anticipate that your approach may mean the loss of whatever satisfaction he was just getting out of his toy. He may decide the best thing to do is flee to a spot where you can't reach him. On the other hand, there won't always be a safe spot available, or there might not always be a route to safety open.

6) In such a case, when you succeed in taking the toy away, you might arouse 'extinction aggression' in your dog. Extinction aggression is a reflex that can occur when a reward or a source of satisfaction is removed, or even at the threat of its removal. Almost all animals have this reflex, not only dogs. We have it, too. It is not learned behaviour. It can take place regardless of environmental circumstances, and regardless of who the dog is facing. In the laboratory, a rat has been shown to attack not only another rat, but even something as big as a cat or a dog in a neighbouring cage when rewards suddenly cease or something the rat likes is suddenly taken away. A bird will, under the same circumstances, attack a cat or a dog in the next cage. A cat will attack a dog or a chimpanzee, and so on. If there isn't any living animal around to attack, the frustrated animal will attack and fiercely bite some inanimate object in his cage. Extinction aggression can be uncontrolled and savage. When you take something away from your dog, don't forget that your hand is the nearest object around, and that you are the nearest living creature. If the dog bites your hand, or if he attacks you, this can be a reflex that is entirely independent of the relative physical powers or social relationship.

I.e., it's not 'dominance' but simple extinction aggression. The fact that most dogs don't do this is thanks to the dog's origin and his general lack of aggression as a species. It is also thanks to how his social system works, and that dogs generally value good relationships and social peace very highly as resources. It's kind of pathetic to kid yourself that this reticence to use violence back at you has anything to do with leadership qualities in yourself, while in fact it's evolution and the dog who are to thank for this.

7) It is, in view of all the preceding, completely natural for a dog to give away some object he has, and just as natural for him not to. What he'll do is dependent on his inner state and valuation of an object at a particular moment, on the social landscape's equilibrium at that moment, on his past history with objects (and with us or other dogs), and sometimes on natural reflexes over which an animal has little control (such as extinction aggression). Don't forget that every time you take something away from him, you are giving him a learning experience that will shape his expectations (i.e. influence his inner state) the next time.

Fact: The more you take things away from your dog, the more you will ruin your relationship with him. This has nothing to do with power and leadership, and everything to do with trust and how dogs organise their social systems.

Myth 59: I should be the one to control the toys, and I should be sparing in allowing my dog to play with them, so he will remember that I am the Alpha leader.

This myth is related to Myth 57, originating in the idea that only the leader of the pack can have stuff — be it food or inedible possessions — lying around all over the place, and still be able to claim his stuff at any and all times. If your dog can always find a toy somewhere in the house, this will supposedly spark the idea in her mind that she is apparently the leader, since her stuff is all over the place. The people who thought up this idea then went on to attribute all kinds of doggy behaviour to the fact that there are toys lying around. For example, they tell us this is what makes dogs beg at the table, bite visitors in their hands and/or ankles, pull on the leash, growl when eating, refuse to obey our commands, and (of course) defend the toys. All these very different kinds of behaviour supposedly share a single cause, namely that the dog has developed complicated (and apparently not very sympathetic) ideas about being the leader, all because her toys are lying around.

The whole idea is rather far-fetched, rather anthropomorphic, and more than a little out of whack with how animals truly think. It expresses a complete lack of understanding about the origins of behaviour in mammals other than human men.

The advice to be sparing in giving your dogs toys is useless. Removing all the toys won't have any effect whatsoever on whatever behaviour problem your dog has, except that it can, in some cases, backfire and aggravate the problem.

If a dog is deprived of toys, and thus of distraction, in her home, she can become bored. Boredom can cause measurable distress in an animal. Boredom is damaging to an animal's mental well-being and can, because of the stress hormones the body produces, damage an animal's physical health. Your dog can become apathetic, having lost all expectation that life will bring her anything fun or exciting. The lack of stimulation will cause various neural networks in her brain to start weakening and even to die off. She becomes dulled, and her capabilities diminish. Some dogs react to boredom by developing obsessive-compulsive behaviour. The dog starts to lick or chew compulsively at some part of her body. This behaviour can be so extreme that she licks parts of her body totally bald, or she licks and chews until open wounds develop. This is similar to the human nail biter whose fingernail beds are completely stripped and painful for the rest of us to even look at. Taking away all your dog's toys can have serious detrimental consequences for your dog's mental and physical health.

Taking away all her toys can also artificially heighten her motivation to keep a toy on the rare occasion she's allowed to have one. This is similar to the situation in Myth 24, where we looked at puppies who were kept in impoverished environments and, in many cases, starved first, in order to make sure they would engage in a conflict about a bone. With nothing to do in the house, your dog starts to suffer mental starvation. She loses the opportunity to maintain her social skills with respect to possessions. You both lose the opportunity to have trust building experiences with possessions. So in addition to her diminished well-being, you are creating a situation of deprivation, in which conflict may become more — not less — likely.

These conflicts can become more intense than they would have been under more normal, less deprived circumstances. If you remove all her toys, your dog may end up very bored. A dog suffers when she's bored. Relief of boredom then produces a feeling of pleasure, as the toys meet various mental and physical needs your dog has. So the more bored she is, the more intense her satisfaction may be on the rare occasion when she does have a toy. Then you want to take the toy away, to show you are the leader. But when we take away a thing or a reward that is giving an animal intense satisfaction, we risk triggering extinction aggression (see Myth 58, paragraph 6). Because your dog is now in a state of artificial deprivation, and because her motivation to keep the toy is now artificially heightened, this extinction aggression can be especially fierce. I mean, these are exactly the techniques scientists use to make sure dogs will have artificial conflicts in the laboratory. Why in heaven's name would it be good advice to do this in your home?

Fact: You don't have to be Miserly Master of the Toys to have a good relationship with your dog. Being miserly with toys will not solve any behaviour problems your dog may have, and it may make the problems worse.

Azrin, NH, Hutchinson, RR, Hake, DF, Extinction-induced aggression, *JEAB* 9, 191–204, 1966.

Catania, AC, Coming to terms with establishing operations, *The Beh Analyst* 16:219–224, 1993.

Davison, M, Baum, WM, Choice in a variable environment: Every reinforcer counts, *JEAB* 74: 1–24, 2000.

Dunbar, I, Bohnenkamp, G, *Preventing Aggression,* Centre for Applied Animal Behaviour, Berkeley CA, 1985 (3rd ed June 1986).

Kelly, JF, Hake, DF, An extinction-induced increase in an aggressive response with humans, *JEAB* 14: 153–164, 1970.

Sidman, M, *Coercion and its Fallout,* Authors Cooperative, Inc. Publishers, Boston, 1989.

Myth 60: If my dog tries to sleep on my bed, this means he's trying to become leader of the pack.

A lot of people, including a lot of dog trainers, will tell you it is of utmost importance not to let your dog lie on elevated resting spots (such as the sofa). Even if you are so stupid as to allow the dog on the sofa, then you still absolutely *must* forbid the dog to lie on your bed! These people will tell you that the moment you find your dog on your bed is the moment you know he has been sneakily, slowly increasing his rank for a long time already, and that he now thinks the time has come to overtly take over the house.

This utterly stupid idea has caused much unnecessary human anxiety, and it has caused much unnecessary canine suffering.

This utterly silly idea is also based — yet again — on the fantasy that the dog is a wolf, and the misconception that we know anything much about wolves in the first place.

Now, we already know that wolves don't allow us to observe them in the wild if they can help it. We also know that scientists solved this problem by occasionally shooting a tranquilliser dart into a wolf, putting a radio collar on her, and releasing her to return to her group. Scientists can then sometimes localize the group by flying around in a plane. They watch what the wolves do from high in the air. But human hunters track wolves from the air, too, and wolves know this. So the main thing scientists see while flying around in their planes is fleeing wolves. These fleeing wolves dive into the cover of the forest as quick as they can. They do not oblige by going to some open terrain and lying around there for the scientist to count who is lying highest (even if he could see that from high up in the air) — or for the human hunter to pick them off one by one as they display their resting behaviour.

Nevertheless, someone thought up the idea that the wolf with the highest rank always sleeps on the highest spot. (Which could make us wonder whether Adolph Hitler had a preference for the top bunk bed — see Myth 10.) The whole idea is a human fantasy and a human projection — an anthropomorphism. But aside from that, the whole fantasy is about wolves, and at this point we know that the dog is not a wolf. He is a species of his own. We know at this point that if you want to know about dogs, you have to look at dogs and not at wolves.

Research on free-ranging dogs in urban areas proved that when a dog wants to rest, he usually goes off alone to find a shrub to lie under or a vestibule to sleep in. If the weather is very hot, a dog will find a spot under a car. Sometimes he shares this piece of shade with a friend, both lying equally high (or low, if you like) on the flat street. Sometimes a dog was seen lying in the sun on top of a car. When groups of dogs were seen resting or sunning, the groups were loose collections of passing acquaintances. Dogs turned out not to live in packs, and not to have leaders, and — relevant here — there was no pattern at all in which dog lay on the dumped sofa (higher) or the dumped mattress (lower) on the vacant lot.

In my own longitudinal study of a group of well-socialised dogs, I found the explanation for why now one dog, now another, would be found on the sofa versus on the mattress at a vacant lot. The dogs in my study lived in the natural environment — that is, together in an ever-changing group of other dogs, and in the presence of various other animals humans keep (in this case, a cat, a rabbit and a free-ranging house rat). These dogs were observed almost twenty-four hours a day, seven days a week, for (so far) fourteen years. It turned out that everyone was allowed to lie everywhere. There is absolutely no sifting as far as how high one or another resting spot might be. Not only that, but anyone who has occupied a spot is allowed to stay there — be it a puppy, be it the cat, be it the rabbit. If a dog approached a spot where he or she wanted to lie down and found it occupied, the dog either went off to look for another spot or, sometimes, gently tried to join the occupant on the resting spot. As soon as the occupant vacated the armchair, cushion, dog bed or human bed s/he had been lying on (for example, to go drink some water), the other dog was free to quickly grab the vacated spot (if he or she hadn't already fallen asleep elsewhere). Now the spot was his or hers, and the first dog would just go lie somewhere else. Research shows, in other words, that dogs live by the rule that a spot belongs to the occupant until he or she vacates it, and then it's up for grabs. Relative elevation plays no role whatsoever.

If your puppy tries to climb onto your bed, this does not mean the dog is 'dominant' or that he thinks he's the crown prince who will grow up to be king in your house. What he is is a *baby*, who is looking for the safety of your smell and warmth, and for the pleasure of your company. Just like he did with his mother. If you find your adult dog on your bed one day, this doesn't mean he's decided now is the moment to take over your house. It just means he chose the place to lie down where a) it's nice and comfy, and b) your reassuring smell is all around him. If you were out when he climbed onto your bed, it doesn't mean he decided to start a revolution while you were away. It means he missed you and looked for the spot where your smell is strongest, so he could feel like you were still with him a little. Even the dog who knows he's not allowed on your bed might, in his loneliness, be unable to resist the need to be near your smell. You shouldn't see this as naughty, uppity or 'dominant', instead you should be touched by how attached he is to you. The same goes for the dog who quickly occupies your spot on the couch when you go to the kitchen for a snack during the commercials. Your spot is all nice and warm, it smells wonderfully of you, and... the dog rule is that a spot is up for grabs when the occupant vacates it for a sec. Your dog has no evil or dangerous intentions.

If your dog growls at you once he's lying on the bed or the couch, then something else is going on. We will handle this in Myth 61.

Fact: There's absolutely no need to fear a household revolution just because your dog chooses elevated resting spots, even if one of them is your bed.

Myth 61: If my dog growls at me when he's lying on my bed, he is trying to dominate me.

There are three domestic canine rules that are relevant to this situation: 1) Everyone is allowed to occupy any resting spot regardless of relative elevation; 2) You don't enter each other's personal zone without permission; and, 3) If you vacate a spot, it's up for grabs. It is a proven fact that a threatening dog is a dog who is feeling unsure about what's going to happen next. She is indicating that she doesn't (yet) trust what the other is planning to do, and is asking the other to keep a little distance for the moment.

Human rules about spots are different. We humans sometimes ask each other to move over on the couch to make some space. We can have possessive feelings about places even if we don't occupy those places at all times. We think of our bed as a very private place. Even our children aren't allowed on our bed, let alone a dog or a stranger. A lot of people believe it's unhygienic if a dog lies on their bed. Other people have been told by a dog trainer that it's an absolute no-no to let a dog lie on elevated spots, and most of all their owner's bed.

Dogs don't understand any of this. All they know is that a spot was vacant. It just so happened to be in your bedroom, where he's away from household traffic and he can have an undisturbed nap. This particular spot has the big advantage that your beloved odour is especially strong there.

So the dog is lying on your bed, you come into the bedroom, and she growls at you. This means nothing more (and nothing less) than that she has learned in the past that people chase her out of the bedroom. To her, this is abnormal and perplexing behaviour, which goes against all the canine rules of politeness and peaceful interactions. She growls because her past experience has taught her to feel unsure about what perplexing and rude — and maybe even intimidating or scary — thing you might do now. Because she is anxious about what you are going to do, she is asking you to keep your distance for the moment. The dog has no idea that you will interpret her simple and polite request to stay out of her personal zone as aggression. It is perfectly normal among dogs to say, 'Not just now, dear,' and curling a lip for a sec or growling is, among dogs, the perfectly polite way for them to do it.

This behaviour can be more intense in a dog who has been treated harshly. Lots of dogs end up in obedience classes where their humans learn to use the choke chain and other painful methods of training the dog. These dogs learn that a human who enters their personal zone is very likely going to hurt them. Lots of people spend their time trying to 'dominate' their dog. These people are constantly doing things the dog doesn't understand — taking his food bowl away, taking his toys away, getting angry at all kinds of things that are normal and innocent dog behaviour (pulling on the leash, dashing out the door, indicating she'd like to turn left when the human wants to turn right, and — yup — climbing onto an elevated vacant spot for a nap). Many people have hit, slapped or kicked their dog for all this innocent behaviour, or they have given a hard and painful jerk on the choke chain. The dog has learned to expect people to be unpredictable and to get angry at strange moments. She has learned that people will hurt her when they do this. She feels defensive at the very thought that you are now going to approach her.

This behaviour can get dangerous in a dog who has first learned that we aren't to be trusted, and then learned that biting is a good way to keep us from hurting her. These dogs can lash out and bite if you disturb them while they are sleeping. Even here, in the dog who is sure of the effect of her bite, 'dominance' still has nothing to do with it. The dog is just plain miserable due to having to be on her guard all the time. Her behaviour is the result of a learning history, which is — at all times — still open to change, if only people will stop hurting the dog.

Fact: Your growling dog in the bedroom chose a spot to rest in all innocence. Unsure of what humans will do, she chose a spot away from human traffic. When you entered the room, she became unsure about what was going to happen next, and she is asking you to please keep your distance. She is not dominating you. She is telling you she doesn't trust you, and you really need to think about the reasons for that.

If the problem is serious, you need the help of a competent behavioural therapist. See Myth 41 for how to find one.

Myth 62: If my dog doesn't obey a command, this is dominant behaviour.

This particular myth is truly sad, because it is a result of how good our dogs usually are. A dog is generally very attached to his human. The basic attitude of the dog's whole species is to value social relationships and to look for compromises that will keep relationships peaceful and intimate. Because the dog is so sensitive in conducting social relations, he learns to pick up on all kinds of subtle signals in his human. He learns how to cooperate in all kinds of things with us, without our having to consciously teach him what we want. We get used to the dog knowing what we want. Comes a moment when we want something else from him, something that isn't part of our usual routine. The dog doesn't do what we want. We don't get it, because he's always so cooperative, so we decide he's now being stubborn. 'He knows what I want, but he's just too stubborn to do it.'

Sometimes this myth is a result of human laziness. We buy a dog, but we don't bother to learn anything about dogs, or about how animals learn or how you can communicate to a dog what you want him to do. You don't bother to go to school with the dog, because you assume anyone can raise a dog. But even if you do go to classes with the dog, you immediately proceed to chat with the person next to you, while the instructor's words fall on deaf ears. You don't bother to practice at home with the dog, expecting the dog to learn what he needs to know in that one short hour a week at the dog school. When the classes are done, you expect the dog to now know what you want — after all, he's had ten whole lessons — and you decide he's just stubborn — i.e. being 'dominant'.

In many cases, the dog school will affirm this myth. Although there are more and more good dog schools, there are still lots of trainers out there who are hanging on for dear life to the old nonsense theories. These trainers have no idea how animals learn. The first thing they make you do is to buy a choke chain, so you can painfully punish the dog for each mistake he makes. This trainer doesn't know that he is ignorant about how animals learn, so when his methods don't work, he blames the dog. This is the point where you get the whole stupid song and dance about pack living, the dominance hierarchy, and being the Alpha leader. You are told that the dog knows what you want, but that he is just too 'dominant' to do it. He's resisting letting you exercise power over him because of his 'dominant' personality. All you need to do is break his dominance, and then all will be well. In fact, this is nothing more than an excuse to get violent with the dog and, in fact, to torture him. Yet again, the dog supposedly knows what you want and is just being stubborn.

What it all comes down to is that we assume the dog can read our minds.

Forget it. Dogs can't read our minds. They are extremely sensitive to body language and non-verbal signals. They can learn pretty quickly to predict our behaviour and how they can adapt their own responses to it. They do this gladly, but it only works as long as things go according to the normal routine. When something in the situation is suddenly different, the dog can't predict it anymore, and our commands don't help him know what to do.

The reason commands don't help him is that dogs' brains are not equipped to process verbal information. It is extremely difficult for a dog to learn human words. To do this, they have to be led through a learning process that is specifically tailored to help non-verbal creatures. First the dog has to learn that a particular behaviour might get him some kind of reward from us at all. He can then learn to do this behaviour when presented with a non-verbal signal — e.g. a certain movement of your hand, or the fact that you get the leash off the hook in the hallway. Once he's learned the non-verbal signal, you can help him associate the signal with a word. He can learn that when you say 'sit', it means the same thing as the hand signal for 'sit'. He can learn that when you say, 'Wanna go out?' it means you are going to get the leash in a sec. He will start to react to the words even before you go get the leash. Eventually, he will — under normal circumstances — be able to understand the word you use as well as he understands the non-verbal signal. But as soon as circumstances change, he'll need you to use the non-verbal signal again, so he can be sure he heard you right and to help him know the word still means the same thing it usually means.

But we're not done yet. Even if you have helped your dog in all the right ways, so that he has learned to understand a number of human words, routine and circumstances continue to play a role in whether he will know what you want him to do. If you ask him to sit in a situation where he usually just stands next to you, this will cause him to feel honestly confused. His entire past and all the environmental signals are telling him to stand. The only thing that is telling him to do something else is that one human word. Because his brain is put together to react according to habit and to be highly sensitive to non-verbal signals, these will all have much greater weight for him than that little word you just said. He is confused, thinks he misunderstood what you said, doesn't know what to do. So he does what he always does in this particular situation, and just keeps standing there next to you. He is not being disobedient or 'dominant.' He just doesn't understand what you want.

If a dog has been trained with a lot of punishment, then you get a different situation. This dog isn't just baffled because he's being asked to do something unusual. The dog has been treated with violence in the past to make him obey commands, and a command has become a signal that violence is imminent if he doesn't guess right (and fast, to boot). The unexpected command frightens him. His fear makes his brain shut down altogether. He's subject to fear-induced deafness, too terrified to hear anything at all. Or he hears the word, but he's too scared to remember what it meant, and — knowing that every small mistake will be harshly punished — is too scared to make even an educated guess. He doesn't even dare try the behaviour he normally does in this situation. So he freezes up and does nothing at all. He might show some stress signals — yawning, suddenly sniffing the ground where he stands — and he looks away, hoping that averting his gaze will calm his human. The owner who has learned to train the dog by punishment interprets all this as 'contempt for me,' and punishes the dog yet again, convinced that violent behaviour is the way to win respect (give me a break!). The dog will end up being even more frightened in the next unexpected situation. He will be even less able to focus and understand a verbal command, and even less able to get over his paralysis and do a behavioural guess. This is a vicious circle that can go on endlessly, with increasing frustration for the dog's owner and increasing suffering for the dog. This dog is not 'dominant', he's just scared shitless.

If you are dealing with a young dog, then there are yet other factors playing. An adolescent dog is in a developmental phase in which it is of great importance for him to interact with other dogs. As he makes the transition from being a pup to being an adolescent, his behaviour goes into temporary chaos, and he needs the help of other dogs to reorganise it into a coherent and polite doggy whole. His body is suddenly full of raging hormones, which cause all kinds of feelings that are new to him. His impulse control is temporarily gone. To the adolescent dog, the urge to interact with other dogs is irresistible — because he needs their help in learning how to take his place as a mature and polite adult in the canine social system. Other dogs teach him anew that he must get his impulsiveness under control. They teach him acceptable ways to deal with his new feelings. They remind him that compromise is still the way to go, despite all the new feelings, and that he still needs to avoid arguments and to inhibit his bite at all times. In fact, you should be glad your adolescent is seeking out these experiences, and you should not be too anxious to cut off the playing and get back home with him again — because he is working on social skills that will be of benefit to your own relationship with him, too. Aside from all this, your adolescent dog is at some distance from you when you call him. He's surrounded by a rush of environmental stimuli in the group of dogs he's playing with. He's paying attention to their signals, there's lots of noise during play, he's concentrating on controlling his own reactions to the various stimuli. If he doesn't obey your command to come to you, he probably didn't even hear it because it got lost in the chaos of stimuli he's in the middle of. Or he did hear it, but is so involved in the lessons he's learning that your request seems less important than the other thing he's doing. I would remind you at this point that a dog is a living being. He has his own motivations, longings and natural behaviours — and he has a right to these. Your adolescent who would rather play than come when you call him is not 'dominant' nor even disobedient. He's just full of adolescent contradictions and, at the same time, full of a young and healthy lust for life.

Who is supposedly the leader plays absolutely no role in any of this. The natural dog lives in constantly shifting, flexibly organised groups, which are based on voluntary friendship. Dogs do not have leaders. Dogs do not give each other commands. The only power one dog ever exercises over another dog is the power to keep the other out of his personal zone — and the power of personal attraction. Dogs do not tell each other to sit or lie down, to come here **right now**, to shake hands, or to go find the ball and retrieve it. A dog has no interest whatsoever in controlling what another dog does, as long as the other stays outside his personal zone. And if a dog wants the other to enter his personal zone, he *tempts* the other dog into coming closer. A canine command to approach does not exist.

Tempt. Here is the key word in all of this. To train a dog, you need some technical knowledge of how animals learn, that's for sure. But training a dog is, above all, learning how to motivate and tempt a dog into cooperating voluntarily with what you are proposing. Violence and 'Alpha leaders' have nothing to do with it. They are just excuses to be lazy and cruel, and they get in the way of what you want to achieve.

Fact: If your dog doesn't obey a command, you need to take a good look at your training techniques and find ways to improve them.

Myth 63: If my dog stands up on her hind legs and places her front paws on me to greet me, she's trying to dominate me.

The funny thing about this one is that it hasn't yet occurred to anyone (including the experts) to cry 'dominant!' when small dogs do this. The fact that we only make this reproach when we're talking about a big dog betrays (yet again) that we aren't describing what's going on in dogs, but rather talking about what's going on in ourselves and then projecting our feelings onto the dog.

When a large dog stands up on her hind legs to greet us, she suddenly seems very large. She might even make us (almost) lose our balance. This may make us feel a bit intimidated, but just because that's how we feel doesn't mean the dog is intending to make us feel that way. Some of us never minded our dogs doing this until we heard the story about the dominance hierarchy. Ever since then, we've been wondering why she wants to get her teeth so close to our face.

Dogs, on the other hand, have never been told about the dominance hierarchy theory. They have no idea about ranks and leaders. They aren't the least interested in power games as long as they trust a person. If they don't, they will want the power to keep that person out of their personal zone. Aside from that, dogs are mostly interested in affirming the peaceful relations with the other. One of the signals they use to do this is licking or nuzzling at the corners of the other's mouth, in particular with others they feel most attached to.

A dog who stands on her hind legs to greet a human is usually trying to get to those corners of the human mouth. She is trying to give us the affectionate and calming welcome she would give to another dog she's intimate with. The trouble is that no one taught her humans would rather she didn't, which we forgot to do because it was so cute when she was little. In fact, many people encourage puppies and young dogs to greet them this way because it looks so cute. A dog has no way of knowing that we'll start to be irritated or scared by the exact same behaviour just because she's gotten bigger now.

As long as you don't have other problems with your dog, you don't have to be worried because she greets you this way. You can teach her to keep all four feet on the floor by taking a treat in your hand before you come in the door, then holding the treat in front of her nose as if it were a magnet and using this edible magnet to move her back down to the floor. As soon as she's on all fours, give her the treat and lots of affectionate attention. She'll learn soon enough what she's supposed to do.

If you do have some other problem with your dog, it might indeed be a good idea not to let her teeth get so close to your face until this problem is solved. However, the solution is the same as in the preceding paragraph — use a treat to get her down on all fours. By doing it this way, you'll simultaneously be working on the other problem, since ninety-nine percent of the problems we have with dogs are due to their having lost their trust in us and feeling worried about what we'll do. Mistrust and anxiety are, after all, the only reasons your dog would ever think of using her teeth against you. (For exceptions to this rule, see Myth 30.)

<u>**Fact:**</u> Licking the corners of the other's mouth is a friendly greeting and a calming signal. You don't have to be afraid of a dog who trusts you.

Myth 64: Mounting the other is dominant behaviour.

This myth is a projection of several human characteristics and feelings onto dogs. 'Mounting' is when a dog stands on his hind legs, embraces another dog (or our leg) with his front legs, and makes a pumping movement with his pelvis, as if he's copulating with the other dog (or our leg). Just for the record, female dogs do this sometimes, too. Nevertheless, when dogs do this, it is always a sexual gesture — and that's where we humans get in trouble, because sex is a difficult subject for us. When a dog does something sexual at an inappropriate moment, we feel embarrassed or ashamed. When we feel embarrassed or ashamed, we also tend to feel dominated. It's then hard for us to suppress the feeling that it must be the dog's intention to make the other feel dominated.

Besides our own embarrassment about sexual actions, it's also a fact that sex is, among humans, all too often all about power. It's a very recent development even in our modern Western societies that women have been allowed command over their own bodies and sexuality. The law in our modern Western societies designated women as chattels (that is, an item of tangible property) until some thirty years ago. Most of the world still gives women the status, in law, of items of tangible property, including our bodies and our sexuality. Despite much progress (in some places), rape, the sexual abuse of children, and sexual harassment in the workplace remain persistent problems for women everywhere in the world. And, as we all know, it's now generally recognised that rape, child sexual abuse, and sexual harassment at work are not at all about sex and desire, but about the exercise and display of power.

It is, then, no wonder that human scientists decided that sexual behaviour among animals was also about power, giving way to the age-old tendency to project the structure of their own societies onto the animal kingdom. It isn't surprising either that our own feelings tell us that a dog's mounting behaviour is power behaviour, especially when it's not really about mating.

The fact remains, however, that dogs don't share our feelings. They are innocent and unembarrassed about their bodies and about sex. If we look at how their brains and bodies are put together, we have to conclude that sex must be pleasant for them, but at the same time we also have to conclude that they aren't capable of having all kinds of complicated thoughts about the whole business. A dog isn't capable of thinking about what would be an appropriate moment, who would be an appropriate partner, or that something like sex would have anything to do with such a totally different subject (and motivation) as power. When a dog mounts another being, this is a simple, direct and honest reaction to certain stimuli, which doesn't mean anything but what it really means. We have made things so complicated in our own lives that it may be hard for us humans to imagine, but in dogs the behaviour is generally motivated by joy.

There are four situations in which a dog might mount another dog (or our leg).

1) **A female is in heat**. In this case, we are dealing with a real sexual act — which, by the way, only takes place if the female concurs voluntarily. Dogs do not rape. Sex has, for them, nothing to do with power.

2) **Displacement behaviour**. Displacement behaviour is what a dog does when

he doesn't exactly know what to do with something he's feeling. Displacement behaviour is sometimes used to gain a moment to think. This is the dog who suddenly stops to sniff the ground or scratch a non-existent flea when we've called him in an angry voice. This is also the dog who goes to grab a toy when you come home because he wants to lick the corners of your mouth but he knows you don't like this, so he figures out some other way to express his joyful energy abut seeing you come home. When a dog is full of joy that he doesn't know how to express, he (or she) will sometimes mount the other. This is often done at a spot that would be the wrong place for having sex — the neck or side of the other dog, or our leg. When a dog does this joy mounting, he gets a truly imbecilic expression on his face, an open-mouthed grin, he pants, and his tongue is hanging somewhere down around his knees. There is no show of teeth nor growling. The dog who does this is in ecstasy, and he is without evil intentions.

3) **When an adult dog meets an adolescent dog.** An adolescent dog's hormones are all in a chaos. Both male and female hormones are present in the body in abnormal concentrations. Some of these dogs have a smell that operates as a sexual stimulus to some other dogs. These dogs often end up being sexually mounted, often by dogs of the same sex. The adult dog who mounts one of these adolescents isn't 'dominating' him or her. He is just confused by the smell the adolescent is giving off. This mounting is the response to a sexual stimulus. It is friendly and joyful, just as real sex is among dogs.

Conversely, many adolescent dogs will go through a phase themselves of trying to mount other dogs, a pillow, their blanket, your leg — of having a sexual reaction to the strangest things at the most inappropriate times and places. This doesn't mean the adolescent is becoming dominant as he approaches the door to adulthood. It is again just the chaos of new hormones and new feelings. A ten-month-old male dog has far too much testosterone in his body. Testosterone levels peak at this age, after which they begin to fall to normal adult levels. By the time he's a year and a half, the dog's behaviour will have returned to normal. (See also Myth 74.)

4) **Castrated males.** It seems that some castrated male dogs have more female hormones in their bodies than others. Some castrated males end up spending their lives being sexually mounted by other males. The adult male will dance around, flirt, pant, make all kinds of play gestures, and he will try again and again to get to the copulating part of the game. The castrated male may not like this, but the sexually excited male has no evil intentions. He is just reacting to the female smell the castrated dog emanates. Mounting is a sexually motivated behaviour, just as it is toward the adolescent dog.

Though mounting behaviour has nothing to do with power or showing who's in charge here, it can become distressing to the dog it's aimed at if the excited dog keeps at it for too long. Dogs are used to others obeying the rules about respecting personal zones. They are used to having other dogs wait for permission to approach, and to other dogs not approaching when asked not to. Their feeling of safety in social traffic depends on others following these rules. Nevertheless, you will sometimes see a dog who is in an ecstasy of sexual feelings persistently ignoring the signals to stop trying to get so personal. This can be confusing and distressing for the dog who is the object of the persistent flirtation.

When you see your dog in a situation like this, and you see it's starting to distress your dog, go help him or her. This doesn't mean you have to get angry at the excited dog (he means no ill, and he'll likely ignore you anyway). This means you ask the other dog's human to leash him so you can leave the area with your own dog. If that person refuses, then leaving anyway often works — when the flirting dog starts to follow you despite his human's calls, the other person will usually revert to leashing the dog after all.

Fact: Mounting behaviour is an innocent reaction to either sexual or joyful feelings. The dog who does this means no evil, nor is s/he trying to regulate a power structure.

Examples from real life

Prins

Prins was a dog I had taken in when the junkie who owned him moved out of the neighbourhood. This dog was used to starving for several days, then getting something to eat, then starving again. The first year I had him, he remained utterly amazed that he was fed every day. He was absolutely joyful about this fact. Every time I fed him he would eat with great gusto and then do a round of mounting a leg of each human in the room. It would be silly to think that this thirty-pound dog was having the following complicated thoughts: a) he had come into our house and taken over, b) that we therefore fed him every day, and c) that he should, therefore, after eating, make sure to display his power to us so we would feed him again tomorrow, and to celebrate his victory over us. In fact, he was just happy that he'd eaten today, since you never know what tomorrow will bring. After a year of being fed daily, he began to feel less surprised about that fact, and he stopped doing the rounds of mounting after a meal.

Fidessa

This was my brother's dog, a delightful and intelligent miniature poodle mix. Fidessa had a litter of puppies before she was sterilised, and my brother kept one of her daughters. Mother and daughter were great friends. They delighted in each other's company and never left each other's side. On occasion, Fidessa would look at her daughter, get a certain joyful gleam in her eye, and run over to mount her. The daughter didn't seem to mind at all, and the mounting sessions would eventually erupt into a session of delighted play. It would be silly to think that these two little friends were having the following complicated thoughts: a) you're my daughter, and even though we get along great, I have to show you who's in charge here, b) well, I'll let you mount me so you know I know you're in charge and then c) we'll play, since now we've affirmed the power relations. In fact, Fidessa was just very happy to have such a good friend of her own size around. Unlike Prins, she never did come to find that fact ordinary. She kept having these outbursts of joy in her daughter as long as she lived.

Myth 65: Standing up and placing the forepaws on the other's back is dominant behaviour.

This behaviour looks very different from the sexual mounting behaviour we just talked about (in Myth 64). The dog will stand up on his hind legs and place his forepaws on the other's back (or on our lap or shoulders). He does *not* make a pumping movement with his pelvis. This is *not* a sexually motivated action. The usual story is that it is *always* 'dominant' when a dog makes himself taller or tries to look bigger, but the reality is (as usual) a little more complicated than that. To understand the meaning of this behaviour, you have to look at the other signals the dog is using when he stands up onto the other like this. You'll see one of the following things.

1) Dog-to-dog climbing

a) An invitation to play. The dog starts squeaking, he turns his ears outward, he wags his tail excitedly, and he does little play jumps toward the other dog. In his excitement, he might rear up on his hind legs and place his forepaws on the other dog's shoulders or back for a sec. His ears are still turned so the openings point outward. This dog's delight suggests that some of the same emotions are playing as in sexual mounting. Standing up for a sec is an invitation to play.

b) Reaction to an abnormal smell. An adolescent male dog can have as much as five times the normal adult level of testosterone in his body. His feelings and behaviour are a temporary chaos, in which he's trying to find his way again. Most adult dogs will tolerate the adolescent's wild behaviour, giving him only an occasional reprimand. There is a group of adolescents, however, whose smell provokes adult males in a different way. And now you need to pay attention, because this looks quite different from the happily pumping sexual mounting or the invitation to play. The adult male's movements are stiff and tense as he rears up to place his forepaws on the younger dog's back. Once up there, he bares his teeth and stares at the back of the young dog's neck. The adult dogs freezes up in this staring posture, waiting to see what the adolescent dog will do. He's not pumping, and there is no delight nor sexual confusion. The adult dog is expressing a high level threat toward the adolescent.

In my experience, this reaction is aroused most often by certain breeds, namely the Labrador and the Golden Retrievers. This suggests that we should suspect a human cause at the root of it. Pedigreed dogs are not products of nature, but of our tampering with canine genes. Our tampering has often caused all kinds of unpleasant side effects. We've created dogs who have problems in their skeletons, dogs who have trouble breathing, dogs whose retinas slowly rot as they get older, dogs whose eyes pop out of the sockets if they get a fright, right on through to dogs with an abnormal chemical housekeeping in their entire body and/or brain. It looks as if the adolescent dog who arouses this threat behaviour in adults must have even more testosterone in his body than the average adolescent. The hypothesis here is that this causes the adolescent to stink so much of maleness that adults dogs find the smell threatening. It looks as if they react to the smell by threatening back, sometimes quite fiercely.

This hypothesis is supported by the fact that the adolescent can't control the situation nor stop the threat by using his calming signals. This means you can't just call the threat 'dominant,' because that would indicate that acting 'submissive' (as misguided people call the calming signals) should solve the problem and stop the threat. This also means that we can't place this threat behaviour in the context of our self-organising systems theory, in which adult dogs sometimes use threats to teach younger dogs how to take part in the social system in the proper way — because, again, there is no social solution for this adolescent dog. It won't help him at all to use signals to indicate he's no threat to the adult dog. He ends up getting a severe symbolic whacking — and sometimes actually being attacked — no matter what he does.

If your adolescent male is getting this kind of reaction, it's not safe to let him interact with adult males until he passes out of this stage of his development. Even if he doesn't get hurt, the experiences can be traumatic for him. As he gets older, his hormones will calm down and his testosterone level will fall to the normal adult level. Adults will start to react normally to him. So the solution to this problem is not to get angry at the adult dogs (which won't help anyway), but to wait.

c) Fighting breeds and other aggressive breeds. If a dog of one of the aggressive breeds starts to show this climbing behaviour toward your dog, he is not particularly reacting to anything in your dog. Rather, he is started to execute a genetically determined program in his brain, which will unfold no matter what your dog does. This dog is preparing himself to deliver the killing bite to the back of your dog's skull. This dog is not being 'dominant,' nor is he trying to teach your dog his 'rank', and he's not trying to teach him social rules, either. The pit bull, the American Staffordshire terrier, the Presa Canaria, the American bull dog, and all of the other breeds who have been bred for aggression, they just want your dog dead and are preparing to make him that way **right now**. This is a life-threatening situation. If you don't interfere immediately, your dog probably won't survive the coming attack. The best thing to do is to shoot over and grab the threatening dog's hind legs, and to whip them into the air in a quick and abrupt movement. No matter what happens next, **do not** let go of those hind legs until the owner of the aggressive dog has leashed him.

I know that the owners and fans of these breeds will object to this information being spread. But I have seen too many dogs maimed and killed to be much concerned about what the owners and fans of the aggressive breeds want us to believe. And when scientists and humane societies try to defend the aggressive breeds, they talk exclusively about whether we can prove these dogs kill humans more than other dogs do. Then when the evidence shows they do, the scientists and humane societies change the subject to whether these dogs 'bite' more than other dogs do. None of these people are interested in whether your dog will die. You are, and it's best to follow the above advice — which, by the way, won't hurt the aggressive bred dog a bit. It's also best to follow this advice before the attack starts, because then you run the least risk of being bitten or attacked yourself.

2) Dog-to-human climbing

So that was dog-to-dog climbing. Sometimes a dog will climb up with his forepaws on a human. To know what he means by this, you have to watch all the other signals, just like you do in dog-to-dog climbing.

a) Love for a human. Sometimes a dog loves you so much that he wants to get up and lick the corners of your mouth. He may put his paws on your lap or shoulder as he tries to get near your face. The fact that he is making himself tall has nothing to do with power relations here, it's just that there's no other way for him to reach your face.

b) Threat towards a human. If a dog climbs up against you and gives off threat signals as he does this (growling, staring at you, baring his teeth, stiffening up or totally freezing up), then we are (yet again) way beyond anything we could call social dominance even if social dominance did exist among dogs. The dog who does this to you is indicating that he's prepared to use real aggression, a thing that does not occur in normal social traffic — and for which there is no social solution. This is a dangerous situation, if only because the dog's teeth are now so close to your face and neck. This behaviour is rare, but it does occur, and (contrary to what the owner might say) it never 'just comes out of nowhere.' It can be anticipated, though humans don't always bother. In the aggressive breeds, the dog is just getting ready to do the task we created him to do, that is, to kill. The dog may never have shown this behaviour before, but it was nevertheless predictable that he eventually would — after all, that's the whole reason the guy bought the dog in the first place. In other dogs, there's always an entire history behind such behaviour, in which the dog has lost all trust in humans. These dogs have been giving clear signals for a long time that they feel tense and worried in the presence of human strangers. Just because the dog's human chooses to ignore this and continue to confront him with strangers doesn't mean the behaviour 'came out of nowhere.' In fact, there has always been an extended build-up to the moment when the dog does decide to climb onto a human and threaten.

The best thing to do when a dog directly threatens you like this is to break eye contact immediately and simultaneously totally freeze up yourself. Don't move a muscle. It's better if the dog's human doesn't touch him (this can act as a trigger) or speak in an angry voice to him (this will only heighten the dog's worry). Rather, he should call the dog in a happy tone, and try to seduce the dog into coming to him. Or he can act like he's going to the kitchen to get a dog treat or feed the dog, calmly saying the things he normally does when he does this. Hopefully, the dog will be distracted and decide to follow his human. Then the human can calmly hook a finger in the dog's collar and take the dog into some other room, putting him behind a securely closed door. Then the human should call a qualified behavioural therapist that very same evening, to start working on the trust issues with the dog. (See the text box at the end of Myth 41 on how to find a therapist.)

Better yet is not to visit someone who has a dog with an aggression problem unless the dog is securely shut away somewhere with something to keep him busy and happy during your visit.

Fact: Rearing up to place the forepaws on the other's back or shoulders can be playful. It can also be a direct threat, and so serious that it falls way outside the bounds of any kind of normal social behaviour.

Myth 66: If my dog won't let me do certain things to her, this means she's being dominant.

At this point we know that dog society is not based on power relations. Domestic dogs live by compromise, and they watch out not to do painful things to each other. We know that the threatening dog is an insecure dog. She's worried about what the other is planning to do and is therefore asking the other to stay out of her personal zone. She isn't trying to exercise power over the other, but over her own personal space — something dogs allow each other to do. It's a fact that most animals try to avoid arguments and fights whenever they can. It's also a fact that all living creatures (except certain humans and the aggressive dog breeds) will, under normal circumstances, do all they can to avoid pain.

Labelling all resistance to our human actions as just some kind of power play in a dog is, thus, lazy thinking. If we want to know what's actually going on, we have to look at our own behaviour from the dog's point of view and try to understand how it looks to her.

Dogs can be baffled by the way we want to just shove into their personal zone no matter what a dog is doing just at that moment. Dogs can be frightened by the fact that we approach without earning their trust first. It's also a fact that we often want to (or have to) do things that are unnatural or painful for a dog. Many a human impatiently combs her dog's long hair, pulling the comb through knotted spots, without thinking for a sec how much this hurts. We're in a hurry, so we get the ear ointment out of the fridge and put it in her ears while it's still very cold. It doesn't occur to us how painful this is. We need to look at a torn toenail, while the dog already knows it's extremely painful whenever anything so much as touches that nail. We want to dry her off after a walk, and as we do this we bend over her and roughly rub the towel over her whole body. Many humans find it perfectly normal to put a choke chain or a prong collar around their dogs' necks, so they can hurt her if she makes a mistake. And of course, much of what a vet has to do can be painful for a dog.

We find it perfectly normal when a cat puts up resistance. But the instant a dog resists, we call her 'dominant'.

This is unfair.

A dog who is always looking for an argument can't take part in canine social systems. Other dogs will start to avoid the belligerent dog because her behaviour causes the social landscape to become unstable. When we want to approach our dog and then we bend over her, this looks to the dog like we are seeking an argument. So the next time we grab a towel, the dog might ask us to stay out of her personal zone. Dogs just do not arbitrarily look for arguments, and they are practically always allowed to protect their personal zone. It's nothing to do with 'dominance', but rather just the normal canine rules of politeness.

A dog sees her human coming at her yet again with the ear ointment, the comb, the choke chain, or the prong collar. The dog has already found out what these objects mean is going to happen next. She's already experienced what happens at the vet's. She knows pain is on its way. Now, Nature had very good reasons for making sure animals would try to avoid pain. Pain is, after all, a signal that the body is being damaged. A species that ignored pain and allowed its body to be hurt would probably not survive for long. So avoidance of pain is a strong natural reaction that is related to self-preservation. In addition, it's an established fact that pain can arouse aggression. This can be an uncontrollable reflex in an animal. So let's give dogs credit for the fact that they are so averse to using aggression and to unnecessary arguing. They show great self-restraint by first just asking us to please stay out of their personal zone. If we ignore the scared or hurting dog's request, we leave her no choice but to force us to stop hurting her (or not to start). It's our own fault if she snaps at us, and it's unfair to then start calling her 'dominant.' It's even more unfair if we already call her 'dominant' while she's still in the stage of just asking us to stay away, because in fact she's doing her utmost to *avoid* aggression.

It may seem strange if your dog then ceases to resist at the vet's as soon as he puts a Mikki Muzzle on her. (The Mikki Muzzle, which is commonly used by veterinarians, is a muzzle in the form of a textile tube that slides over the dog's snout, as opposed to the muzzles that are more like a cage around the dog's mouth.) The vet will probably say something like, 'See, see, the muzzle calms her because it imitates the dominant father grabbing the puppy's snout to show her her place.' This is utter nonsense, which ignores a general biological phenomenon. Freezing up is a reaction that many species have when confronted with an inescapable threat to their lives. Freezing up or playing dead sometimes saves an animal's life. So your muzzled dog isn't feeling 'dominated', nor is she suddenly aware of her lower rank due to some kind of father grab. She's just in a frozen panic because of the thing on her face. She's so scared that a kind of general paralysis sets in. On the other hand, you will sometimes meet a dog who doesn't freeze up in panic when the vet shoves this tube-shaped muzzle onto her face. Occasionally a dog will go into wild frenzy of fear. She suddenly seems like a wild animal, and the muzzle doesn't make you or the vet feel safe anymore. It's silly to think that this dog is taking the time to think about everyone's respective ranks. Nonsense. The dog is just convinced that she now has to fight for her very life. She's sure she's going to die in a minute.

Unfortunately, we don't always have a choice. There are times when the only way to save a hurt or sick dog's life is to do something painful to the dog. Sometimes it's not possible to anaesthetise the dog (though you can always ask your vet if there isn't a way to reduce the pain of any treatment, just in case). You are not to blame if you have to do whatever it takes to make your dog undergo the treatment. It would, however, be gracious of us if we would understand her panic reaction instead of calling her names. It would also be gracious of us to understand her temporary mistrust of us after the fact, and to give her time to get over the experience and learn to trust us again.

Then there's one more rather strange point here. Many authors write about resistance in a dog being 'dominant' behaviour, and then proceed to prescribe trust building exercises as a cure for the problem. All of them admit that trying to 'dominate' the dog back will only make the whole situation worse. They are aware that the dog will only resist all the more if you try to 'dominate' her (that is, show all kinds of threatening signals and behaviour toward her). The first step all these authors prescribe is to avoid any kind of confrontation with the dog. During therapy, the human learns how to approach the dog in a non-threatening way, while the dog learns to trust what the human is going to do. It remains a riddle why these authors, who do recognise that the dog is threatening because she is frightened, nevertheless go on talking about 'dominance' and 'ranks.'

<u>Fact:</u> It's completely and utterly normal that a dog puts up resistance against things that worry her, scare her, or cause her pain.

Myth 67: Sitting or lying down are submissive attitudes — *unless* my dog turns his back on me. Then he is being dominant by showing his back (or, worse, his anus) to me.

The first mistake here is that sitting or lying down aren't 'submissive' attitudes. They are just comfortable positions a dog will adopt when he has to wait for something. In other situations, the dog uses these postures as calming signals, a way to tell another dog that his intentions aren't scary or evil. See Myths 11, 12 and 13.

As far as his anus goes, please read on.

When dogs meet each other, the anus is about the first place they want to smell each other. They have no idea that an anus could be considered disgusting. On the contrary, it smells wonderful. A dog shows all parts of his body to others quite freely and in all innocence, just as he innocently and freely burps or lets out a fart in our living room. This is true of all non-human animals. Humans are the only animals who feel like some parts of their bodies are filthy and disgusting and shameful, or that we can show contempt for each by turning our backs on someone or mooning him. A dog has no idea that his back or his anus could be insulting to us.

Besides his innocence about his own body, a dog who turns his back on the other is using many calming signals simultaneously. By turning away, he avoids eye contact. Instead of showing his weapons, he keeps them as far away from the other as he possibly can, even pointing them in the other direction, away from the other dog (or the human). By showing his back, he makes himself vulnerable. The other can now approach from behind without feeling worried. It's sad that we would see contempt in this, because in fact the dog is showing sensitivity to and respect for the other's anxieties and personal boundaries.

People who tell you this silly myth will generally be trying to convince you that you should train your dog by using lots of punishment. This myth betrays the fact that this person feels very small inside and perceives 'dominance' in practically everything a dog does. If you train a dog with lots of punishment, however, you end up with a dog who is scared of you. The dog has no idea why his human is so often angry and so harsh, and dogs are oriented to avoiding arguments — so the dog tries turning his back, to tell the human that anger isn't necessary, because the dog's intentions aren't scary or evil. The dog is hoping to calm the ever-angry human. He wants to see his human smile at him again. The more you punish the dog, the more scared he'll get, and the more often he'll turn his back on you in the hope of avoiding your anger. Contempt has nothing to do with it.

Fact: None of a dog's attitudes express power relations. There are no 'dominant' attitudes nor 'submissive' attitudes, and there certainly aren't attitudes of contempt. If you stop scaring your dog, he'll stop turning his back on you.

Rugaas, T, *Calming Signals*, Legacy By Mail, Inc., Carlsborg, WA, 1997.
Semyonova, A, The social organisation of the domestic dog; a longitudinal study of domestic canine behaviour and the ontogeny of domestic canine social systems, Carriage House Foundation, The Hague, The Netherlands, 2003. www.nonlineardogs.com.

Myth 68: Dogs can be insistent nags, trying to make us do what they want when they want it. This is dominant behaviour.

Dogs do indeed sometimes do things that feel to us like insistent nagging. She keeps laying the stick in front of your feet during the walk in the park, even though you aren't in the mood to throw the stick for her. You're sitting on the couch watching TV and eating some potato crisps. The dog comes and sits in front of you, folds her ears in her neck, and proceeds to stare intently at your hand every time it moves from the bag of crisps to your mouth. As soon as she sees you answer the telephone, she goes and grabs her ball. She proceeds to lay the ball between your feet again and again, nagging you to play with her just when you want to concentrate on your telephone conversation.

These are moments when we feel like the dog is trying to make us do what she wants, when she wants it. This is the moment when experts who think dogs are secretly wolves will tell you that the dog is trying to dominate you. Subtly and non-violently, but all the same, the dog is trying out who is boss around here. The reason these experts believe that is that they have poor understanding of training techniques.

Because the truth is, persistent behaviour that feels to us like nagging is a result of a very specific training technique.

The technique starts with rewarding the dog every time she does a certain behaviour. She will start to do this rewarded behaviour very often. After a short while, you skip a reward or two. The dog doesn't know you're skipping the reward on purpose. She thinks you're just making a mistake and failing to notice she's doing this thing you reward. So she'll try again later, in the hope this time you'll remember to reward her. After a while, she figures out it pays to keep trying because you do sometimes give her the reward. At this point, you can start to increase the number of rewards you skip. You only reward every seventh or eighth attempt, later every fourteenth or twentieth attempt, and so on. Then you make the rewards totally unpredictable. You reward her second attempt, then the sixteenth after that, then the third after that, then the twenty-ninth, and so on. This technique of unpredictable rewards, with sometimes a long interval in between (and sometimes a short one) teaches the dog that it's definitely worth the effort to keep trying. The reward may take a while to materialise, and it may be unpredictable when this will happen, but it *will* happen. This is a powerful training technique, which produces extremely persistent behaviour.

In humans we call this a gambling addiction.

Back to your life with your dog. After your dog made eighteen attempts at a certain behaviour, you've probably thrown the stick for her after all, or given her a crisp or (perhaps unconsciously) kicked the ball away for her. You were probably hoping to get her to stop nagging. In fact, by letting her repeat her request eighteen times first, you have unwittingly applied the technique of unpredictable rewards and created persistent behaviour. You have actually unwittingly taught your dog to keep trying at least eighteen times, and maybe more.

Don't feel too bad about it, though, because you are in good company. The best trainers use this technique *consciously* when they train for competitions, because you aren't allowed to reward the dog during an exercise at a contest. They use this technique during training to teach the dog to keep up a behaviour for a long time even though she's not getting a reward for it yet. The dog will go through her paces at the contest, used to the fact that she sometimes has to follow twenty commands before a reward comes. Once off the contest field, the trainer gives her her reward. This keeps the dog's faith that it pays to persist. People win prizes with this technique. If you have inadvertently trained your dog this way — by occasionally throwing that stick or giving her a crisp — she's just doing what you taught her to do. There's no way she can know that you now find her persistence irritating.

Besides, the dog is not the only one who has been trained here. You love your dog. You often like to do what she asks, and you enjoy throwing the stick or sharing your crisps or kicking the ball for her. Her pleasure is a powerful reward for you. You're not as tireless as she is, so after a while you've had enough of it. You want to walk a while without bending down for the stick, or watch your TV show without being stared at, or concentrate on your telephone call. You feel uncomfortable about not doing what your dog is asking you to do, because you love her so much (otherwise you wouldn't have given in sometimes in the first place). You know what she wants and you feel a little guilty about not giving it to her. And there is the punch line. It's our own slightly guilty feeling — and not the dog's behaviour — that makes us feel nagged.

Fact: Persistent behaviour is the result of unpredictable rewards, a technique you may have applied unconsciously. It feels like nagging because of our own feelings, and not because a dog is playing power games with us.

So what do I do about it now I've trained it?

If you have inadvertently expertly trained your dog to persist in a behaviour, there are two possible solutions.

One is to start rewarding every attempt again for a while. This will get your dog used to getting a quick reward again. After about three weeks, you can then just stop giving the reward altogether. If you do this, it's very important to completely ignore your dog when she does the behaviour you want to be rid of. Don't look at her, don't laugh or scold, just pretend you don't see her. If necessary, get up and walk away without making eye contact. Above all, don't give in after the third or fourth — or eighteenth — try, because you'll be back to training her that it pays to persist. If you choose this route, be aware that the behaviour will get more intense for a short while before it starts to die out. The dog is sure you just aren't noticing that she's brought the stick, is staring at your crisps, or has put the ball near your feet. So she may do it a little more emphatically. The stick may be laid right in front of your line of motion instead of next to you as you walk. The staring dog might scoot up a little to stare at you from closer. The ball might suddenly be put on your lap instead of between your ankles. Don't let this temporary intensification worry you. This is called an 'extinction burst,' the intensification of a behaviour immediately before the behaviour starts to die out (or 'extinguish'). This is intensification is irritating, but it's a good sign: it means the behaviour is getting ready to start dying out. If you have retrained every-time rewards, then persist in withholding rewards altogether, the behaviour will extinguish.

The second possible route is to immediately start ignoring the inadvertently trained behaviour, without first training every-time rewards again. The main difference is that it will take the behaviour longer to extinguish.

Myth 69: My dog shakes his coat out after I pet him. This is dominant behaviour: he is symbolically proving his independence by shaking off my touch.

In one of the shelters I went to work at, it turned out there was a raging discussion going on about this particular myth among shelter personnel. Since everything a dog did had to be either 'dominant' or 'submissive', there was now this problem of how to classify their behaviour of shaking out their coats.

Flabbergasted, I decided to give the answer non-verbally. I walked up to the head of the dog wing and messed up his hair. He couldn't resist the urge to smooth his hair back into its normal shape instantly.

And there you have it. Each hair is anchored in a little hair sac in the skin. The hair sac is surrounded by tiny muscles. The hair and its muscles are used to being in a certain position. When we pet a dog and mess up his hair, his skin feels uncomfortable because of the hairs and the muscles being in a different position. The urge to smooth his hair back into its normal shape is irresistible.

That's all that's going on.

Fact: Your dog isn't symbolically shaking off your touch, it's just that messed up hair feels uncomfortable.

Fact: This particular myth is an excellent example of how weird things can get when people believe in the dominance hierarchy theory. This theory basically teaches us that we have to watch the dog at all times so he won't 'dominate' us. We end up behaving like paranoid maniacs, worried about every little thing a dog does, constantly looking over our shoulders and seeing danger everywhere.

Fact: This is utterly silly. Most of us get a dog because we want a friend, and if only we build our relationship on trust rather than coercion, a friend is exactly what we get.

Little Wolfie

Sylvia had recently lost her small dog to a disease, and had missed this dog terribly. To comfort herself, she bought a German Shepherd puppy. Her first big dog, she decided she had better go to school with him.

At the dog school, she was told that this tiny, innocent looking animal, weighing all of fifteen pounds and basically still nothing more than a round belly on tiny little legs, was soon going to develop into a dangerous animal. After all, getting a German Shepherd is serious business, because we all know that German Shepherds are super-dominant. If Sylvia didn't immediately start to oppress the puppy, she'd end up with a tyrant in her house who ruled her by threat and might kill her one day. What it came down to was that the puppy was a sort of Trojan horse. She had inadvertently let The Enemy into her house. The dog school advised Sylvia to buy a choke chain and start harshly punishing the puppy right now, because that was the only way to avert this horrible future danger. By the time she got home from the first class, Sylvia was so taken aback that she decided she wanted to get rid of the pup. She felt frightened even having him in the house. She called the society for the prevention of cruelty to animals, who referred her to me.

Thank heavens. Basically, the dog school was doing its best to saddle Sylvia up with their own self-fulfilling prophecy. Indeed, if you take a puppy and start being harsh to him immediately, you will be teaching the pup that we hurt him and aren't to be trusted. You will, indeed, end up with a dog who wants to keep you out of his personal zone (because you are dangerous), who defends his food and toys against you (because you are anti-social), who is worried when visitors come to your house (because you never know what a human will do next) and so on. And then the instructors can say, 'See, we told you so!' This is a form of insanity. It's sick to start out by torturing an animal, and then to blame the animal for what it does in response to torture. However, given the origins of the whole theory, this is not really so surprising.

Sylvia and I decided to work with little Wolfie on the basis of treat training and trust building. He turned out to be a delightful, intelligent, cooperative little creature. He grew up learning that humans are the source of delightful things, and that he is safe with us. Wolfie turned out to be an affectionate and trusting adult dog. He adores Sylvia and is happy to do anything she asks. He is always watching her, not because she's the 'Alpha leader', but because every move she makes might mean something great is going to happen.

In addition to the treat training and trust building, Wolfie took part in my own group of dogs several days a week as he grew up. They taught him the rules of canine politeness, how to use his body language, and how to seek compromises. Although he is now a hundred-pound adult, Wolfie is perfectly willing to wait until the other dog feels secure and quite willing to help the other dog by making all kinds of reassuring gestures. If another dog growls at him, he backs off cheerfully, well aware that the other dog just needs a little more space to feel comfortable, -- yes, even if it's a mini-Yorkshire terrier.

Getting to this happy ending was sometimes a struggle with the paranoid myth this chapter is about. Once planted, the seed of paranoia did sometimes sprout a little. The question arose as to what all the puppy biting meant — whether Wolfie wasn't practicing to take over later (see Myth 6 on what puppy biting is really all about). Sylvia was, at one point, worried about why Wolfie always wanted to play with her favourite alarm clock — as if he chose that particular object as a toy precisely because he knew it was the one thing she didn't want him to play with (in fact, the clock had all kinds of interesting things sticking out of it and made a very interesting noise once in a while). Sometimes paranoia arose when Sylvia had once again been lectured to at a park. Watching her puppy obey her so well, other dog owners warned Sylvia that she would, like the rest of them, run into problems when the dog hit adolescence. She would come back to me feeling a little unsure of herself. Happily, she always accepted my explanation that these other owners were basically gritting their teeth with jealousy and hoping she'd end up having the same hard time they were having with their own punishment-trained dogs.

Sylvia never did have those problems, because she was willing to believe me and not look for dominance in everything her young dog did. The one who convinced her most, of course, was Wolfie himself. Not exposing him to the old self-fulfilling prophecy allowed his true, wonderful nature to emerge.

Myth 70: If you want to be the leader of the pack, you always have to be the one to take initiative. You, not the dog, must decide what happens and when it happens. In other words, never acquiesce in any request your dog makes.

This myth is a corollary of the postulate that wolves and dogs have leaders, and that only the leader ever takes initiative. In Myth 51, we saw that wild wolves most definitely do go their own way and initiate their own activities when they feel like it. It's not only the parent animals who do this. But we have now also seen that the dog isn't a wolf anyway, that he is a semi-solitary scavenger who doesn't live in a stable group, let alone having a leader of any kind.

This particular myth is also connected to Myth 68. There are moments when a request from a dog makes us feel like the dog is trying to make us do what she wants, when she wants it. We end up projecting and thinking that the very asking is 'dominant'. Many trainers and behavioural therapists will affirm this projection (see Myths 95, 96, and 97). This is because they have been taught to see a dog as a sort of dominance machine.

A dog is not a dominance machine. A dog is a living creature with her own feelings and longings. She has a right to those feelings and longings. She comes to you with her longings because she has learned that you love her and will try to satisfy her needs. You are her source of pleasure in life.

But there's more. The reality is that our dogs are completely at our mercy. She can't eat unless you feed her. She is confined to your house and can't just go out and look for diversion when she's bored. She can't even go out for a pee unless you open the door because she can't open it herself. You even have the freedom to kill her (or have her killed) if the whim should arise. A dog is truly dependent on us for all things in life. She can't meet her own needs. She needs us to do this. It's a bit unfair to turn things around so that her very dependence on us — her seeking the pleasure of our company or trying to tell us what she needs — is supposedly an expression of 'dominance'. In fact, I find this a bit cruel.

Your dog has no choice but to ask you for the things she needs. You don't always have to say 'yes', but you should recognise her dependence rather than getting into all kinds of paranoid and illogical fantasies about power relationships.

On the other hand, if you have accidentally applied the technique of unpredictable rewards (see Myth 68), your dog just might be nagging so often and so persistently that you are actually hampered in leading your life. So you go to the dog psychologist, who says, 'Always be the one to take initiative. Never acquiesce in any request your dog makes. Then you will be the leader of the pack, and she will magically understand that you — not she — decides what happens and when it happens.'

It works. After a while, your dog stops nagging. The trouble is, it doesn't work because you are now the 'Alpha leader', nor because your dog has become less 'dominant.' It works because you have stopped rewarding the asking behaviour you had been rewarding up to now. And if you've read this far, you know that behaviour will die out on its own if only it goes unrewarded long enough. The dog eventually learns it's no use asking you for anything because you won't meet her needs anyway. She gives up. She spends her life lying in a corner, not moving until you say or do something. You think you are now the leader of the pack. In fact, all that's happened is that the dog doesn't see you as a source of pleasure anymore.

The technique 'ignore all requests' can be useful if you've inadvertently created a constant nagger. However, it's better to be selective about which requests you ignore. Remember at all times that your dog is entirely at your mercy and helpless in life without you. Remember that she is a living being who has a right to long for something. Ignore the requests that have become unbearable nagging to you, but be merciful and do meet your dog's needs at other moments. This will bring your relationship with her back into balance — both you and the dog happy.

Fact: 'Ignore all requests' can, under some circumstances, be a useful training technique, but it has nothing to do with leadership. Be wise in applying this technique because if you take it to extremes, you will lose a thing of great value in your relationship with your dog.

Myth 71: I know I'm leader of the pack when my dog watches me breathlessly at all times.

Because dogs have no such thing as leaders, there are two possible reasons why your dog would be keeping a sharp eye on you at all times.

1) Someone has been using punishment training with the dog. Someone has used a choke chain or a prong collar or a head halter, with which the dog's head and neck were jerked around. Someone has been throwing tin cans of coins at him, or key chains, and yelling at the dog, slapping him, kicking him, beating him, giving him electric shocks, and all the other things some people call 'training techniques'. All of this has very likely been done rather clumsily (see Myths 95 and 96), so that it is unclear to the dog how he can avoid yet another punishment. Sometimes he's punished because he does something, sometimes because he unknowingly omitted to do something. Somebody saw both doing and not doing as 'dominant', all according to the human whim of the moment. The dog has learned that humans are unpredictable, unpleasant and even dangerous. The dog who has been through this kind of 'training' lives in permanent anxiety. He is at your mercy, can't just go live somewhere else, might even have a microchip in his body that'd make sure he was delivered back to you anyway. The dog who lives with a punishing human has no choice but to keep an eye on that human at all times because otherwise some small or large disaster might overtake him any second. Some people don't see the fear in the dog's eyes. Other people see it but don't mind it at all because they confuse fear with 'submission.' They kid themselves romantically that this means they are the Alpha wolf.

2) You have trained your dog with rewards and treats, and without punishment. You dog has learned, just as my dogs have, that wonderful things can happen any second of any day when you are around. He feels safe in your presence. He knows that many of your movements don't mean anything, but you never know... He keeps one eye (or ear) on you at all times just to be sure he doesn't accidentally miss a signal that something great is going to happen now. He adores you. He doesn't adore you because you are the Alpha wolf. In his eyes you just have what we normally call charisma.

Fact: Dog number one watches his human in the breathlessness of worry or fear. Dog number two keeps an eye on his owner with always-pleasant anticipation. Both dogs know their human is a human, not a wolf, and neither dog has any idea of anyone being the leader.

Myth 72: If I dominate my dog and make sure I'm leader of the pack, then my dog won't develop behaviour problems of any kind.

This is a fantasy many people have been taught to rely on. We've already looked at various parts of this fantasy. Seeing this fairy tale summarized in a single sentence, it should strike you that it's actually quite a strange way of reasoning.

Even when humans are interacting with each other (and not with a totally different species), the definition of a 'behaviour problem' is quite subjective. A person might behave in a way that you or I can't stand, but which someone else thinks is perfectly normal or even cute and charming. We all have our own ideas about what's normal and what's a problem. So how could anyone imagine that dominating a dog will mean the dog is never a problem for *anyone* anymore, given all our various and often contradictory criteria and wishes? This fantasy is, in the first place, a good example of sloppy reasoning. It's magical thinking.

It becomes even worse when we try to apply the idea of 'behaviour problems' to interactions between two different species. Each species has its own natural behaviour and will very likely find some aspects of another species' behaviour baffling or revolting. From the dog's point of view, it's very impolite when we want to enter their personal zone without permission. It's socially unheard of that we want to take away their toys or (worse yet) their food. It's baffling that we want to chase them off a resting spot and do things to them that hurt, and the amount of violence we use toward them is — in their eyes — utterly insane. It's difficult for a dog to adapt her natural gait to ours. She has no idea of physics and doesn't know that her slight pulling on the leash arrives at your shoulder magnified many times by the length of the leash. We like to survey a landscape with our eyes as we walk through it, but a dog sees the world best through her nose. She doesn't feel like she's really seen something until she's had a good sniff. So there she goes, zigzagging over the pavement in front of your feet from one smell to another — yet another behaviour problem in our eyes. A dog has all kinds of natural longings that aren't always convenient for us, so we experience them as a problem.

This myth says that if only you can assert some kind of imaginary status as 'leader' (a thing that doesn't exist in the eyes of dogs), then somehow all these inter-species differences will be solved. Suddenly a dog will magically understand all of our highly personal and ever changing human rules. She will suddenly be able to read our thoughts and do the right thing with all of us at all times. She will become a sort of machine with no longings of her own, who will automatically do things the way we want her to.

The whole idea is a bit weird to say the least.

Besides all of this, there's also a language problem. Humans often either don't understand dog language at all, or they misinterpret it as being all about 'dominance' and 'submission.' In fact, dog language serves to exchange information about each party's inner state, so that each dog can take the other dog's feelings into account as the two of them look for a mutually satisfying balance in an interaction. Their language functions to generate enough mutual trust that the dogs feel safe interacting with each other.

A threatening dog isn't being 'dominant' or exercising power over you. She is exercising power over her personal zone, a thing the dog rules give everyone a right to do. A threat is nothing more (and nothing less) than a statement that she feels unsure and worried about what the other is going to do, and a request to the other to keep a little distance for the moment. The signals we are taught to call 'submissive' aren't submissive at all. The dog who uses these signals is reassuring the other. She is telling the other that her own inner state is such that she's not going to seek a conflict or do anything scary or unpleasant, and that the other doesn't have to feel worried. Dogs use their language to make themselves predictable to each other. They exercise great discretion in their interactions with each other, ever aiming at that mutually satisfying equilibrium.

We, on the other hand, are taught that it's all about power. And because we are taught to interpret a threat signal as 'dominance,' we fail to establish adequate communication and healthy interactions with our dogs. We don't have a tail we can lower, nor ears we can fold back against our neck, but we can — if only we are willing — give off some of the calming signals that dogs understand: standing still rather than approaching, maybe even taking a step back, averting our gaze, yawning, licking at the air, turning sideways, squatting to make ourselves smaller and less intimidating. Unfortunately, we often aren't willing. On the contrary. All too many of us go into the 'What? Growling at *me*!' mode and become — in our eternal ignorance — violent because we believe — in our eternal, specifically *human* projection — that violence is the same as 'dominance' and that 'dominance' is what it's all about. Dogs are utterly baffled by this, and they are absolutely right to be worried about what we are going to do.

Our social rules are different and much more complicated than the three simple rules dogs follow in their social interactions (see Myth 11). Our wishes are much more complex. They are often related to very complex thought processes, like our understanding of the value of money and the principles of economics, our rules about noise, our ideas about sex and virtue, and so on. A dog has no idea how much the new couch cost, nor that if she lies there every day she will eventually make a dirty spot where she always lies. She has no idea why we would object to such a dirty spot, or even to her tearing the couch apart in her panic if we leave her alone for an hour or two. She has no idea the neighbours might call the police because she's barking. A dog can't know how embarrassed we feel about our sexuality, or that a woman might feel publicly molested (or a man worried people will think he's homosexual) if the dog grabs our leg for a happy pump. Jerking savagely on the dog's neck with a choke chain, beating her, shocking her, taking away her toys and then always being the first to go through a door and the first to eat — none of it will make a dog any wiser.

Fact: 'Behaviour problem' is a subjectively defined concept. It is also a species-specific concept. 'Dominance' had nothing to do with it and is most definitely not a cure. In fact, exactly the opposite is likely. The more you try to 'dominate' your dog, the worse the behaviour problems will become.

Myth 73: The cause of a behaviour problem is always in the dog, never in the human.

In Myth 72, we saw that 'behaviour problem' is a subjective term. What's normal to one species may be abnormal or totally insane to another species. If we look at it this way, we could say that the *source* of a behaviour problem is in the dog, i.e. in his natural, species-specific behaviour — which is to say, the problem is in the fact that he is a dog in the first place. It's because of his being a dog, after all, that he believes (for example) that we should respect his personal zone when he asks us to. We don't do this, because our rules are different. If this scares him and he bites, well, there really is a problem.

All the same, the *cause* of the problem is not in the dog. After all, it's us who want to push into his personal zone without first building trust. We are the ones who approach without giving off calming signals, and often with intentions that go way beyond what a dog can understand.

Here, we have to preview Myth 97 (behavioural therapists). Dog behavioural therapists are taught that the cause of a problem is always in the dog, and that they should never tell the human that he or she is the problem. So the therapist merrily goes seeking the cause in the dog, sincerely believing this is the right place to look. Once she's found the cause in the dog, the therapist apparently fails to notice what she does next. Namely, the behavioural therapist always (but always) then proceeds to help the human to change his or her behaviour toward the dog. Once the human's behaviour has changed, the dog's behaviour begins to change, too, and the problem is often solved. If the human doesn't succeed in changing his or her own behaviour, then the problem does not get solved. So apparently, and regardless of what the therapist believes, the problem was actually in our own behaviour, and not at all in the dog. And apparently she knows this on some level, since we are the ones she works on changing.

Now we skip to Myth 96 (police-dog trainers). We don't teach our dog anything, then we blame him for not knowing. Or we don't know how to teach him (Myths 95 and 96), so we decide he's either stubborn or 'dominant' (Myth 62). We torture him (Myth 84) and call this training, then we decide it's a problem when he resists being hurt. If a dog doesn't know what you want him to do, or if he feels he has to defend himself against what you might do next, the cause of the problem isn't in the dog. The cause is our own violence and our lack of expertise about what a dog actually is and about how animals in general learn.

Sometimes a dog can have a behaviour problem that isn't directly caused by his human's behaviour, but rather by human dog-breeding policies (see Myths 18, 38 and 39). This is usually about behaviour that evolution and natural selection had weakened or eradicated in the domestic dog, behaviour that made it impossible for the carrier of certain genes to live near humans. The killing bite (in the aggressive breeds), the obsessive herding of sheep (in the Border Collie), the inability *not* to follow a scent (in the Pointers and the tracking dogs) — these are qualities that are, indeed, genetically anchored in the dogs themselves. They will be there regardless of how we behave toward each of these dogs. It's a problem when a dog bred for killer aggression attacks other animals or humans. It's a problem when your Border Collie tries to herd children in a school playground, or when your Pointer or your beagle is constantly getting lost due to having picked up a scent. Still, the cause of this behaviour is not in the dog, but in the breeders. After all, it isn't the dog who decided it was a good idea to revive archaic behaviours and then exaggerate them even more. The cause is also in the breeder's customers. If you have one of these dogs, it's because you took a look at the breed standard and consciously chose a dog with certain artificially exaggerated behaviour. It's quite logical that behaviour that made it impossible to live near humans 10,000 years ago would again make it impossible to live with us now. It's not fair to point our finger at the dog, since we are the ones who came up this bright idea.

In the end, the solution to canine behaviour problems always lies in us. We have to change our own behaviour if we want to solve the problem. We need to throw out all the nonsense about dominance and start building on trust with our dogs. We need to stop relying on punishment and hurting our dogs, and instead learn how to train him with rewards. It falls to us to stop breeding dogs for archaic behaviour that makes it impossible for them to live with us, and to stop buying dogs from breeders who persist in doing so.

Getting rid of the silly belief this chapter is about is extremely important, because it often leads to the death of innocent dogs. When a dog comes into our home at the age of eight weeks, eighty percent of his brain still has to develop. Unless he has been bred specifically for aggression, he is, at birth, already designed to learn about flexible and peaceful social relationships with almost any other living creature. Nature designed him for taking part in social traffic based on trust and treating each other with discretion. If things go differently than Nature planned and we end up with a different kind of adult dog, this isn't his fault. Even an adult dog is malleable, as long as he hasn't been bred for extremes in behaviour. We can quite often still correct our mistakes, if only we are willing.

Placing the cause of a behaviour problem in the dog is often nothing more than an excuse for getting rid of him or killing him without a guilty conscience. It's true that not all dogs can be salvaged. Sometimes a dog has been given such a set of genes or been so badly mistreated that it is impossible to keep him among us. It can be too dangerous to try to retrain the dog, or his behaviour can be so extreme that it exhausts even the most patient human or makes the dog himself miserable. Sometimes (though not as often as we pretend) we genuinely have no choice but to kill a dog. In these cases, it's important to do so with appropriate feelings of sadness and to be fully conscious that it's we who have failed — because otherwise this tragedy will continue to repeat itself.

Fact: The cause of behaviour problems in dogs always lies, in the end, in humans. The solution to behaviour problems in dogs is to change our own behaviour — be it with one dog, be it in how we breed dogs in general.

Myth 74: If my male dog has behaviour problems, castrating him will solve these problems.

Whether or not this is true depends on just what the problem is.

1) **He growls or snaps at members of the household.** This kind of aggression is usually a result of insecurity or anxiety in the dog. Castration won't remove these feelings. The solution to this problem is to change human behaviour and start building trust with the dog instead of trying to dominate him. Sometimes the person the dog threatens most has never tried to dominate the dog. This doesn't matter. The solution is still for those who do try to dominate the dog to stop this and start behaving in a predictable and trustworthy way. (But do go back and take a look at Myth 31, the spoiled little yappy dog.) It's quite possible that the dog doesn't feel anxiety anymore because he has discovered that snapping at people works so well. Now he casually snaps anytime he wants to get his own way. This behaviour is a result of learning. Castration won't erase learning.

In both of the above cases, the solutions lies in re-educating the dog — that is, doing behaviour therapy with him. Castration can be a help sometimes, but only because castration slows down his entire metabolism and (for reasons we don't yet understand) makes *some* dogs *somewhat* less quick to bite. The dog's general reactivity is lessened — he will react less quickly, less intensely and less persistently to many stimuli. This can make him less 'touchy.' But castration alone is not the solution where learning has caused a problem, and it would be dangerous to depend only on castration while leaving out the behaviour therapy.

2) **Aggression between two resident male dogs in the household.** The domestic canine social system is based on all its members being willing to seek compromises with each other. In a normal situation, a dog learns at a young age to be reticent about using aggression and to solve conflicts in other ways. The trouble is, a puppy (or a young dog) only learns this if he gets plenty of chances to interact with adult dogs without human interference. Many puppies and young dogs are 'protected' as they play in parks with adults. They end up never learning about how to reach compromises. Many people 'protect' a new pup from their adult dog's attempts to parent the pup and teach him the canine rules. In such cases, the pup can develop anti-social personality traits. It's completely normal that the adult dog resists the pup's anti-social behaviour and keeps trying to parent and teach the pup, who in the meantime has become an adolescent. People keep interfering, 'protecting' the younger dog, maybe later switching to 'protecting' the older dog. Canine conflicts keep occurring, and they get more and more serious as time goes on.

A second common situation in which two male dogs sometimes have ever escalating arguments is when the human has acquired two brothers from a single litter. The two pups grow up together, often without being exposed to a parenting adult dog in the household, and often without being exposed frequently enough to adult dogs outside the household. 'They have each other', their human thinks, 'What do they need other dogs for?' This is rather like locking two teenage hooligans in a train compartment and hoping they will teach each other civilised manners.

In both of the above situations, the arguments can escalate to the point where they are no longer ritual conflicts. In both of the above situations, it's important to take measures *before* the dogs start to actually wound each other during their arguments. As we have seen, the doggy rules require that real aggression not be used. So once a dog has wounded another dog, the whole system starts to topple. The wounded dog will start to see a real, life-threatening enemy in the other dog (and rightly so). Next time they argue, he'll fight for his life, wounding the second dog. It becomes a spiral of violence. This can reach a point where a calming signal during an argument doesn't work anymore — the one dog just wants the other dog out of his life. At this point, flopping onto the back to expose neck and belly can have the effect of provoking a killing bite instead of the normal response of stopping all threat behaviour. Once it's got to this point, the best thing to do is re-home one of the dogs. If you decide to re-home the more aggressive of the two dogs, then it is wise to look for a home where he's the only dog.

However, if it hasn't reached this point yet, then this is a problem that can be helped by castration. It turns out that this reduces the inter-male aggression in about half the cases. The now castrated dogs become less reactive, and they probably both smell less strongly male to each other — and both factors help decrease the intensity of their reactions to each other. This reduction in intensity then increases the chances of success for a behaviour therapy. With the help and supervision of a behavioural therapist (you cannot do this alone!), you can start to guide the dogs in having pleasant experiences with each other.

3) Growling and snapping at (or even biting) strangers on the street or in the home. This is an anxiety problem. Experience has proven that castration does not have much impact on this problem. The solution here is behavioural therapy.

4) Aggressive behaviour towards strange dogs outside the home. If this problem suddenly started when your dog reached adolescence, and if his aggressive behaviour is exclusively aimed at other males, then castration might help. It appears that castration reduces a dog's reactivity, including his inclination to revert quickly to biting. In addition, castrating your dog will make him smell less strongly male to other dogs, who will then be less touchy about his behaviour. So besides what it does to his own hormonal balance, castration will give your dog a chance to have more pleasant learning experiences with other dogs.

However, if your dog has already seriously wounded one or more other dogs, then castration won't solve the problem. If your dog has made more than a tiny, superficial fang-hole in the skin of any other dog, this means he has not learned to inhibit his bite. By the time he's an adolescent, it's too late for him to learn this because it is too dangerous for other dogs to try to teach him. The only solution here is to keep him away from other dogs at all times.

If this aggressive behaviour is directed at both male and female dogs, then castration won't solve the problem. Your dog may be inadequately socialised. An operation can't take the place of learning experiences. Your dog may have had one or more traumatic experiences with another dog (or dogs). Castration won't remove the legitimate fear that results from a trauma. In both of these cases, you may need to contact a behavioural therapist. This problem can be a result of your choice to buy one of the breeds that have been bred for aggressive behaviour. In this case, castration won't solve the problem. Behavioural therapy won't solve the problem, either. His genes and the brain and body they made him grow will remain what they are. The only solution is to keep your dog away from other dogs altogether.

Problems castration usually does help

1) A dog who compulsively sets out urine flags inside the home.
2) A dog who disappears to go chasing females in heat.
3) A dog who engages in constant, compulsive sexual mounting behaviour (toward your leg, toward the cushion on the couch, toward other dogs, toward the table leg — i.e. toward practically anything he can hug).

Castration solves these problems in 70–90% of cases.

It remains unclear what role castration plays in solving even the problems it does help to resolve. Often we suspect that castrating the dog just gave his human enough renewed confidence (and fresh hope) to work anew on training the dog. Sometimes a behavioural therapist was called to the scene, who — besides advising castration — simultaneously started teaching the dog's humans how to do treat-training and trust building (whether between the dog and humans or between him and other dogs).

Fact: If there's a problem, don't just depend on castrating your dog. Whether castration will help depends on what the problem is. In most cases, it can't hurt to spend money on a behavioural therapist, since learning plays a role in almost all behaviour problems in dogs.

Askew, HR, *Treatment of Behaviour Problems in Dogs and Cats: A Guide for the Small Animal Veterinarian,* Blackwell Science, London, 1996.

Borchelt, PL, Aggressive behaviour of dogs kept as companion animals: Classification and influence of sex, reproductive status, and breed, Appl *An Ethol* 10: 45–61, 1983.

Hopkins, SG, Schubert, TA, Hart, BL, Castration of adult male dogs: effects on roaming, aggression, urine spraying, and mounting, *JAVMA* 168:1108–1110, 1976.

Overall, KL, *Clinical Behavioural Medicine for Small Animals,* Mosby, Inc., Missouri, 1997.

Palmer, H, Appleby, D, ed, *The Behavioural Effects of Canine Castration: An Owner's Guide,* Pet Behaviour Centre, Defford, Worcestershire, 1993.

Peremans, K, *Functional brain imaging of the dog; single photon emission tomography as a research and clinical tool for the investigation of canine brain physiology and pathophysiology,* Universiteit Gent, Faculty of Veterinary Medicine, Gent, 2002. http://www.uznuclear.ugent.be/research/phd_dissertations/Functional_Brain_LowRes.pdf

Van Den Berg, L, *Genetics of aggressive behaviour in Golden Retriever dogs*, Utrecht University, Utrecht, 2006. http://igitur-archive.library.uu.nl/dissertations/2006-0427-200041/index.htm.

Part 6

Myths about how dogs learn

Myth 75: It's perfectly all right to combine punishment and reward in training a dog.

When people say 'punishment' they usually mean doing something unpleasant or even physically painful to a dog. They often mean jerking with all their might on the choke chain or prong collar, hitting or slapping the dog, kicking her, or throwing something at her. Technically, this active presentation of an unpleasant or painful stimulus is called 'positive' or 'active' punishment.

Even scientists believed for a while that this kind of punishment would make an animal learn faster. An active punishment — most commonly an electric shock — would make an animal avoid doing certain things. We could (they thought) decrease the animal's repertoire of behaviour until only the desired behaviours were left. Then we reward only these desired behaviours. It may seem logical that decreasing other choices would speed up learning, but we now know that it doesn't work that way. A typical experiment shows us that something else happens instead. The experiment goes like this:

Step 1: We teach a caged rat to press a lever for a grain of food. Once he's learned to do that, we shock him each time he presses the lever. We also turn the lever off so it stops giving him the grain of food. After the first two shocks, the rat turns out to hesitate before pressing the lever again. Each time he's shocked for pressing the lever, he hesitates yet longer before doing it again. Nevertheless, he does press the lever an average of twenty-six times before giving up altogether and trying something else. By this time, the rat has become somewhat fearful of his surroundings, so he hesitates constantly as he searches for new behaviour that might get him food. All the same, he does eventually discover that pulling a chain now gets him a grain of food. He is still hesitant — after all, you never know when you will suddenly get a shock from a thing that was previously harmless. But eventually he seems to forget his fear and go to the chain whenever he's hungry. It looks like punishment worked, because now he never presses the lever but always pulls the chain. But we can't draw any conclusions until we've done step two of this experiment.

Step 2: We teach a different caged rat to press a lever for a grain of food. Once he's learned to do that, we turn the lever off so he no longer gets food when he presses it, but we don't add the electric shock. The rat turns out to press the lever more and more quickly and intensively, until — after the same average of twenty-six tries — he decides it doesn't work anymore and goes to look for an alternative. He doesn't hesitate to explore his surroundings or what happens when he pushes or pulls on things, so very quickly discovers that he can now pull on a chain for food. He immediately proceeds to do so without hesitation whenever he's hungry.

Conclusion: Both groups of rats tried the lever an average of twenty-six times before giving up. Because the non-punished rats didn't hesitate, they went through their twenty-six attempts quicker than the punished rats. They then explored their surroundings faster and learned the new trick faster. It turns out that behaviour doesn't die out because of punishment, but because the reward is removed. It also turns out that punishment slows down the process by causing anxiety and hesitation. We now know that this applies to mammals in general, including humans and dogs. Punishment causes distress, and distress always slows learning. This fact has been known since 1938, and has been proven many times since then. It's time to start using this knowledge.

If you want your dog to stop doing one thing and start doing another, punishing him will only slow his progress. You need to remove the reward he gets for the old behaviour — don't leave tonight's steak on the kitchen counter, don't give him attention when he barks, walk away if he's nagging you. At the same time, you reward the behaviour that you do like. Expect him to look on the kitchen counter (or bark, or nag) twenty-six times before he stops, knowing that he will then switch to the behaviour you now do reward. Or — if you don't reward anything new — knowing he'll quit anyway and just go lie on his bed.

Fact: The less you punish the dog, the quicker this switch will take place.

Newman, G, *The Punishment Response*, J.B. Lippincott, Philadelphia, 1978.
Sidman, M, *Coercion and its Fallout,* Authors Cooperative, Inc, Publishers, Boston, 1989.
Skinner, BF, *The Behaviour of Organisms: An Experimental Analysis*, Appleton-Century-Crofts Inc, NY, 1938.

What science tells us

Active punishment has, in the course of time, been extensively researched. For some reason, we humans — including scientists — keep hoping punishment will turn out to work. The fact remains that punishment does not change behaviour. What happens is that behaviour is interrupted or temporarily suppressed — but this is a different thing than getting an organism to permanently make a different choice. Here, we will review a number of proven facts about punishment.

One of the most important discoveries is that punishment has to be traumatic if it is to have any lasting impact at all on behaviour. If a punishment is traumatic enough, it can even lead to suppression of behaviour that is necessary to sustain life. Please note: *the punishment has to be traumatic enough.* Even those scientists who are trying to make a career by claiming that punishment works admit this fact. This means that if we depend on punishment, we have to cause a trauma each time that we want to change the behaviour of a human or canine animal. Now, some people may be willing to do that, but read on, because it isn't so simple.

Even if the punishment is traumatic, it still has to be applied every single time the organism tries out the behaviour. If we fail to punish an attempt and the behaviour ends up getting its reward, the punishment doesn't work anymore. Behaviour does not die out forever unless you permanently remove the reward. But if you do this, you don't need to add punishment. And, as we have seen, punishment can even slow the process.

Then there's another scientific conclusion. Even if a punishment is so traumatic that an organism doesn't try out a behaviour again, it's still not the punishment that caused the behaviour change. Punishment generates fear. If you are afraid and you find some way to decrease your fear (for example, avoiding the lever that shocked you), this reduction of fear is a powerful reward.

Before you say, 'Well, I wouldn't mind traumatising my dog and changing his behaviour by fear reduction, if only the behaviour will go away', there are other facts you need to know.

First of all, punishment has side effects. It leads to an anxiety about exploring and trying out new things. After all, you have learned that traumatic things happen, and you never know what else is hiding a shock under a seemingly innocent exterior. Exploratory behaviour ends up suppressed along with the punished behaviour. This leads to slower learning. Punishment can lead to a generalised anxious attitude in life. The animal becomes guarded and suspicious in dealing with her surroundings — a thing we call paranoid neurosis when we see it in a human. An animal can start to develop a stereotype behaviour (doing a certain thing compulsively all day, be it licking her paw or chasing her tail). In humans we call this an obsessive-compulsive personality disorder. Punished behaviour can simply shift to another target instead of disappearing. A punished animal can go into regression and start to display infantile behaviour, or she can start to develop physical complaints (a result of stress hormones in the body). You can end up with a complete behavioural depression — the animal stops behaving altogether, withdraws to a corner somewhere, and can even stay there until death comes. An animal can go into sudden and total panic, or can develop ADHD-like behaviour. Punishment without side effects doesn't exist. We can't predict which side effects a particular animal will show. We don't find this out until we've already punished and, of course, by then it's too late.

A second point is that punishment only works when you have a prisoner. Otherwise the animal will just leave the punishing situation. In fact, the most important discovery all the punishment-loving scientists made in eighty years is that the behaviour of fleeing can be trained extremely quickly by punishment. It's not that the animal learns to do something else, but that she learns to be somewhere else — namely, anywhere where she's found out she doesn't get a shock. This is the dog who comes when you call her, but who stays just out of your reach, moving away if you walk toward her.

The third fact everyone needs to know involves aggression. Let's look at another famous experiment in the lab. Rats are shocked in various situations. Some rats are alone in their cage and can't identify anyone as the cause of their pain. These rats will attack and bite some object in their cage. Some rats aren't alone, and these rats will immediately attack some other animal that just so happens to be nearby. If the other animal is in a neighbouring cage, the rat is willing to learn all kinds of complicated tricks to be able to get to that other animal and attack her. The attack is vicious and uncontrolled, and takes place even if the other animal is much bigger. All mammals have this reaction. Back to dogs: a punished dog often can point to the cause of her pain, and even if she can't, you are the animal standing most within reach. Think about this before you hurt her.

When it's clear who the punisher is, and when avoidance or escape isn't possible, punishment will generate counter-control. The punishee tries to gain some kind of control over the punisher. In humans, this can be complicated behaviour — teasing, manipulation, lying, simulation, passive resistance and so on. In dogs, whose thought processes are much more limited, counter-control generally means that one day they bite back (or, if you're unlucky, that they go into a full attack). For example, it's generally known that when you use a shock collar on a dog, you have to be very careful that she doesn't figure out you're pushing the button, because a dog can then launch a life and death attack on you. Much of what the uninformed call 'dominance aggression' is really counter-control.

In a nutshell: watch out, because torture always has its price.

Aside from the various dangers, those who maintain that punishment works have failed to understand the real mechanism. Avoiding a punished behaviour is, in the end,not because of the punishment, but because of the reward of fear reduction. An animal will cease to behave because of the reward not behaving produces. No matter which way you look at it, rewards are the only thing that exercise real and sustained power over behaviour.

Punishment reduces the quality of an animal's existence and introduces the risk that an animal will strike back at some point. A punished animal doesn't develop an aversion to her behaviour, but to her punisher. Punishment has no real power over behaviour. As long as the reward for the behaviour continues to be available, suppression is conditional and temporary. The only way to make a behaviour disappear for good, and to get rid of the impulse toward that behaviour, is to remove the reward once and for all. If you want quick change, omit punishment and — instead — actively reward some other behaviour you do like.

More thoughts on punishment

It has been so exhaustively proven that punishment is ineffective while at the same time causing serious diminishment of the quality of life, that such great scientists as B. F. Skinner and Murray Sidman totally abandoned the idea of punishment. The question arises, then, as to why some scientists have been so anxious to go on experimenting with punishment in the hope of showing that it does work.

Some of this has, of course, to do with the wish to build a career by brilliantly proving the Great Names to be wrong, upon which you then become a Great Name yourself. Another reason is that research funds are hard to come by, and many a scientist is prepared to design any kind of experiment if it will only get him some money.

I personally believe that there is a third factor in play. Punishment is ineffective if you want to change behaviour. Even if you do make it highly traumatic and create a complete behavioural depression, punishment is still inefficient — there are easier ways to achieve the same thing. So, I believe that the fascination with punishment is because it is so very satisfying to us as revenge, never mind whether the targeted behaviour changes.

Scientists are human beings. In the course of their daily lives outside the laboratory, all kinds of things happen, and they sometimes will — just like the rest of us — experience how rewarding it is to get small or large revenge for the small or large wrongs that are done us. Since they are, just like the rest of us, subject to the laws of behaviour, I believe that scientists are then, on an unconscious level, subject to a desire to find out that this powerful reward is somehow objectively justified. How could a thing so deeply satisfying not have some universal and objective justification? Disbelief is due to our own emotions. In other words, continuing attempts to prove that punishment works are actually an attempt to find objective justification for an emotional fact. This emotional fact (the satisfaction revenge gives us) is a particularly human response. Other animals don't have it. The scientist unconsciously projects this inner emotional (and particularly human) experience onto the outside world as he formulates his research question. Therefore, in the light of all that has gone before, I assert that the very research question itself is a form of unconscious anthropomorphism. It is scientists looking for a way to project a deep human wish onto the outside world, at the cost of much suffering.

Myth 76: Punishment does work if you apply it the very first time a behaviour occurs, that is, before the behaviour has ever been rewarded at all.

This statement is a result of not understanding the mechanism behind suppression of behaviour. If a behaviour has never been rewarded, and if you do punish it the first time your dog tries it, he might possibly decide not to try it again. But this isn't because punishment works, and you need to consider the following before you follow some unknowing trainer's advice to try it.

1) It has been proven that dogs do not make a connection between their own behaviour and a punishment. Rather, they tend to associate the punishment with something that just so happens to be nearby at the moment the punishment took place. If you punish your dog the very first time he looks on the kitchen counter, it may look like he learned 'looking on the kitchen counter isn't allowed'. In fact, he's probably learned to be scared of the counter because something bad happened to him when he was near it. He may therefore avoid the kitchen counter in future, with the side effect that he doesn't look to see if there's any steak there. You can punish him the very first time he jumps up to greet visitors and he may never do it again. But he hasn't learned 'jumping isn't allowed'; he just found out that something unpleasant happened when visitors arrived. He may avoid visitors in future, with the side effect that he doesn't jump at them anymore. Read further before you think, 'Well, that solved my problem, didn't it?'

2) One problem is that you can't tell exactly what an animal will connect with the punishment. In both of the above examples, the dog might just as well end up scared of a vase that happened to be standing on a table nearby.

3) Punishment has many side effects. Some of these are predictable. Punishment predictably arouses aggression, avoidance behaviour and/or fear. Some side effects aren't so predictable. Lots of punishment can create an ADHD dog, or it can create a totally passive and depressed dog. We don't know in advance which a dog will end up becoming.

4) Avoidance behaviour can have strange consequences, which aren't always predictable in advance. The dog ends up refusing to go into the kitchen altogether. Because that's where his food is, he starts to associate food with the fearful experience. In the end, he is incapable of eating, even in another room. The dog can start to avoid visitors, since he is now a bit scared of them. No one notices that he's avoiding, so a visitor approaches to greet the dog — and the dog bites (the old, 'He bit me for no reason' story). The dog can learn that the doorbell means visitors, so he starts to be extremely stressed and growlly at the very sound of the doorbell. He might start biting passers-by out on the street who try to pet him, and maybe even those who just pass too close. And so on. Avoidance behaviour is not something you want to get into with your dog.

5) When people try to punish a behaviour the very first time, they are generally too late. The dog has already got a bite of the steak, or the visitor has already petted the jumping dog. Once a behaviour has been rewarded *even once*, punishment

becomes totally and absolutely useless. Look back now at Myth 75. Punishment will now only slow down learning what we want the dog to do.

6) Once a behaviour has yielded a reward even once, it will continue to come back. Punishment can interrupt or temporarily suppress the behaviour because of the anxiety punishment causes. Still, after a while, the anxiety will fade out and the behaviour will come back. This is called spontaneous recovery. It's as if the dog suddenly remembers, 'Oh yeah, that's what I used to do...' and there he goes again. As we saw in Myth 75, some trainers will assert that this can't happen if only you make the punishment severe enough (in other words, traumatic enough), but this is a bad idea. The worse the punishment, the greater the chance of serious side effects. And the worse the punishment, the greater the damage to the dog and to his quality of life. Besides, it doesn't work. A traumatic punishment may suppress behaviour a little longer, but if the reward stays in place, the behaviour will return. So all your effort, and all the damage you do, will be for nothing in the end, anyway.

7) People who punish their dog risk getting into a cycle of violence with their dog. Punishment can interrupt or temporarily suppress a behaviour, so it looks — at that moment — as if it worked. This is a powerful reward for the dog's human. And of course the laws of behaviour dictate that rewarded behaviour ends up being repeated. Since it's a fact that we humans are subject to the laws of behaviour just like any other animal, the chance that you will punish your dog again is increased. When the behaviour resurfaces (spontaneous recovery) you risk thinking, 'Okay, now I just need to punish it even more severely'. (You are now having an extinction burst — see Myth 68 — perhaps paired with a bit of extinction aggression — see Myth 58, paragraph 6.) This second punishment again temporarily suppresses the behaviour, so it seems as though it worked. The behaviour comes back again a little later, so you punish even more harshly. The behaviour is again interrupted, so it seems the punishment worked again. The trouble is, the punishment is *not* working to change behaviour — otherwise the behaviour wouldn't keep coming back. But the human owner fails to notice this because the interruptions are so rewarding to him. The punishment becomes ever more severe, and in many a case this has led to criminal abuse of a dog, sometimes by people who normally would never dream of hurting an animal. Because we aren't aware of the laws of behaviour acting upon ourselves, the escalation of our behaviour often takes place unconsciously, and before we know it — and totally unaware of it — we are seriously hurting an animal.

The solution to this problem is to think ahead, so that you can make sure that a behaviour you know you won't like never gets rewarded in the first place. Don't leave steak on the kitchen counter, but let it thaw in one of the cupboards. Teach your dog to sit-stay for a treat when there are no visitors around, and then reward him for sit-staying when someone comes in the front door. If he jumps up, keep turning your back on him so the behaviour doesn't get him the attention he wants. If behaviour has, unfortunately, been rewarded even once, remove the reward once and for all. Unrewarded behaviour will die out on its own, without us having to hurt or traumatise a dog or deal with the side effects.

Fact: Active or severe punishment has such serious side effects that its better to scratch it altogether. Withholding the reward is harmless and much more effective to boot.

Myth 77: I should never punish my dog in any way whatsoever.

To deal with this myth, we have to take a more advanced look at what we mean by punishment. We will also take into account how old a dog is and what history she has.

When people say 'punishment', they usually mean something violent or painful for the dog. Stuff like jerking on the choke chain or prong collar, throwing a can of coins or marbles at her face or head, delivering an electric shock, beating her, kicking her, shoving her nose in the poop she just deposited on the floor, and all kinds of other things humans have thought up. In Myth 75 we saw that these are all forms of positive or active punishment — actively delivering an unpleasant or painful stimulus to an animal. This kind of punishment interrupts behaviour for a moment but doesn't change behaviour, and it has serious side effects. It diminishes a dog's general well-being, even if no visible side effects show up. It is better never to use any kind of positive punishment with your dog. This is true no matter what your dog's history or how old she is, and no matter how obnoxious her behaviour.

There is, however, a second form of punishment: negative or passive punishment. Instead of actively introducing an unpleasant stimulus, we remove a pleasant one (such as a toy). Even this kind punishment can have nasty side effects. If you take things away from your dog, you are breaking the canine rules of politeness and showing that you aren't trustworthy. She may start to mistrust what you are going to do when you approach her. In the end, she might get defensive about possessions when a human is anywhere nearby. This form of punishment is, nevertheless, useful if you have a dog who compulsively lays toys on your lap in an effort to get you to play. When the dog does this, she has voluntarily transferred possession of the toy to you. Now you can stand up and put the toy somewhere out of her reach. (Don't look at her or grouch at her, just make the toy disappear.) If she returns with another toy and transfers possession to you again, you repeat this. After several tries, the dog will stop putting toys on your lap.

Another kind of passive punishment is not giving the dog a reward she has learned to expect. We use this technique quite often in behavioural therapy. A dog who nags all day, shoving her nose under your arm, putting her paw on your lap or barking to get attention, is completely ignored for a change. Sometimes this means literally walking away when the dog starts to nose, paw or bark. Usually she will show signs of bafflement or frustration, and often she will intensify the behaviour at first — but in the end, if you are persistent in totally ignoring her, the behaviour will die out. The main danger in this technique is that once you start, it is crucial that you keep it up to the bitter end. Otherwise you end up applying the technique of unpredictable rewards and training intensification of the behaviour you didn't like (see Myth 68).

Then there's a verbal correction. You suddenly 'bark' at the dog: 'No! Bad dog!' By suddenly raising your voice, you startle the dog and interrupt whatever behaviour she was doing just at that moment. This can be an unpleasant stimulus for the dog, but I don't think of it as a punishment. Rather, I see this as a social signal. You are giving the dog information about your inner state, and doing it in a way that dogs often do among themselves ('protest barking').

Whether this is damaging for your dog will depend on her history and on what you do next. Your raised voice was intended to interrupt some behaviour. The dog has now received a signal that you object to what she was doing, but she doesn't know what you'd like her to do instead. It is extremely important for your dog to know that your 'bark' will not be followed by violence of any kind. An adult dog with a history of being beaten can go straight into such a state of stress at the sound of your raised voice that she can't learn a thing anymore. In some cases, a dog could get defensive and, expecting another beating, suddenly bare her teeth at you (or worse). On the other hand, another adult dog who has never been abused will be able to just turn around and look at you to see what kind of social signal you give next. This is the moment to ask her for some other behaviour and reward the other behaviour in some way. But the truth is, in most cases it's best to just distract an adult dog if she's doing something you don't like and get her interested in doing something else.

With puppies and adolescent dogs, the yell can be very useful (again, if the pup or adolescent has never yet been beaten, slapped, jerked, shocked, or had her nose pressed in poop). The young dog is startled when you suddenly 'bark.' She stops what she was doing, and you can praise her or reward her for this (they aren't the same thing!) Or you can ask her to do something else, and then reward her for doing it. This method imitates the behaviour of adult dogs when they parent a younger dog. They bark (or growl-bark) to let the young thing know she's gone over some social boundary. Because you don't proceed to physical punishment after barking, and because you praise or reward something else, the young dog learns that she can make a very pleasant world for herself by exercising polite social behaviour. She learns to control her impulses and to keep an eye on others' boundaries. At the same time, she learns that she can control what happens next (and her own life) by adjusting her own behaviour (as opposed to the beaten dog, who learns that she has to control you and make you adjust your behaviour).

Active punishment has many horrible side effects. Dogs don't punish each other this way. Among normal dogs, it's all a just a show and a ritual, in which they watch out not to hurt each other or cause serious pain. All they actually do is exchange information about each other's inner state. Puppies and adolescents are sometimes subjected to what you could call intimidation. This is, however, never truly violent, and it stops as soon as the younger dog adjusts her behaviour. It's all right, and sometimes necessary, to raise your voice at your dog — as long as this is not paired with any kind of violence, as long as you do reward other behaviour, and as long as you don't misuse this chapter as a licence to use only yelling to train your dog. In fact, it's better to save your 'bark' for emergency situations, when it is absolutely necessary to interrupt the behaviour of, say, running toward a busy street and get your dog to do something else (like stopping in her tracks).

Fact: Some punishments do more damage than others. Passive punishment can be useful when used intelligently and sparingly. But never forget that punishment, even just yelling, only teaches your dog what you *don't* want. The only way to let your dog know what you do want is to actively reward the behaviour you like.

Myth 78: My dog knows what this command means because he's already done it right three (or five, or ten) times.

Once a dog has followed a command successfully a few times, people conclude that the dog now knows what the command means. This is a human projection.

Our species learns relatively quickly, we are good at words, and we are able to think in abstractions. You only need to tell us once or twice, or we only need to go through an exercise once or twice, and we can draw a general conclusion: 'Oh, so *that's* what I'm supposed to do'.

Dogs learn in an entirely different way. Sounds do mean something to them, but not the way they have meaning for us. A puppy will be alert to your tone of voice. He knows that intonation conveys relevant information. However, he does not have an area in his brain for speech like we do. He does not know that such a thing as words exists. Before a dog can pay attention to our words, he first has to figure out that one particular sound we make means something different from the other sounds we make. In fact, he has to work out that our sounds (as opposed to the tone) have any meaning at all. Even when he's realised this, it's still difficult for him to unravel verbal structures and understand words.

However, he can — with much effort — learn to recognise a number of our words. Let's suppose he's learned that when you look straight at him and say a word, you probably want him to do something. He has no idea what you want him to do. If you are using rewards to train him, then he won't be afraid to try out various things — coming over to you, nose-nudging your hand, tapping you with a paw, barking. First he'll try out the actions you have rewarded in the past. Then he'll try out others. He's guessing. He knows this is a game and that if he guesses right he gets a treat. At some point, he does guess right, and you reward him. This is the point where you are at risk of thinking, 'Okay, now he knows this new command'.

Don't think this. The dog didn't understand the word you said, because it was new to him. He did not hear it as a discrete, recognisable sound (dogs find this difficult). You looked at him, made a sound, he knew you wanted something, and he guessed. Even if he did hear the new word, a dog isn't capable of drawing a general conclusion about what it means just because he guessed right once. It takes a dog many successful trials to draw a general conclusion about anything at all. All he knows is that it was the right guess this time. The next time you give the command, he'll start guessing all over again. And the next time, and the time after that. After many successful practices he may be able to consistently recognise the word you are using and to couple it to some specific thing he is supposed to do. He starts to always get it right on the first try — in the living room, at any rate.

As soon as you use this word somewhere else, he starts guessing all over again. This is because dogs can't be sure so quickly about what the relevant factor is. Your dog may have concluded that 'sit' in the living room means he should put his backside on the carpet. Or he may have concluded that it means he should put his buttocks on the floor next to the coffee table (since the table is in the middle of the room, he's next to it no matter where he sits). But now you're outdoors and he doesn't see a carpet anywhere, or (in the other case) the coffee table. He doesn't know that 'sit' now means he should put his buttocks on the *grass;* or he may start looking around for a coffee table. To him, the word is not as yet a meaningful thing in itself, without all the other familiar parts of the situation he did the first learning in. That the word 'sit' would apply only to the position of his buttocks is still a bridge too far for him, because he can't think so abstractly. So there he goes again, trying out all kinds of things you have rewarded in the past, including — eventually — putting his backside on the ground. After lots of successful trials, he figures out that 'sit' means the same thing in this second place. 'Aha, so it also means bottom-on-grass!' or 'Next to the swings'. But to a dog, this doesn't mean it works that way in a third place (e.g. bottom-on-concrete; nothing to be next to). He finds this out by guessing all over again in the third place. And so on. After you've practiced with him in lots of different places, after literally hundreds of successful attempts, a dog can finally draw the conclusion that 'sit' means the same thing everywhere and under all conditions, that he's supposed to do something specific with his buttocks, no matter what other things or stimuli are around, no matter what surface he's standing on, and no matter which other behavioural choices are open to him in all these various places.

If you conclude too quickly that he already knows a command and start to punish him for not obeying, then you will slow down the learning process. The less free your dog feels to guess, the less quickly he'll discover which thing you want him to do, and the longer it'll take him to learn what the command means.

Fact: Animals learn differently to humans. Dogs draw abstract conclusions only after hundreds, sometimes thousands, of successful tries.

Myth number 79: If I jerk on the choke chain, the moving ring pinches my dog's skin just behind his ear. This imitates the mother's corrective bite from my dog's puppy days.

This myth is still part of a lot of clubs' training dogmas. As with most dogmas, it's not based on facts. Most likely someone (we'll never know who) made up this one to get suspicious students to toe the line. Students who were training at a club for the very first time and who were averse to the idea of causing their dogs pain. If the trainer tells them they're being overly sentimental and that he's just telling them to do what a dog's mother does, well, it's hard to resist. Hearing their hesitation ridiculed in front of the whole class, most people will be intimidated into going along with it. In fact, the trainer is being a bully and the story is a fiction.

Most of us have seen an adult dog discipline a puppy. It happens with lightning speed and it can look scary. The problem is, it happens so fast that you don't see what really happened unless you tape it. The video shows that the adult dog bares her teeth right next to the puppy's neck, switching from side to side so the pup sees those big teeth flashing by, but she doesn't put her teeth on or into the pup. Sometimes the grown-up will bump the pup with her teeth, without closing her jaws. Sometimes she will nip a pup, but even then she grabs a bit of skin on the pup's back, and not behind his ear.

A mother dog, in fact no adult dog, uses her teeth to hurt pups. They don't pinch the skin behind its ears. If they want to move a pup, they pick it up by taking its whole abdomen in their mouth, sometimes you'll see a pup dangling with its thigh in the mother's mouth. They don't pick a pup up by the skin on the back of its head or neck.

Dogs aren't only careful using their teeth with pups, by the way. If you watch playing dogs or arguing dogs, you'll sometimes see them grab a fold of skin and pull on it — but they go (carefully, even in an argument) for the loose skin on the neck and shoulders of the other dog, not for the tight fitting skin at the back of the head.

This whole idea is yet another human fabrication, and a dangerous one. Any effect the choke chain has is not a result of the moving ring, but of the whole chain suddenly tightening around the dog's throat. By suddenly jerking on the choke chain, you deliver a blow to the dog's pharynx and/or larynx. Together, these organs form a delicate system that controls both vocalisation and the complicated motion of swallowing. A lot of choke chain dogs end up with chronic coughs. Some end up extremely short of breath. I have seen some have trouble swallowing food. This is all due to damage to the pharynx and/or larynx. But this isn't all a choke chain can do. When the chain tightens suddenly, the entire neck gets a blow. This can cause damage to the *medulla oblongata*, a part of the brain that extends into the highest vertebrae at the back of the skull. If you damage this, your dog can end up with various degrees of paralysis.

Fact: The 'mother's corrective bite just behind the ear' is a fiction. A choke chain is *in no way* related to anything a mother dog does to her pup. The trainer who says it is, is just looking for ways to justify bad training techniques. A dog school that still uses the choke chain is a throwback left over from the cave days of dog training. As soon as trainer tells you to buy a choke chain, it's time to go looking for another trainer.

Myth 80: A choke chain will teach my dog not to pull on the leash.

When a trainer tells you this, the main information contained in the statement is that the trainer doesn't understand how dogs learn. You will also hear this myth at the pet shop, where staff are concerned, above all, with transferring your money from your pocket to their cash register.

The idea is that every time the dog pulls on the leash, the chain will choke him. This hurts. Animals try to avoid things that hurt. So, says the theory, the dog will stop pulling in order to make the choking stop.

Experience shows that this is not how it works. The dog goes right on dragging the human along, panting, gasping, coughing, but not slowing down one little bit. The dog does this because:

1) Dogs do not associate punishment with their own behaviour (see Myth 76).
2) He has four legs and his natural gait is therefore faster than yours (see Myth 51).
3) Because he is full of lust for life and is anxious to explore all the smells and colours this world offers (see Myth 51, especially in reference to adolescents).
4) He gets used to the choking and thinks it's the price this world charges for a walk.

The weird thing is, I see people who have been walking their dog on a choke chain for years, but the dog is still pulling. If I ask why the dog's on a choke chain, they'll explain that it is teaching the dog not to pull. So I say, 'But he's still dragging you down the street, isn't he?' Surprised looks. 'Ah, now you come to mention it, the pulling hasn't changed a bit!' It's as if the theory acts as a barrier that keeps reality from getting through to our perceptions.

Sometimes the dog with the choke chain around his neck is an old dog. When asked, the owner says the dog finally stopped pulling on the leash when he got to be about eight years old. The owner believes this is because the choke chain finally did work after all those years. Let's ignore for the moment the fact that all dogs slow down when they get old and suppose, for argument's sake, that it is the choke chain that did it. Even if this were the case, which it isn't — a technique that takes eight years to work is not what anyone would call 'effective'.

In the meantime, all that choking is damaging the dog. His carotid arteries are pinched shut. His brain ends up with an oxygen shortage. The blood pressure in his skull rises and can cause permanent damage to the optic nerves. The choking can damage the delicate organs in his throat and his *medulla oblongata*. This is serious stuff.

Fact: Don't fall for this one. A choke chain has never prevented a single real, live dog from pulling on the leash in all of history. As soon as a trainer starts to tell you this, it's time to start looking for a different trainer.

Myth 81: A prong collar will teach my dog not to pull on the leash.

A prong collar, also known as a pinch collar, is a differently designed choke chain. It's made of larger links, with blunt or pointed spikes sticking out of each link on the inside of the chain. When you put the collar on the dog, the spikes are on the inside, aimed at her skin. When the collar tightens, these spikes grab folds of skin and pinch them. Blunt or sharp, the point is to cause pain, and the spikes often pinch the skin until it bleeds. The prong collar is yet another instrument recommended by trainers who don't understand how dogs learn (see Myth 96), and by the pet shop that wants your money any way they can get it.

There is a bitter advantage to the prong collar: it doesn't choke the dog. The spikes that poke into her neck and damage her skin can't embrace the neck in a way that cuts off circulation. The spikes do leave enough space for blood to get to the dog's brain. On the other hand, these collars can cause serious wounds. The dog's trachea or larynx can be punctured. Tendons and muscles around the neck are damaged. Sometimes you'll see a dog with a necklace of crusty, infected wounds around her neck.

A prong collar causes severe pain. Some dogs just learn to live with the pain (after all, they have no idea where it's coming from), while they keep on pulling on the leash. Some dogs can learn that if they move very carefully, they can avoid the pain — until something happens that makes them forget themselves for a moment. The dog pulls again for a moment to get to an interesting smell, or (if she sees a cat or another dog) she suddenly throws herself with all her weight into the leash. She gets a sudden, awful jolt of pain in her neck.

What does a dog learn from this? That taking a walk with you is unpleasant and even dangerous. She becomes hesitant, full of anxiety. The sudden pain might arouse aggression, as pain tends to do. She might, in an unthinking reflex, direct this aggression toward you. The pain is so severe that the dog screams (at this point, the owner is thinking 'Good, that's what you get for pulling!'), sits down for a moment in pain and amazement (owner: 'See — it works!') and then turns around and bites the person holding the leash (owner: 'Oh my God, this wasn't supposed to hurt *me*!') Or she might bite someone else, depending on who is standing closest to her. Everyone ends up thinking the dog is aggressive, when in fact lashing out is a perfectly natural animal reaction to sudden pain.

What a dog doesn't learn is not to pull on the leash. The moment you put some other kind of collar on the dog, she'll immediately proceed to drag you down the street again. Or over to the cat or the other dog whom, by this time, she really does want to murder (see Myth 82). A prong collar won't teach a dog to walk calmly on the leash. It will wound her and make her fearful. It also risks causing her to develop serious aggression problems., not because she *is* aggressive, but because aggression is a normal pain response in all animals.

<u>Fact</u>: There are lots of merciful ways to teach a dog to walk on a leash. If your dog is pulling or lunging on the leash, what you need to do is contact a good dog school (one that trains with rewards). If you don't need all the other lessons (your dog already does a good sit, down, stay), you can arrange for a private lesson or two, aimed specifically at this problem.

Alternatively, you can buy Turid Rugaas's book, *My Dog Pulls. What Do I Do?* Dogwise Publishing, 2005. ISBN 978-1-929-24223-8.

Myth 82: The prong collar will teach my dog not to lunge at other dogs, cats, people, or anything else during our walks.

So you put the prong collar on the dog and there you go. At some point in the walk, your dog sees a cat or another dog and tries to lunge at it. When he gets to the end of the lead, the prong collar delivers a sudden, severe jolt of pain. The dog screams. He sits. He looks around in utter amazement. You think, 'Ha! It works!' and continue on your way. In the next block, your dog sees another dog or cat, and this time he lunges with yet more fury. As he throws himself into the leash, he gets another severe pain jolt. He screams again, and sits down with a surprised look on his face. You think, 'Ha! It worked again!' The third lunge is more furious yet. Your dog looks hysterical, he barks and growls and jumps around at the end of the leash, but the pain doesn't seem to be getting through this time. So you add to it by giving a jerk yourself. The dog screams, sits down, and looks around, this time with a look of panic in his eyes. You think, 'Ha! It works if I increase the pain'.

But your dog keeps lunging, so you keep increasing the pain. Your dog starts to have the hysterical reaction to a cat or another dog at an ever-greater distance. One day (and it usually doesn't take so very many days), your hysterical dog suddenly turns around and bites your hand or your arm. He starts to get hysterical and attack other dogs even when he's not on the leash. You're sure he will now kill a cat if he ever gets hold of one — and you're probably right. Now you think, 'What a horrible dog! I must've chosen the wrong puppy at the breeder's'.

You didn't choose the wrong puppy. Your dog wasn't born aggressive. Owners who put a prong collar on their dogs are, by doing so, creating aggressive dogs regardless of what Nature or genes would've made the dog become. This is how it works:

1) A dog does not associate the pain jolt with his own behaviour. He associates the pain with something that just so happens to be in his surroundings when the pain occurs (see Myth 76). In this case, the dog associates the pain with the cat or dog he lunged at. The increasing lunges are actually attempts to chase the other animal away before the pain comes, in the hope of avoiding the pain.

2) Sudden pain can arouse aggression, sometimes very serious aggression. This is a general animal response to pain. Your dog doesn't bite your arm because he knows you are causing the pain, but because any animal will choose the closest animal available to execute this reflexive pain response upon. In this case, that just so happens to be you.

3) Your dog will quickly learn to see a cat or another dog as a signal that predicts a jolt of pain (just like the bell that rings or the light that goes on two seconds before the lab rat gets a shock). This very expectation arouses aggression in your dog. Because he isn't capable of making the link with the pinch collar, he will have this same expectation when he's off leash and sees the signal. This expectation will now be enough to arouse the aggression response. Because the pain aggression response is a reflex, your dog will attack so quickly that he'll probably never get

the chance to learn that other dogs do not predict pain when he's off leash. Rather, he's likely to attribute the lack of pain to the fact that he attacked in time.

4) If you get angry at him and punish him for the attacks, you will be affirming the fact that other dogs are a signal that something horrible is going to happen. If not the pain in his neck, then your fury. Your dog may end up killing another dog one day.

Fact: A prong collar will not cure your dog of lunging at other creatures when he's on the leash. It will make the lunges ever more aggressive, and you will end up with a dog that is really dangerous for other living things.

Does it always work this way?

Some of the people who read this book for me before publication were a bit sceptical of whether it always works this way. Always is a big word. Whether a dog will always end up attacking? No. The degree of pain-induced aggression will depend on the individual dog and the individual situation, but some kind of aggression is almost always the result in the end.

The tale of aggression I tell in this myth is not a theoretical story. It's one I have seen happen too many times, in exactly the progression I describe above, for me to have any doubts about what the prong collar does to dogs. The cases where a dog didn't develop an aggression problem were not due to my being wrong. They were due to the owner abandoning this instrument in time because s/he saw what the collar was doing to the dog. Or because the dog wasn't pulling or lunging hard enough for the pain to get really serious. Or because the owner managed to make the dog so frightened that the dog didn't dare behave at all, let alone lash out (this is called learned helplessness).

I have had dogs in therapy who'd undergone this kind of training, who really tried to kill other dogs when they were let loose in parks. I have seen many dogs lash out and bite (or even attack) the person who was walking them on a prong collar. As pointed out above, it wasn't after the first jerk on the leash, nor the second, but sometime between about the fifth and the thirtieth pain jolt. I have seen dogs attack when the owner went to the hallway to get the leash (no, the dogs hadn't figured out it was the prong collar, they'd just learned to hate walks so much that they'd attack to avoid them).

So yes, prong collars will — if used long enough, and it doesn't take very long — almost always create aggression problems with your dog. Almost always means there will be some exceptions, but why take a gamble that your dog is one of them, especially since there are so many other, non-damaging ways to solve the problems of pulling or lunging on the leash?

Myth 83: I don't have to train with food treats. My pleased tone and a pat should be enough of a reward for my dog.

This myth is tightly tied to the idea that you are supposed to be your dog's leader, and that a dog is so anxious to please her leader that every sign of approval will work as a strong reward. At this point we know that dogs don't live in hierarchies and don't have leaders, and that they most certainly don't have 'the will to please' (see Myths 7, 10, 11, and 48). No animal exists that lives only to please another animal, not even a leader. An animal lives for the quality of its own life. A mentally healthy human does this too, by the way. So why would your pleased voice or a pat be a reward to a dog? There are two possible reasons:

1) If we are training with punishment. We do what our trainer tells us to do, not asking the dog to sit, but telling her to. We use a firm, commanding voice when we speak a command. Now the dog has enough experience to know that after we use this tone, we are likely to jerk on the choke chain or the prong collar. Our tone has become a signal that something painful is about to happen. She can't leave, because we have her on the leash. She tries one thing, tries another, and finally, after a process of lighter or heavier torture, she discovers that if she sits, the pain doesn't occur. We say, in a pleased tone, 'Good dog!' and maybe pat her chest. The dog learns that our pleased tone is a signal that she is, for the moment, out of danger. Our pleased tone gives her the reward of anxiety reduction.

2) If we are trying to train without punishment. We hope our happy tone will be enough to motivate the dog. We are still hoping that an animal will do anything for us just out of love. Because our relationship with the dog is good, and because she enjoys our company, our voice and our touch are indeed pleasant for her. The trouble is, they won't be so pleasant that she will be willing to work hard for them. Our pleased voice and our pats won't be able to compete with other, stronger rewards like the dogs playing ten yards up, or the bread someone threw in the bushes for the birds.

Training only with your voice and a pat will always progress more slowly than training with food rewards. There are good reasons for this.

If a dog has learned that a command is, in fact, a threat, your pleased voice loses the power to relieve the dog's fear entirely. She knows another threat will be coming soon. She learns that training means pain. Though she eventually figures out that a certain voice means she's supposed to do something, every new command means a process of guessing exactly what she's supposed to do and finding out by being hurt many times before she guesses right. Training feels dangerous and, because she doesn't have a speech area in her brain, the whole process feels difficult and unpredictable to her. As soon as you put on your training voice, your dog will feel distressed and anxious. And it is a natural law that distress and anxiety slow down learning processes. Anxiety diminishes an animal's capacity to take in and process information from the environment (i.e. from you). On top of this, if you are punishing wrong guesses, you are in fact punishing the dog for trying to get it right! So as much as your dog might want to get it right, she has learned that trying to do that is dangerous. The dog will become hesitant to move at all and might be keeping the eagle's eye on you that your trainer wants to see, but you shouldn't kid yourself that this is because she loves you or because you are the leader. She's just extremely worried about what you'll do next. Then there's this: as soon as you unleash your dog, your voice loses its value even as a threat. Your dog can (and will) avoid your punishment by staying out of reach. Your blood pressure rises as you get angrier and angrier, convinced your dog is taunting you. Of course you can teach a dog that escaping will, in the end, produce an even worse punishment, but training remains a torture for the dog and a frustrating business for both of you.

Even for those of us who train without punishment, our voice remains a relatively weak reward for our dogs. Don't forget that training is hard work for your dog. The things we want her to do don't fit into the way she naturally experiences the world. She isn't verbally oriented, so it's hard for her to learn words. She has to concentrate — first to figure out what we want, and then to attach a word to the action. Even if your dog loves you very much (see Myth 43), this doesn't mean she'll be willing to overcome all the frustration these difficult tasks involve for her just to see you look pleased at the end. 'Good dog!' or a pat doesn't greatly increase the quality of her life, despite her love for you. A piece of unusually delicious food has more power. Food appeals to the dog's strongest sensory organ (smell), and it hooks nicely into the dog's evolution as a natural scavenger that spends its days searching for small tidbits among human rubbish piles.

Experience shows that a food reward is more effective in motivating a dog and keeping her interested in the lesson than a pleased voice or a pat. This is especially true in the phase where the dog has to learn something new. Food can motivate a dog to overcome frustration and keep looking for what we want (without feeling afraid!). Many dogs learn to like solving these puzzles for their own sake, because they have learned that puzzle solution yields something, in the end, that has meaning *to them*.

Fact: In competitions, it's the trainer who trains with food rewards who wins. Her dog is relaxed, learns like lightning and works with great pleasure. She has a tool that is effective even if the dog is far away from her, and that can compete with all kinds of other interesting things that are going on. Her dog not only wins, but has also fun.

BUT FOOD ISN'T ALL THERE IS

Some dogs are not so interested in food or treats. Some dogs would rather you throw a ball for them or give them access to some other toy they like, or some activity they enjoy. Some dogs who are normally interested in treats won't be so in all situations. They might need something that distracts them more actively or gets them moving around — again, a ball or a short play session. The point of this chapter is not that food is all there is. The point is that you have to find the rewards your dog likes to work hard and long for, and that your mere approval will not be one of them unless you first make your dog fear you.

Myth 84: If you punish a dog enough, this will teach him that you are the Alpha leader and he has a lower rank. Once he's understood this, he will obey all commands and let you do anything you want to him without resisting. He will become the perfect dog.

Too many trainers still swear by this myth, from the local dog school right through to many a police K9 unit. However, this myth is based on a number of misunderstandings. It started early in the nineteenth century with the rise of the robber baron industrialists, who propagated the idea that the strong rise to the top and have a natural right to lead. Then came the Nazis, who fantasised that the animal kingdom organised itself by violence into rigid hierarchies, following exactly the rules that the Nazis hoped to impose on all of us. Back then, people also believed that animals and children learned best by punishment. The assumption grew that animals and children can read our thoughts — they know what we want, and if they refuse to do it, it's just rebelliousness. The final phase was the rise of consumer society. There is a huge advertising machine that trains us in instant gratification. Success means getting yourself into a position where you can order others around, having your needs and fancies satisfied *right now* and preferably without having to work too hard at it. If we are 'worth it' (and who wants to believe s/he isn't?), we have a right to be catered to and a right to be frustrated and angry if we aren't.

If you've read this far, you now know that dogs don't live in a dominance hierarchy (see Myths 10 and 11), and therefore can't possibly understand such a thing as 'rank' — no matter how often or hard someone beats him, kicks him or shocks him.

Dogs also can't read our minds and rarely know why we are punishing them. But even if a dog did understand, he still doesn't know just by looking at us what other thing we want him to do instead. The only way a dog can learn what you want is if you give him a signal he can understand — a reward — when he guesses right. Even if he got it right three times yesterday, or if he always gets it right elsewhere, this still doesn't mean he knows what you want today or in this new place (see Myth 78). Beating him, taking things away from him, even always being the first to go through the door — none of these things will bestow telepathic powers on your dog.

A lot of the things we want to do to dogs are scary or painful to them — combing their coats, looking at the torn nail on their foot, drying them with the blow dryer. Pain avoidance is, in all species (and excepting some people and all fighting dog breeds) a natural behavioural response. It's also a healthy behavioural response. It's not likely that punishment will teach a dog to let you do scary or painful things to him without resisting. He might learn that he has to bite you, because you persist in scaring or hurting him so often, and because you become violent yourself when he tries to tell you you are scaring or hurting him.

As for the consumer mentality, our Myth 84 is just as much wishful thinking as the idea that finding just the right deodorant will suddenly make you managing director.

Fact: It would be nice if life were so easy, but it isn't. The only way to achieve such wishes is to put in the work.

A real case

If nothing else works, then I should lay my dog on his back and strangle him until his tongue starts to turn blue. This will teach him that I'm the Alpha leader. He will become an obedient dog.

I received a call one day from a very upset housewife who'd had a crisis with her Border Collie the night before. The dog had bitten her son on the Tuesday and on the next evening had attacked her husband when he tried to leave the dog in the yard and go back into the house. The attack was so scary that Dad literally fled into the house. After some discussion, he went out and put a muzzle on the dog. The dog went into a fury, so Dad fled back into the house again. Every once in a while, they'd look out the window to see how the dog was doing. When the dog saw their faces, he flung himself at the window in what seemed to be an insane rage. They called the local Animal Ambulance, which took the dog to a vet. The vet injected the dog with a tranquilliser and kept him for the night. When they went to get the dog the next day, the vet advised them to put the dog down since he obviously had some kind of inborn defect.

The housewife (I'll call her Jenny), whose dog it really was, loved the dog and never had a problem with him herself. Jenny was reluctant to have him killed, so she called the society for the prevention of cruelty to animals and was referred to me. Here's the history I ended up taking, and the observations I made to get the story no one was telling.

This family had previously had two dogs, both of them very small. Jenny felt competent to raise small dogs without help, so she hadn't gone to a dog school with these dogs. Both turned out to be sweet dogs, compliant, pliable and trusting. Jenny's two children were small during the lives of both these dogs and didn't get involved with raising or training them, though they had a fond and cuddly relationship with the dogs. When these two dogs died, the family decided to get a Border Collie. Because this was a larger dog, Jenny decided it would be a good idea to go to a dog school with him. Since her son was now thirteen, she figured he was old enough to get involved with training the dog.

At the dog school, Jenny (and her son) heard the story about the dominance hierarchy for the very first time. When the dog didn't obey a command, this meant he was contesting his low rank, and the right thing to do was (for example) jerk on the choke chain or throw a bunch of keys at his head. That would teach him who was the leader. Jenny's gentle nature didn't allow her to do this kind of thing to a dog, so she left it to the men in the house. Dad had a very busy construction company, so he didn't have much time to be involved with the dog; but the thirteen-year-old boy didn't have to be told twice about power relations or that he was allowed to bully the dog to arrange them. He enthusiastically stepped into the role of dog punisher in the family.

Everything seemed to go fine for about eighteen months. The dog was reserved and hesitant in his contact with the boy, but the family interpreted this to mean the dog thought the boy had a high rank. Then one day the dog was on his way upstairs when the son started to come down the stairs. Stuck on a narrow passageway with the boy, and with only a difficult flight route left open to him (it's hard for a dog to turn around on a staircase), the dog growled at the boy as the boy approached him. This was the first time the dog had ever growled at anyone, so the family was quite dismayed. They decided to call the dog trainer. The trainer told them the dog was obviously at an age when he was starting to challenge the person he saw as the Alpha in the house and trying to become the Alpha himself. He told the family to keep the choke chain and the leash on the dog indoors. Whenever the dog did something they didn't like, they were to give a mighty jerk on the leash. This would, again, teach the dog who was who in the house and solve all the problems.

The son enthusiastically followed this advice, but it didn't solve the problems. In fact, the dog's threat behaviour toward the son worsened. He started to growl anytime the son approached him. The family decided to call the breeder they'd bought the dog from. The breeder (a woman) told them they weren't being strict enough. She advised them to take the dog and lay him on his back whenever he growled, to strangle him, and not to let go until his tongue turned light blue. This would teach him his rank. And once the dog knew his rank, all the problems would be solved.

Jenny and her husband thought this was strange advice, but like most people, they thought that trainers and breeders are experts. And again, since Dad wasn't around much, he only did this to the dog once in a while. It was the son who ended up taking responsibility for regularly strangling the dog. This went on for about three and a half years. During this time, the dog started to develop other 'strange' behaviour. He began to be fearful and growlly around men who came to the house. He'd be fine all evening, then suddenly, when the son (who was now dating) came home, he'd start to prowl around the living room, growling and showing his teeth as he slunk around the perimeter. He started approaching the son while the family watched television, sitting down in front of the son, staring at him, and growling. When the family loaded itself into a van to drive off for a holiday, they'd put the dog in last, sticking him in a small, enclosed space between lots of luggage and supplies and the family members. The dog started to have panic attacks if the son reached into the back to get a sandwich or a magazine, retreating into a corner at the back, snapping at the air, growling. The whole family would have to get out of the van and let the dog calm down before they could drive any further. The dog also panicked if Dad raised his voice at one of the children during the drive. The family had been willing to live with this behaviour until the crisis came that made them call me.

As I asked for details about both attacks, the story turned out to be different from the one Jenny had told me on the telephone. The son said he had been sitting at his desk in his room, door closed, with the dog sitting behind him in a sort of bottleneck between two wider sections of the room. He'd got up to leave the room and had to pass the dog. The dog had suddenly lashed out and bitten him without any provocation, then ducked under the bed. The boy demonstrated for me how he'd walked past the dog — sideways, with his hands held in the air up near his ears. There was one problem with this story, and that was the wounds. The bruising and small puncture wounds were on the boy's thumb cushions and the forearms just above the wrists. This suggests that in fact the boy had had his hands extended toward the dog when the dog lashed out. Not only that, but the wounds told that the boy had his hands extended toward the dog's face or neck when the dog lashed out. It was clear that the dog had bitten the two body parts that had been closest to his teeth — left, right, in a lightning move, just enough to open a retreat to a safe hiding place.

The telephone story about the later attack on the father turned out not to be complete either. Like the son's, Dad's wounds were on one of his hands, one on the thumb cushion and one just above the wrist. When I asked about the details of what had happened, it turned out Dad had strangled the dog out in the yard until the dog's tongue turned light blue. When he'd let go, the dog had lashed out and bit his hand, then fled. As Dad walked toward the house, the dog had come back and bit at the tails of Dad's coat. The dog did allow himself to be muzzled several minutes later. It wasn't until the muzzle was on his face that he'd gone into a 'fury.'

None of the women in the house had ever had a problem with the dog.

Analysis: This family did not have trouble with dogs until they were told the myth about the 'dominance hierarchy'. This led the men in the house to treat this third dog differently than they had treated the first two. The adolescent son in particular had enthusiastically punished the dog and regularly strangled him, in my opinion much more often than he admitted to his parents. The whole family was unable to make the link between their own behaviour and the dog's responses. This is illustrated by their bafflement that the dog had bitten the father. If I hadn't asked detailed questions, they wouldn't have thought to mention that Dad was in the act of strangling the dog when the dog lashed out.

Diagnosis: The dog's initial threat behaviour was caused by anxiety. Adding yet more punishment and pain increased this anxiety. The biting incidents were a result of repeatedly putting the dog in a situation that was literally life threatening (the strangulations). Nevertheless, the dog was still desperately trying to salvage the relationships. His bites remained well inhibited, and he never bit more than he needed to to open up the option of fleeing (which he then did). His approaching and growling at the son when the family watched television were not 'dominance' or deranged behaviour. These were repeated attempts to get the boy to show a normal response (this is, the dog was soliciting non-threat signals from someone who seemed dangerous and unpredictable, but with whom he had no choice but to share a space — see Myths 12 and 13). His reaction to the muzzle was a perfectly normal reaction in a dog that had never so much as seen a muzzle before, let alone been trained not to panic when it was put on his face. The problem was not in the dog, who had accepted even strangling for five years before he finally bit anyone. The whole problem here was the magical thinking 'dominance' involves (see Myths 72 and 84), and the presence of a bullying adolescent no one in the family was capable of criticising or disbelieving.

Therapy: The family was to stop all punishment. They were to study my booklet on dog body language so they would be able to see when the dog was feeling anxious and how to respond to this. They were to start training the dog with treats. This was partly counter conditioning to build up new, positive associations with the men in the house. Partly it was to create predictability for the dog by teaching him a number of responses he could know would always be safe and would never lead to a strangulation. When visitors were in the house, the best solution was to avoid the problem. I advised this family to get the dog used to spending a half hour alone in a room every day, and then to confine the dog to this room with some edible toys a half hour before visitors came. This would spare the dog a stressful situation, and it would make sure visitors did not make mistakes that would revive the dog's fear. I also advised them not to take the dog on vacation with them anymore.

Results: The therapy worked. In fact, given the dog's history, it worked amazingly quickly. The dog continues to have periods of being nervous around the son, but I suspect this is due to the son not being able to resist at least teasing the dog when his mother isn't looking. But even if I'm wrong, it's not because this dog is 'dominant'. Sometimes a person has just hurt a dog so badly and so frequently that real trust can never be restored.

Myth 85: You should hit a dog with a newspaper rather than with your hand.

Despite the fact that ever more people are now using modern training techniques that are based on knowledge about how dogs learn, there are still a lot of people who believe you have to use physical punishment with dogs. Apparently many of them do in fact realise that physical punishment arouses anxiety, because they will tell you that a dog will become hand-shy if you hit her with your hand. This is true. The dog will learn to expect a blow when she sees a hand suddenly coming at her. She might take this from her owner — since she is totally at his/her mercy and has no choice — but she might not take this from a stranger. This is the dog that snaps at the extended hand of a passer-by who tries to pet her on the street.

It is also true that a smack with a newspaper is much more merciful than many of the other things people have thought up to discipline dogs — though if you aim at the dog's nose, you can cause extreme pain even with a newspaper. But assuming you don't do this, and that you are using what seems like symbolic violence rather than real violence, the dog still learns to expect a blow. The fact that you end up making the dog afraid of newspapers instead of your hand doesn't make this a better way to raise a dog.

A dog is always learning, from every experience she has. However, she isn't always learning what we think she is. As we try to teach a dog commands, for example, she is not only learning the words we use. She is also learning whether it's safe to try guessing what we want or not, whether training is fun or distressing, and whether to trust us or fear us. If training hurts, she may not be able to figure out that it's the choke chain doing it — though I have seen dogs conclude that the owner grabbing the leash is a sign now painful things are going to happen (she still doesn't know it's the choke chain, as such). If she's had keys thrown at her face, she'll start to cringe or look at you anxiously every time she hears that jingle (though she still doesn't know what a key is). See also Myths 16, 25, 28, 56, 58 (paragraph 5), 61, 68, 82, 86, 45, 46, and the text box at the end of this chapter about all the things dogs learn that we don't notice we're teaching them.

You may avoid your dog becoming hand-shy by hitting her with a newspaper, but you are still teaching her she can expect to be hit. This can have surprising results. One day a visitor comes to your house. Your dog welcomes the visitor and then settles down somewhere on the living room floor, pleased to take part in the fun of having someone over. Once your guest is also settled in, you go to the kitchen to make some coffee or pour some drinks. Your guest sees the newspaper lying on the couch and picks it up to read the headlines while s/he waits for you to come back. Your dog, who was enjoying the guest's presence up to now, thinks the visitor is suddenly planning to hit her. This is baffling to her because all she's doing is lying there, not bothering anyone. She jumps up and, with a short growl, grabs your visitor's arm for a second. She immediately lets go, but she remains standing in front of your visitor, waiting to see what this person will do next. Your guest cries out, 'Ow, she bit me, totally out of the blue!' and you come rushing back from the kitchen to see what's going on. You are startled and embarrassed. You forget what you normally do to the dog with the newspaper. You fail to notice that there is nothing more serious than a bit of dog saliva on your guest's sleeve. You agree with your guest that your dog 'bit out of the blue.' You start to fear that your dog might not be trustworthy (or, worse yet, that your dog is 'dominant-territorial').

You are now in danger of either becoming unnecessarily wary of your dog or of getting into a spiral of violence with her.

Even if you use a newspaper instead of your hand to hit your dog, you are still teaching the dog that violence is part of the relationship with us. If you don't hit her hard in the face, you may feel you are sticking to the dog rules by using only symbolic violence — but if the dog uses symbolic violence back, we are shocked and alarmed. It's better to raise a dog so that she knows even symbolic violence is not part of the way our two species relate to each other.

Fact: It's better not to hit your dog at all, not even with a newspaper.

Feel free to generalize this lesson. When I was working in the shelter, a dog came in whose owner I had happened to work with some months before. This woman had been kind to her dog, but her boyfriend used to take the dog out for 'punishment training' when he felt frustrated with the dog. He'd walk up and down outside the house, jerking on the choke chain no matter what the dog did or didn't do. As usual, the idea was to show the dog who's boss around here, in the presumption that the dog would then magically be able to guess and fulfill all human wishes and whims. When this dog was brought into the shelter, a female member of staff took the dog over from the owner first. The dog just stood there. When a male member of staff took the leash to take the dog back to the kennels, the dog stiffened and started to panic. The female staff had enough presence of mind to grab the leash right away, saying, 'Apparently the dog likes me more.' The dog calmed down again. Everyone was baffled by this response until I explained the dog's history.

Something like this was probably also the explanation of why a Doberman pinscher had attacked a male staff member several months earlier as soon as he took over the leash from the dog's owner. I've seen dogs flee or freeze up ready for fight or flight when I picked up a stick or a shoe. So it's not just violence with newspapers. There are many things a dog can learn to understand as a signal that something awful is about to happen.

Myth 86: If your dog hides under the couch, you can lure him with a sweet voice and a treat. When he comes closer, you grab him and punish him for what he did. That will teach him not to try to escape his just punishment.

This myth might seem strange to many readers, but I run into it so often that it needs to be addressed.

Other myths are at the root of this one. The first is that a dog knows when he's been bad (see Myth 47). The second is that the dog stays out of reach specifically to taunt his owner (see Myth 83). The third is that a dog learns from punishment (Myths 75, 76, 77, and 85). In fact, maintaining or increasing distance is a calming signal. When a dog decides to hide, it's because he has learned that his calming signals won't work to defuse his owner's anger, and so the only thing a dog can do is flee (or fight back, so you should be glad he's chosen to hide). Hiding under the couch reveals that the dog has been harshly punished in the past, and that he is frightened of his owner.

The dog under the couch is, thus, not taunting anyone. He's lying there with a fearfully beating heart, feeling utter terror. He has learned that, once his owner is angry, there is no way to stop it or to get peace back into the situation. Since he doesn't want to fight or bite and is utterly powerless to disarm the situation any other way, the dog is hoping that if he just stays out of sight for a while, his owner's baffling anger will subside with time. Or that someone else will get the beating this time.

It's cruel to trick a dog who is feeling so frightened. He hears his owner's voice calm down, he sees a treat being offered. He hesitates, but his fear is dying down and he is starting to feel some hope. Finally, he decides to trust the situation. He meekly creeps out from under the couch — and the result is that he gets the beating after all.

His owner thinks, 'So there! That'll teach you not to hide from me!' But this isn't only cruel, it's also short sighted. The owner is usually very surprised when this trick works once or twice and then stops working altogether. To the rest of us, this was predictable, because we know dogs are always learning as they go.

Besides creating a dog that stays under the couch for hours, this person is also creating a second problem: he's teaching the dog that a human is never to be trusted. The dog is learning that a sweet voice and a treat can be signals that a beating is coming. He will start to retreat whenever anyone talks kindly to him. He might start to show his teeth to anyone who offers him a treat. He may freeze up when a passer-by in the park tells him what a sweet dog he is and wants to pet him. His tension can escalate to the point where he snaps at this passer-by.

This dog is now afraid of humans. When visitors come into the house, he might need to test them before he can feel safe in the same room with them. He wants to reassure himself that they won't touch him. He approaches the guest, showing his uncertainty with his body language. He's hoping the guest will ignore him while he checks the person out and then retreats again. Some dogs are so mistrustful that they'll lie down at a guest's feet, planning to keep the guest from moving until s/he leaves. The visitor doesn't know how to read the dog's signals, so s/he tries to pet him, putting on a sweet voice and looking straight into the dog's eyes. The dog gets more and more tense. He might growl, he might snap at the petting hand. Later, the supposed 'dog expert' comes and declares that the dog is showing pathological behaviour by both approaching and growling (see also Myth 97). The dog ends up dead.

Luring a dog to punish him isn't about teaching the dog anything. It's about revenge. Dogs don't understand revenge, and they don't learn anything good from it. All it does is teach the dog that we are literally never to be trusted. He can only feel safe when we are totally and utterly ignoring him.

Fact: Dogs are always learning. The only thing a dog learns from this myth is that we are especially dangerous when we make an effort to sound or look friendly.

Myth 87: You can teach a dog to swim by throwing him into deep water. Dogs don't drown, because swimming is instinctive in them.

It's better not to try this one. It's not only incredibly cruel to a creature who is utterly in our power, it's also dangerous. An adult dog who has never swum will not automatically make the right movements to keep herself afloat. If you throw a dog into the water like this, an awful lot panic. I've seen this happen many a time. The dog tries to keep her head above water by trying to reach for the ground with her hind feet, so that her spine ends up pointing at the bottom. She'll wildly beat the surface with her front paws, as if she's trying to climb into the air. If you don't help a dog who is doing this, she'll drown.

Swimming is learned behaviour in a dog. The best time for her to learn it is, like so many other things, in her puppy days. A pup has proportionately more fat and less muscle, so she'll float more easily than an adult dog. Until about her twelfth week, a pup is not inclined to be afraid of new things. If we put our hands under her belly and gently lay her in the water, she'll make a walking motion with her feet. Then you can slowly remove your support. The pup discovers that she not only keeps floating, but that she can even move around in water by using her feet. At this age, the knowledge will become anchored in her growing brain as a normal part of 'how the universe works'. These are dogs who jump enthusiastically into the water wherever they are, then proceed to cut efficiently through it like a well-designed boat.

A young dog can also be taught to swim without being afraid during her first experiences in the water. Young dogs don't yet have complete control over their impulses. You can take her to a beach or a lake where the bottom slopes gently down toward deeper water. First, practise playing with her in the shallows, so she gets used to standing in the water. When she does this without hesitation, get her used to running and jumping and getting splashed, then you can start to move slowly toward deeper water, playing all the while. Eventually, you walk out just past the point where the dog can keep her feet on the bottom and still follow you. She'll hesitate, but don't give in to the temptation to force her: that might make her frightened of water for the rest of her life, besides damaging her trust in you. Just keep on playing with the ball where you are, not bothering about the dog. Most young dogs will, in the end, be unable to control the impulse to join in the fun again. She's relaxed in the water anyway, and will give in to the impulse to take one or two more steps. She'll discover that her head is still above water, even though the ground is gone from under her feet. After a while, she'll start swimming with great confidence.

Adult dogs have more trouble learning to swim. They don't float as easily as a puppy, and they have learned to look before they leap. They have learned to avoid anything that makes them feel apprehensive. If you don't succeed in getting your adult dog to take that last step into deep water, you can try helping her. Like the pup, you first let her float with your hands supporting her under her belly, until she feels confident doing this with you. She will most likely be making the walking movement with her feet while you support her. When she's relaxed enough, you can remove one hand, then (carefully) the other and let her make the discovery that she is now swimming. Walk ahead of her back towards shallow water, constantly telling her what a great dog she is. She'll discover she can swim back to shallow water, where her feet can touch the bottom again. Be happy with her and show it. Once you've repeated this enough times, the chances are good that your dog will dare to follow you out to the deeper water of her own accord. The more patiently you do this, and the less anxiety the dog feels while you help her, the greater your chances of success will be.

But we can't always teach a dog to swim. I have two dogs myself who have decided, once and for all, that they are not going to swim. They'll go up to their chest in the water, but they can't bring themselves to take that last step they need to take to reach the ball that is floating just an inch out of reach. On the beach, they both panic when I take that last hand out from under their bellies. However much fun it would be (for all of us) if they could swim, I'm not going to force them. Their trust in their well-being and me are too important; they are entirely in my power, and I don't believe in abusing power.

Fact: Swimming is not instinctive in a dog, and your dog may well drown if you just throw her into deep water.

Part 7

What goes in and what comes out:

Eating, drinking, peeing and pooping

Myth 88: You should feed a dog his entire daily ration in one large meal once a day. This is good because it imitates the fasting-feasting rhythm of the wolf.

This is a dangerous myth.

Your dog is not a wolf. He isn't even a hunter. His stomach is made to process the small quantities of food that he finds in the course of the mornings and evenings while rummaging around the rubbish dump, after which he mostly lazes around. The dog's stomach is not like the wolf's. It is not designed to process huge amounts of food in one go, and it is not designed to stay stable if the dog runs and jumps around while his stomach is full.

If your dog goes out for an energetic romp with a full, heavy stomach, it can make a flip inside his belly. This can also happen if the dog eats to much in one session. The stomach can become so full that it revolves on its axis inside the abdomen. Either way, this revolution of the stomach makes a twist in the entrance to the stomach (the oesophagus) and the exit (the small intestine), which seal the stomach closed. It's rather like bending a garden hose so that no more water can come out. The water pressure will then build up in the hose behind the bend. If the dog's stomach turns on its axis, fermentation gasses can't escape anymore. Pressure in the stomach will start to build. The stomach will expand and start to push the other organs in the abdomen aside, damaging them in the process. The expanding stomach may press against the great arteries in the abdomen, sending the dog into shock. Meanwhile, the stomach acids can't escape, so they begin to eat away at the stomach wall, dissolving the stomach itself. If you don't recognise what's going on and get to a vet like a shot, your dog will die a painful, screaming, torturous death.

The symptoms of a turned stomach (known as gastric torsion or organoaxial gastric volvulus) are as follows. A little while after he's eaten, the dog gets restless. He may stand as if he's feeling uncomfortable. He may walk back and forth, cough, salivate profusely, and he might try (without success) to vomit. If you see him doing this, feel his belly just behind the ribs. If the belly is starting to swell, take him immediately to the vet. Phone the vet before you leave so the operating room can be prepared. Gastric torsion is always a life-threatening, acute emergency.

Don't be fooled, either, by the fact that a wolf uses its stomach as a shopping basket, running with a gorged stomach back to the den to regurgitate for the pups. Dogs don't have to bring food to their pups, and they don't travel large distances with a full stomach. Research shows that free-ranging domestic dogs spend about eighty percent of their time lazing around, sunning or sleeping. They rummage the dumps throughout the day. They do most of their travelling in the dusk hours, just before sunrise or just after sunset, when their bellies are fairly empty. When a dog has just eaten a big meal, his loosely anchored stomach has more mass and weight than it usually does. If he jumps around with other dogs, chases balls or other such activities, the mass in his stomach bounces around in his abdominal cavity. If it so happens to make a 180-or-more degree swing, you've got an acute emergency.

Fact: Prevention is better than a cure. A gastric torsion can damage a dog's insides so much that a vet can't save his life, even if you get there quickly. Divide your dog's daily ration over several smaller meals in the course of the day. For most dogs, two is enough. If your dog is especially active, or if he's had a flipped stomach in the past, then dividing the food over four or more meals will greatly decrease the chance of an accident. Don't feed your dog just after a romp. Make him rest at least a half an hour before you feed him. After you've fed him, make him rest an hour or two before you take him out to do anything more than a slow paced walk on the leash. Best of all, take him to the park with an empty stomach and feed him a half hour after you return. You'll have a dog who is glad to come home after his run (yay, dinner time!), and who will happily settle down for a nap after he eats, thus taking care of his stomach the way Nature meant him to.

Special note about puppies: Pups are even more vulnerable than adult dogs. Their little stomachs can't handle large quantities of food. A pup should be fed five or six very small meals during the course of the day — and, just like an adult dog, not allowed to romp or play until an hour after he's eaten. Starting at about four months of age, you can start giving four small meals a day, tapering off to two or three as you see him grow.

Myth 89: I should make my dog fast one day a week. This imitates the fasting-feasting rhythm of the wolf, and it's good for my dog's intestinal flora and his metabolism.

The dog is not a wolf, not a hunter. She lives on human leftovers and has no idea of the hunter's irregular feeding patterns. The dog spends her days calmly scavenging the rubbish dump, or trots along at her ease browsing through the waste bins in the alley. When she's had enough to eat, she goes to lie in the sun somewhere. She can always get another snack later, and she knows there will be food again tomorrow.

Research shows that the domestic dog does not go through a cycle of starve-then-feast. They always have a small stream of food coming in. In some geographical areas, it's always enough. In other areas dogs suffer hunger. But even where free-ranging domestic dogs do know hunger, it's not feasting and fasting, but chronic undernourishment. There is still a constant stream of leftovers, just not enough. The food is still eaten spread over the course of the whole day, every day. Just as the dog's stomach is not made to process huge quantities of food in one go, it is also not made for periodic fasting.

You won't be making your dog any happier by making her fast one day a week. Her intestines, their flora and her metabolism don't benefit from this in any way, either.Worse still, you could risk generating a couple of problems you wouldn't otherwise have.

The day after she's had to fast, your dog just might be inclined to gorge if she gets the chance. For example, she might try to tear open the sack of dog food while you're out, which she wouldn't otherwise do. Fasting can, in other words, increase the risk of a gastric torsion (see Myth 88).

A second problem is that your dog might become insecure about getting enough to eat. This could lead to aggression problems around the food bowl, or to aggression when she's found something edible on the street and you want to take it away from her.

Fact: It isn't normal for a dog to go a whole day without food. It may sound romantic, but it is both outside dog reality and — possibly — dangerous to treat your dog like a wolf in this way.

Beck, AM, The ecology of 'feral' and free-roving dogs in Baltimore, Ch 26 in Fox MW (ed) *The Wild Canids,* Van Nostrand Reinhold Co, MY, 1975.

Beck, AM, *The Ecology of Stray Dogs: A Study of Free-ranging Urban Animals,* York Press, Baltimore, 1973.

Boitani, L, Francisci, F, Ciucci, P, and Andreoli, G, Population biology and ecology of feral dogs in central Italy, in Serpell, J, ed. *The domestic dog; its evolution behaviour and interactions with people,* Cambridge University Press, Cambridge, 1995, 217–244.

MacDonald, DW, and Carr, GM, Variation in dog society: between resource dispersion and social flux, in Serpell, J, ed. *The domestic dog: its evolution behaviour and interactions with people*, Cambridge University Press, Cambridge, 1995, 199–216.

Myth 90: Raw meat is better for a dog than cooked meat.

This is an idea that prevailed before the Second World War, before the manufacture of pet food became big business. In areas where people made their dogs' meals themselves, the question of raw or cooked was (to some) a burning one. Most people probably don't think about this nowadays. Some people still believe in giving a dog raw meat at least occasionally, because they think the domestic dog is a hunter. Other people believe that giving a dog raw meat will make him aggressive, giving him a 'taste for blood' (see Myths 31 and 32).

The domestic dog isn't a hunter. After all, he became domestic in the first place by giving up hunting to trail around scavenging our dumps. The species has been living on our leftovers, including cooked meat, for thousands of years now. Many dogs won't even eat raw meat unless you starve them first.

This is a good thing. Raw meat can carry various harmful bacteria and parasites that can harm or kill a dog. It can be just as bad for them as it is for us. Sometimes it's even more harmful to them. Pork is a case in point. The meat of a pig is sometimes infected with a virus that causes Aujeszky's disease. This virus is harmless to humans. Pigs don't always die of this disease. Pigs can even be infected without showing any symptoms, so occasionally a sick pig will be brought to slaughter without anyone knowing it. What you need to know is that the Aujeszky virus is *always* deadly for a dog. If a dog takes so much as a single bite of infected meat, or even licks it, this marks the end of his life. No veterinarian can help him. Death will ensue within about seventy-two hours. It's not a nice death. One of the symptoms can be an itch all over the entire body, an itch so intense that it drives the dog to desperation before he finally dies. It's better not to feed a dog pork at all, but if you must, don't let him smell or lick it before you cook it, and make sure the pork is well cooked all the way through before you give it to your dog. There is some evidence that this virus can even spread by air, infecting a dog who sniffs too closely on a piece of infected raw pork.

It's not good for a dog to eat too much protein. The dog's evolution prepared it to eat a varied diet, not one consisting mostly of meat. The dog needs carbohydrates and various vitamins and minerals, which he won't get enough of from a diet too heavy on meat. He gets too much of one thing and not enough of the others, which can shorten his life in the long term — even if he doesn't die sooner of a parasite or Aujeszky's disease. Too much protein can eventually cause kidney problems. Too much protein can lead to an unnecessarily high level of urea in the blood. The kidneys end up exposed to too much of this protein by-product, accruing damage through the years. This is one reason why old dogs and dogs with kidney problems are often put on protein-light diets.

Fact: Eating raw meat can be bad for your dog. It can be acutely deadly, or deadly over time. The best thing to do is feed your dog a reputable, good quality commercial dog food. These are carefully composed so that they contain everything a dog needs, all in the right balance, and without the risk of making him ill.

Myth 91: We don't have to buy dog food. The dog can live perfectly well on our leftovers.

This is a myth because of the words 'perfectly well'. It's a fact that the dog's ancestor became a dog because he learned to survive by eating our leftovers instead of travelling and hunting all day. It's true that a domestic dog still can survive by eating our leftover food, and that this would be better for them than living on a diet comprised solely of meat, as some dogs do in some parts of the world.

The trouble is, the dog needs a different balance of nutrients than do humans. He needs a little more protein, a little more fat, and a little less carbohydrate than we do. The dog has different vitamin needs. For example, his intestines make vitamin C themselves, so he doesn't need to eat fruit. Some of the things we eat are poisonous for dogs. Chocolate, onions, garlic, grapes (including raisins) and raw bread dough can, even in small quantities, kill a dog.

Besides, survival isn't the same as optimal living. Dogs who live free at a garbage dump, Inuit dogs (who eat only meat and fish) and the livestock guarding dogs in developing countries all have a pretty short life expectancy. If a pup manages to make it through his first two years alive, he can expect to live for about another four years. This is partly due to the enormous parasite load these dogs carry, but it is partly due to nutrition.

Our own species is a case in point of what kind of impact nutrition can have. Our life expectancy rose dramatically in the twentieth century, but the medical sciences aren't as responsible for this as you might think. Our increased life expectancy was mostly due to the construction of sewage systems and, even more, to an increase in the quality of our nutrition. The same goes for the domestic dog. If he gets the right diet, he can expect to live twice as long as his free-ranging relatives.

The dog food industry has studied long and hard the question of what a dog needs, investing huge amounts of money and pinning their reputations on the quality of their products. The best thing to feed your dog is a good quality commercial dog food, one that has the words 'nutritionally complete' on the label. If you do this, you don't need to add extras like dog vitamins, 'nutritional' treats, calcium supplements or other such stuff. These supplements can even be harmful — an overdose of certain vitamins or too much calcium can damage your dog's organs or skeleton.

As long as your dog is eating nutritionally complete commercial food, it can't hurt to give him occasional leftovers from the kitchen. After all, a little variety improves the quality of our lives, too. The thing is to keep out the poisonous stuff (chocolate, onions, garlic, grapes, raisins, bread dough) and not give him so many leftovers that he starts to get fat. Extra weight is an extremely bad thing for a dog. Overweight causes a strain on his skeleton and his organs, just as it does with us. But the dog has an added disadvantage: he is very good at holding onto heat and very bad at getting rid of it. Each extra pound has a huge, disadvantageous effect on his ability to lose enough of the heat that builds up when he uses his body, much more so than the extra pound on a human.

Fact: A dog can survive on our leftovers, but he won't live 'perfectly well' on them, nor as long as he could if fed a good, nutritionally complete commercial dog food.

Myth 92: I should supplement her food with extra calcium and vitamins, especially if she's still a puppy.

In Myth 91 we already saw that the best thing to feed a dog is a reputable commercial food that is labelled 'nutritionally complete,' and to watch out that she doesn't gain excess weight. It's actually better not to add any supplements to a complete commercial food, since vitamins can be poisonous if you or your dog take too much of them. It's possible that the shop owner will tell you otherwise, but don't forget this person is guarding his or her own financial interests: after all, that's what business is all about. In addition, the shop's owner gets information from the manufacturers, who are also in business. Why just sell you food if they can sell you something else as well? So don't expect to get objective or expert advice at a shop, nor necessarily advice that is primarily aimed at benefiting your dog.

For a puppy, it's not only unnecessary but also can cause permanent damage if you add supplements to her nutritionally complete dog food. A pup is growing at a fast rate. Too much calcium and/or too much vitamin D can cause distorted growth in her bones and joints. The dog is then damaged or even crippled for life, since her skeleton can't be changed back once it's grown.

The basic rule is: no nutritional supplements without veterinarian approval. If your dog is living on human leftovers, or if you make her meals yourself, you can consult with your veterinarian, who will sell you the right supplements if s/he thinks it's necessary. The only exception to this rule is the older dog who is developing, or who already has, arthritis. Typical of early arthritis is for a dog to be stiff when she's just gotten up from her bed, then start to walk more easily after a minute or two. Later, an arthritic dog will always walk stiffly. For these dogs, it's safe and therapeutic to add glucosamine to their otherwise nutritionally complete meals. Glucosamine often works wonders with the arthritic dog, just as it does with the arthritic human.

You can buy dog foods that have glucosamine added, but these are generally exorbitantly expensive for the amount of active ingredient the manufacturer has included. It's rather like the sugar on pre-sugared corn flakes, which has turned out to be the most expensive sugar (per pound) that you will ever buy. Since glucosamine won't damage your dog even if you give her a slight overdose of it, it is safe to buy it at a discount drug store or via the internet. Of course, you can also buy it from your vet.

Fact: Except for glucosamine, it's better not to add any supplements to the nutritionally complete commercial dog food you give your dog, unless your veterinarian has told you otherwise.

FOOD SCARES AND SCANDALS

There have recently been a number of scares and a number of real scandals about what the manufacturers put into their commercial dog food. There have even been scares and scandals about what they put into human foods. Some people have become reluctant to feed their dogs commercial foods. There is nothing wrong with making your dog's meals yourself if you do it with knowledge and care and consult with your vet — but this still means being very cautious about giving your dog uncooked meat.

Myth 93: It's all right to limit how much a dog drinks so you won't have to walk him as often.

It's both dangerous and damaging to limit how much a dog is allowed to drink. Water has several important functions in an animal's body. Water is necessary for almost all the chemical reactions that take place in our (and dogs') bodies as life is sustained. Water is also the main transport medium in our bodies. It makes up the largest part of our (and dogs') blood, of our (and dogs') lymph fluids, bringing the useful stuff to the places it needs to be and taking waste to the right places to be dumped. The kidneys are constantly removing all kinds of wastes and poisons from a dog's blood, and *they need water to do this*. If there isn't enough water in the blood, the kidneys can't remove the wastes and poisons because the necessary chemical reactions can't take place. These wastes and poisons end up re-circulating throughout the whole body, passing through all the organs on their way, repeating whatever damage they do, then coming past the kidneys again. If there's still not enough water, the kidneys will again not be able to do the chemical reactions they have to do to get rid of the waste, so they send it on for another damaging trip through the body.

This danger is heightened if a dog is taking medicine. Medicines are, by definition, foreign substances to the body, and they can damage the body if they are not eliminated as quickly as they were intended to be. If your dog is taking medicine and he is unusually thirsty, you should take this as a sign that his body needs the increased flushing. It may be a pain to take him out more frequently, but it would be dangerous to limit his water intake just to save ourselves the effort. Not only normal body waste, but also the foreign substance ends up passing all the dog's organs again and again. So if your dog is on medication, it's important to let him drink as much as he wants to, unless your vet specifically tells you otherwise.

If he's not on medication, drinking a lot can be a sign that your dog is ill. Diabetes is one of the diseases that typically cause a dog to suddenly drink a lot and then need to pee a lot. It looks to us as if the dog needs to pee so much *because* he's drinking so much, but the causal chain goes back a few steps further. The kidneys need water to bind and get rid of each sugar molecule. Logically, they need more water to deal with the heightened sugar in a diabetic dog's blood. So he drinks more and pees more — but the real cause of the need to pee so often isn't the drinking, but the illness that is making his body need so much more water. Limiting his water intake will, yet again, make the waste products stay in his body too long. Rather than attacking the cause (the disease), it only attacks a symptom (peeing a lot), and meanwhile it damages your dog.

In addition to transporting foodstuffs and waste, the water part of our (and dogs') blood also plays a crucial role in regulating body temperature. When it's cold out, the water in a mammal's blood brings heat from the warm abdomen to the extremities, lessening the risk that they'll freeze. When it's hot out, the body dumps excess heat by the evaporation of water. We do it by sweating; dogs do it by panting. If you deprive your dog of water, the regulation of body temperature can crash. As it tries not to, all the above processes can take place, causing damage to all kinds of organs.

Then there's the question of suffering. Imagine that you are very thirsty, but you can only drink when I decide it's time to, because I want to save on toilet paper.

Dogs are utterly in our power. It's not fair to abuse this fact just to save ourselves effort.

So what's normal? This depends on how active your dog is and how hot or cold the ambient temperature is. The more active a dog is and the hotter the weather, the more water he needs. It also depends on what he eats. A dog who eats dry food will need to drink more water than a dog who eats tinned food (since tinned food is about eighty percent water). All we need to do is make sure his water bowl is never empty and leave the rest to him.

Fact: Dogs generally drink exactly what they need to stay healthy. If your dog suddenly starts drinking a lot more, it's a sign that his body needs more water. Maybe it's hot out, or maybe you shifted to dry food — but it can also be a sign that something is wrong. Taking his water away won't solve the problem, and it could damage him or even shorten his life.

Myth 94: Since she is able to hold her pee for 10 (or 12, or 24) hours, it's okay to walk her only every 10 (or 12, or 24) hours.

Before you consider restricting her drinking water to extend this even further, please read Myth 93. That said, and assuming we are talking about a dog who is allowed to drink what she needs, we can move on to this myth.

Dogs can, if necessary, often hold themselves for quite a long time. Dogs who live with us inside our homes generally have to, and do, hold their urine eight to ten hours at night, depending on the rhythm their human lives by. This isn't such a problem because as we mammals sleep, our bodies go into a slow mode of operation. We don't eat, so the body doesn't have to process all kinds of substances coming in. Our muscles produce fewer waste products because they are pretty much inactive. The process of flushing waste through can and does slow down. We lose less fluid by evaporation, so we aren't thirsty and don't drink. All in all, it's usually no big deal to wait until the morning to empty the bladder.

The daytime is a different story. An animal eats, walks, runs, plays. Activity leads to thirst, so the animal drinks. Both digestion and muscle activity produce waste. All kinds of stuff has to be removed from the blood, and there is more water coming through to do this. The transportation of waste and water to the bladder is faster than during the night. If the bladder can't be emptied, the urea levels in her blood rise. If this goes on too long, we get the damage described in Myth 93.

But aside from any physical damage, there's also the question of a dog's well-being. We all know how it feels to desperately need to pee but to have to hold it. A dog feels the same distress if we make her wait too long. Don't forget that dogs are at our mercy. They can't open the door themselves, and even if they could, being out on the street without us is dangerous for them. It's a bit ungrateful to take advantage of their goodwill and their willingness to hold their pee as long as they possibly can for us. When you can't help it because of an emergency, that's one thing — but it's unkind to do this just out of laziness, and dogs don't deserve it.

Fact: A dog will hold her pee for a very long time if you demand it of her, but that doesn't mean she doesn't suffer by it.

Part 8

A few myths about who knows what

Myth 95: Dog trainers know what they're talking about.

Not all dog trainers have had any real education about animal behaviour. Many start out by taking their own first dog to a club or school to find out how to train it. They get along great with the teachers. They do as they are told without asking too many questions about the techniques they're learning. They learn these techniques quickly and enthusiastically. Because they are such good and obedient students, they are eventually offered the chance to become a trainer. These people have learned everything they know at the club: their entire knowledge about dogs consists of the club's story. This is usually a story about ranks and dominance and the choke chain. Sometimes it's a story about how to give a reward at exactly the right moment and getting a high rank for yourself by psychological tricks. The club story is a sort of Holy Revelation. No one knows where it came from. All they know is that it's been handed down for years and years, and that everyone believes in it, and therefore it must be true. And because their own dog sits when they say so, these trainers are absolutely sure they know all about dogs and all about how animals, and dogs in particular, learn.

These clubs are often closed cliques. They often discourage students from looking for knowledge outside their own circle. To have any hope of being allowed to join the trainers' ranks, you must never contradict the trainers. You must never ask difficult questions or challenge anything they tell you. People who do ask questions are often belittled and bullied. If they persist, they are thrown out of the club. The club's Holy Revelation ends up never being revised, corrected or updated.

Some of the so-called positive trainers do this, too. It's just that they so happened to link up at the beginning with a different club than the choke chain club. Positive dog trainers base their training mostly on rewards, using treats, the clicker and other friendly techniques. The cute thing about these people is that they are basically doing the right thing, but they have no idea why their tricks work (see also Myth 70). It's good luck if the dog school you picked out in the Yellow Pages uses so-called 'positive' training. Many of these trainers will still tell you the same fiction the choke chain clubs tell, all about ranks and dominance, but this isn't immediately of crucial importance. Your dog will be trained according to a scientifically sound system — rewarding behaviour you like, giving the dog lots of space to make mistakes without being punished as she searches for the right response. As long as this is all that happens, your dog can be trained here without ending up damaged.

However, the 'positive' in some positive trainers disappears as soon as the dog does something unexpected, or as soon as the trainer starts to get frustrated. If these trainers don't understand why their methods usually work, they then also don't understand why their techniques sometimes don't work. This is the moment when they start telling the story about ranks and dominant personalities in dogs. This is the point where some 'positive' trainers might decide it's time for punishment. They don't tell you to get a choke chain; instead, they have you jerk the dog's head upwards with some kind of head halter to force your dog to sit. They don't know that this is much more dangerous for the dog's spine and brain than jerking on a choke chain — it's just their way of kidding themselves that they still aren't using punishment. Sometimes they'll tell you to throw a can of coins or marbles at the dog, or your key chain, again pretending this isn't really punishment because it isn't painful. They forget that you are taking the risk of wounding the dog if you aim wrong and hit, for example, an eye. Or that even if you don't accidentally wound your dog, he will still develop a fear response to the sound. Sometimes they'll tell you to use the plant spray to aim a jet of water right at the dog's face when he does something you don't like. There are lots of punishments that 'positive' trainers can use when the going gets rough, all the while kidding themselves that they are still better than the other club and unaware that these punishments can also have serious side effects — as all punishment tends to do.

So the main problem with dog trainers is that they are all too often the product of small, closed clubs whose members constantly reassure each other back and forth that they already know everything about dogs — it's all to be found in the club's Holy Dogma. In their self-satisfaction and conceit, they will not allow others to contradict them. This is a result of various aspects of human psychology that are beyond the scope of this book. (When a person becomes convinced, for whatever reason, that s/he already knows everything there is to know, they stop looking for new knowledge. They are unaware that this attitude always marks the beginning of true ignorance.)

Not all trainers reject continuing learning. Many genuinely are trying to keep up and constantly improve their understanding of dogs. But they run into another obstacle, namely the fact that new knowledge is often fragmented, spread around in specialised scientific journals, many of which are inaccessible to the general public owing to extremely high subscription fees. There is also the problem of judging the value of a scientific work. After all, many scientists are, just like the layman, stuck in the old myths that Lorenz spread around (see Myth 10).

That's why this book is so important.

There are many dog trainers who have no idea what they're talking about, no matter how strongly they believe they do. These trainers learned a club dogma, which they pass on to their students. Sometimes one dogma is accidentally less damaging to our pets than other dogmas, but even then, some trainers don't even know why.

Fact: Be wary of every trainer who urges you to use physical punishment of any kind with your dog, or one who wants you to rely on doing unpleasant things to him. One good test of a trainer is whether s/he can teach a new trick to an unleashed dog. Because the fact is, a good trainer doesn't only not need a choke chain, s/he doesn't need a leash at all. If a dog is loosed and free on the field, a good trainer is able to get and keep her attention and knows how to seduce her into voluntarily taking part in an activity. If you are working with a trainer who can't do this, if your trainer becomes helpless when you take away the leash, then it's time to look for a new trainer.

Fact: Another sign that it's time to look for a new trainer is if yours is not willing to answer any and all questions you have without making you feel belittled, bullied, stupid or ridiculous. You have a right to ask questions and to understand what you are doing with your dog. You have a right to express doubts and get a serious answer. There is no such thing as a stupid question, and you shouldn't be made to feel there is.

Askew's view

'If there is one major difference between today's academically qualified veterinarian, psychologist, or biologist practitioners and the academically unqualified dog trainer who advertises his or her services as a "pet behaviour therapist", "dog psychologist", or "canine behaviourist", it is the following: while academically qualified practitioners know that true competence can only be achieved by a combination of extensive counselling experience with a comprehensive knowledge of the interdisciplinary scientific literature, dog trainers are confident that they have learned everything they need to know about how to solve dog behaviour problems in their obedience schools'. (*Treatment of Behaviour Problems in Dogs and Cats:* p.59)

An exception to the unleashed-dog trainer test

If your dog has an aggression problem, it is perfectly legitimate for the trainer to ask you to keep the dog leashed for a while, until a number of trust-building exercises have been completed and it's safe to unleash him. However, the leash is purely a safety measure for the humans involved. The leash is kept limp at all times, except when the dog tightens it by lunging or pulling in an attempt to lash out. The leash is not used to jerk the dog around, hurt him, force him to follow anyone, force him to cooperate, nor in any other way as a tool in the training itself. The dog should be unaware (as much as possible) that he is leashed at all. After all, the whole point of training is to get a dog to regard humans as the source of good things, and to get him to the point where he both wants to cooperate and feels safe doing so.

Askew, HR, *Treatment of Behaviour Problems in Dogs and Cats: A Guide for the Small Animal Veterinarian,* Blackwell Science, London, 1996.

Personal experience with tens of trainers and clubs, internet forums, discussion groups, all of which experience support Askew's (and my own) remarks about club trainers and dogmas.

Hild, R, Cults in dog Training, http://www3.sympatico.ca/tsuro/_articles/cults_training.html, accessed 12 January 2009.

Myth 96: Trainers who specialise in training dogs for police and guard work know what they're doing. In particular, the police dog trainers are real experts.

It may seem self-evident that you should believe this myth. After all, these people (who are mostly men) work all day, every day with dogs. They can order their dogs to attack and sometimes they can even make the dogs stop again. They do difficult work — catching criminals, controlling riots, various guard and surveillance work — and their dogs do it with them. When there's a problem with a civilian dog, a canine unit policeman is often the one we ask for advice. These men are supposed to be able to judge both the character and the behaviour of dogs. Everyone seems to agree that these men must be real experts.

But there is another story behind this myth. Police dogs are often first trained at hobby clubs (see Myth 95), then bought by a police force after they've passed an exam. These particular hobby clubs are even more closed than the average trainers' clique. The training usually takes place on rural fields or in closed halls, and spectators are generally not welcome. It's often difficult for an outsider to find out what goes on during the training of these dogs. This raises the question of why the training has to be so hidden and secretive if these people are so proud of their expertise about dogs.

The answer is depressing. In 2000, the Hondenbescherming (the Dog Protection Union) in the Netherlands commissioned research on the effects of electric shock collars on dogs. The study, done at the University of Utrecht, turned up another, unexpected result: it became clear that most of the police dog trainers had very little knowledge about how dogs actually learn. Worse still, it turned out that they hadn't even mastered their own training techniques. These consist mainly of punishment, with some verbal 'rewards' here and there. (See Myth 83 about the value 'good dog' has for a dog.) There is a lot of physical, sometimes brutal, violence toward the dogs — much of which is administered in such an incompetent manner that the dog can't learn a thing from it or figure out what he did wrong. It seems that these trainers know their practices won't bear scrutiny, because the scientists were only allowed to tape the training sessions after signing an agreement that the tapes would never be shown to anyone else, under any circumstances.

We are, however, allowed to cite some of the written conclusions this study draws:

1) The trainers and handlers often use a single command with a different meaning at different times. Sometimes the command 'here' means the dog should come to his handler, sometimes it means the dog is supposed to walk to the other side of the field at a distance from the handler. If the dog now comes to his handler, he's punished. But if the dog doesn't come to his handler the next time, when the handler uses the word 'here' with a different intention, then he's punished, too. This makes it utterly impossible for a dog to figure out what 'here' is supposed to mean. 'Heel' sometimes means the dog is supposed to sit next to his handler's knee and wait for another command without moving, even if the handler walks away. The next time the handler says 'heel', he means the dog is supposed to walk away with him. Again, it is a difficult task for a dog to figure out what 'heel' means, since it means both 'follow me' and 'stay here'. This trainer ignorance

makes it impossible for the dog to avoid the (sometimes brutal) punishment that a mistake brings.

2) The commands, the rewards and the punishment are badly timed. They are either too early or too late, or they are given under such differing circumstances each time that it remains unclear to the dog what it is he's being rewarded or punished for. Sometimes an electric shock is delivered so quickly after a command that the dog gets the shock even if he obeys the command.

3) One of the handlers who took part in the study told the researchers that his dog had never been given an electric shock during training. When the dog's behaviour proved this wasn't true, the handler laughed and said, 'Well, yeah, but she's forgotten all about it', totally missing the fact that her behaviour showed she hadn't, and that she still expected a shock after a command. In other words, the handlers turned out not even to be able to observe their own dogs' behaviour accurately or understand what it meant.

This study showed that most of the police and guard dog trainers are using outdated techniques to train their dogs. It showed that they are incompetent even in the use of their own techniques. But there is more.

Many of these clubs waste the dog's socialisation period. The handlers are told to allow their pups to 'grow and expand'. This may sound strange, since puppies will grow and expand even if you try to stop them, until we are told what this instruction means. It means that you must not teach the puppy anything, including impulse control and social boundaries. This is the period when eighty percent of the growth of a dog's brain takes place, a period in which we can teach a pup most of the basic commands he'll need (even for police work) with gentle methods. If you use this period well, you will end up with a gently trained dog who nevertheless has the commands so firmly anchored in his brain that he will be a trustworthy ally even during a riot. This period is consciously thrown away. The chance to spare the dog future beatings, shocks and various other antiquated training techniques is missed.

When the dog reaches the age of six months, they decide it's time to start teaching him a thing or two. He's fitted with a prong collar, with prongs or spikes on the inside, aimed at the dog's neck, which pinch and pierce his skin if pressure is put on the collar, often until blood is drawn. The men (and the occasional woman) line up in a row with the dogs at their sides, proudly ready to start the dog's first class. They put on their best strict voices and say, 'Heel!' — a word the dog has never heard before. At the same instant, they start walking, making a beeline across the field. The young dogs have no idea what they're supposed to do, or even that something is being demanded of them. So they end up being dragged across the field on the prong collars, getting jerked about and shouted at all the way. They are subjected to extreme pain, without any idea how to avoid it or make it stop. You'll see them creeping across the field, screaming from their pain, baffled, and so frightened that they lose control of their bladders. Never mind, even if the dog is lying on his back, peeing, not obeying the command is still rebellion that has to be broken — 'dominance'. So go on dragging him, that'll teach him his rank, and once he knows his rank he'll magically know what to do (see Myths 72 and 84). At many clubs, these dogs are lifted into the air and suspended by the neck on the prong collars for mistakes during the training, supposedly to teach them who's the Alpha. They are hung if they try to resist what is being done to them (the common term for this is 'helicoptering'). Their natural reflex to bite back is wrongly attributed (again) to 'dominance', since the handlers forget they haven't taught the dog any other way to make the pain stop, and since the handlers fail to see that the dog is terrorised and desperate. Sometimes dogs are literally hung on trees and beaten as they hang, supposedly to teach them a lesson about something they did a half hour before. The list of weird human behaviour goes on and on...

It's no wonder these clubs are so secretive about their training sessions. One glance shows they have no idea what they are doing. That leaves us with two questions: why are these clubs so reluctant to learn more modern, scientifically based training techniques, and why do police forces continue to buy dogs from these clubs, knowing full well that many of the training techniques are crimes under the laws governing animal abuse?

There is yet another problem, one that touches the rest of us. Many of the dogs who are used for police and guard work come from kennels where dogs are specially bred for this work. As they breed dogs, these kennels are selecting for nervousness and a low bite threshold in their dogs, trying to produce dogs that will be more quick to bite than most dogs are. These dogs are then subjected to the training practices mentioned above, on the training field, in the presence of other dogs. We've already seen (in Myth 76, second paragraph) that dogs don't associate a punishment with their own behaviour, but with something that is present in the environment when the punishment occurs, and indeed there are huge problems with dog-to-dog aggression on the training field. Dogs frequently get into fights that end with the death of one if the handlers don't intervene. The dogs are also taught to attack a trainer's assistant, who plays the villain during the training sessions. The behaviour chain is taught incompetently by trainers who have never heard of Premack or Pryor. (Premack and Pryor were essential in developing scientific trainings methods. Any competent trainer will know and understand their work.) Then, since the dogs were first taught to bite fast and hard (or be shocked) and only later taught the command for letting go, it is very difficult to get them to cease an attack. This failure to let go is the number one problem, and the number one reason for delivering shocks during training. Logically, this produces dogs who are also difficult to control during the real work out on the streets.

The policeman gets used to interacting with this kind of dog. He starts to believe that all this is normal dog behaviour, and he moves in a world where everyone else believes this, too. Since canine unit handlers are often asked to judge the characters of civilian dogs, this raises the problem of distortion. As the Utrecht study showed, in a rare glimpse into this world, these handlers aren't competent in reading their dogs' body language. The men get used to seeing dogs that show extreme fear but don't recognise it as such. They are taught that unbridled aggression is just part of being a dog. These are the people who tell us it is 'normal' canine behaviour for a dog to attack a child or another dog with the intent to kill it: 'dogs will be dogs'. In fact, it is doubtful whether these men (and the occasional woman) can accurately judge the temperament of the civilian dogs that live among us, tell us whether a dog is displaying normal behaviour, or judge whether a dog is too aggressive to be kept alive.

In the end, like all too many trainers, the police and guard dog trainer already knows everything, so don't try to tell him anything. He doesn't know that in some places the service pup lives with her handler in his home during her puppy days, where her early life is used to teach her much of what she will need to know in a more gentle, comprehensible way. He doesn't know that there are places where service dogs live in the handler's home with his wife and kids, no problem. The dog doesn't bite unless she's told to, and she lets go when told to.

Of course, some services (the army, the air force) want aggressive dogs that will be loose cannons, attacking viciously and not stopping. Dogs who are too dangerous to live with humans or interact with anyone but their handlers. Dogs who have learned that other dogs and humans are signals that life threatening events are about to happen, and who will go into the raging aggression an animal uses to fight for its life. The trouble is, after they have artificially produced such dogs, they then proceed to claim this behaviour is just doggy nature, and that they are the only Real Trainers because they interact with these dangerous dogs.

But this was just one study

It's true that the cited study was done in a single country. However, dog training is an international scene, where organisations all over the world share and use the same techniques, meet at international congresses and so on. You can consult many a book on so-called police or guard dog training and find many of the same techniques. Message boards on the internet also show that the beliefs and practices cited in this myth are widespread among canine units and guard dog trainers over the whole world. And the military services in many countries uses the same techniques to create savagely aggressive dogs. This is not to say that all police and military dog trainers and handlers do this. There are exceptions. But exceptions are not the rule, and in most places these people need more basic education about animals, dogs and the laws that govern behaviour.

The myths within the myth

There is another myth enclosed within the myth this chapter deals with: that people who have the most aggressive dogs must be the greatest experts on canine behaviour. 'Gosh, if you can live with, deal with and control a dog like that, you must really know what you're doing.' This myth is one of the reasons the owners of pit bulls and the other aggressive breeds think they are greater experts on dogs than anyone else. It's one of the reasons those breeds are so popular — to prove to all the world that you are the one True Expert. You see it on message boards all the time: 'I live with five pits, so don't try to tell me anything about dogs'.

The underlying belief here — a second myth enclosed within this chapter's myth — is that aggression is the core, typifying characteristic of the domestic dog, who as a hunter is mostly concerned with dominance all day long — when he's not out killing something. So you only really understand dogs if you live with an aggressive dog and have (so far) kept him from attacking or killing you. Or if your dog is always trying to attack other dogs, but you've (so far) stopped him from killing one. Supposedly you then know more about dogs than the rest of us, with our wimpy dogs who aren't constantly in danger of exploding.

If you have read this far, you now know that these beliefs betray great ignorance about what the domestic dog really is.

Real expertise

Real expertise means (among other things) understanding and acknowledging what is normal, what is not, and how the abnormal has been brought about. People who tell us that dogs are naturally aggressive, who deny that their dog's aggression is abnormal, who don't understand why their dogs are so aggressive, who deny the human role in bringing this about (be it by breeding or training) — well, they are anything but experts on the domestic dog or how to train one.

Fact: Police and guard dog trainers are anything but real experts. In fact, they may well be more ignorant than your average club trainer.

Askew, HR, *Treatment of Behaviour Problems in Dogs and Cats: A Guide for the Small Animal Veterinarian,* Blackwell Science, London, 1996.

Borchelt, PL, Voith, VL, Punishment, in Voith, VL, Borchelt, PL, eds, *Readings in Companion Animal Behaviour,* Veterinary Learning systems Co. Inc., Trenton, NJ, 1996: 72–80.

Brinkhorst, LJ, brief aan De Bond tot Bescherming van Honden, 30 November 2000.

Coppinger, R, Coppinger, L, *Dogs: a startling new understanding of canine origin behaviour and evolution,* Scribner, New York, 2001.

Overall, KL, *Clinical Behavioural Medicine for Small Animals,* Mosby Inc., Missouri, 1997.

Powell, D, Francis, MJ, Francis, J, Schneiderman N, Shock-induced aggression as a function of prior experience with avoidance fighting or unavoidable shock, *JEAB* 18: 323–332, 1972.

Reid, PJ, Borchelt, PL, Learning, in Voith, VL, Borchelt, PL, eds, *Readings in Companion Animal Behaviour,* Veterinary Learning systems Co. Inc. Trenton, NJ, 1996: 62–71.

Sanders, C, Understanding Dogs: Caretakers' attributions of mindedness in canine-human relationships, *Journal of Contemporary Ethnography,* 22 2: 205–226, 1993.

Scott, JP, Fuller, JL, *Genetics and the Social Behaviour of the Dog,* University of Chicago Press, Chicago IL, 1974 (published in 1965 as *Dog Behaviour: The Genetic Basis*).

Schilder, MBH, and Van der Borg, JAM, Training met behulp van stroombanden: een schokkende ervaring voor de hond? Hoofdafdeling Geneeskunde van Gezelschapsdieren, Universiteit Utrecht, 2000.

Semyonova, A, The social organisation of the domestic dog; a longitudinal study of domestic canine behaviour and the ontogeny of domestic canine social systems, Carriage House Foundation, The Hague, The Netherlands 2003. www.nonlineardogs.com.

Sidman, M, *Coercion and its Fallout,* Authors Cooperative Inc Publishers, Boston, 1989.

Skinner, BF, *The Behaviour of Organisms: An Experimental Analysis,* Appleton–Century–Crofts Inc, NY, 1938.

Skinner, BF, *Contingencies of Reinforcement,* Prentice-Hall inc Englewood Cliffs, NJ, 1969.

Veerman, CP, brief aan de Tweede Kamer 4 mei 2005.

Myth 97: My dog behavioural therapist knows what he's talking about, because he solved my problem with my dog.

A legitimate animal behavioural therapist will usually have had some kind of real education about animals. S/he will know more about behaviour and about how animals learn than the club trainer or the police dog trainer. S/he will know all about operant conditioning (the technique of rewarding desired behaviour and getting unwanted behaviour to extinguish) and will be able to help you use it skilfully. This is the reason why s/he probably was very good at solving your dog's problem in a humane way. There is no problem with this part of the therapist's knowledge.

However, most therapists are still trained by a fairly small group of college professors and/or graduates and have learned outdated theories about what dogs are. And once they've got their degrees or certificates, they enter a world where, again, everyone is constantly affirming each other that they know all there is to know. (This is why they are always listing all their titles and certificates, to make sure everyone understands that.) In Myth 95, we saw what this belief does to people. This is the reason many of these college educated and otherwise certified therapists will still tell you that a dog is a kind of wolf, including all the myths and fables that go with this story. The college educated or otherwise certified therapist has been given a different collection of Holy Dogmas, some based on fact and others on fiction. There is, all too often, still the old taboo about questioning any of these beliefs.

Armed with degrees or certificates, the therapist informs you about leadership. Yours is a domestic dog, but s/he starts talking about wolves. You are fed the story about rank (the higher ranking wolf ignores the lower ranking wolf, so the lower wolf is always the one to approach the higher wolf). The therapist tells you you must eat before you feed your dog (even if it's only a dry cracker at the counter, because the dog must see you eat before he does). You always have to be the first one through a door and walk at the head of all processions. You always have to be sitting higher than your dog. The therapist tells you to make your dog sit or lie down to get a treat, because these are 'submissive' postures. S/he tells you that often assuming these postures will make your dog start to perceive himself as having a lower 'rank' in the 'pack'. The success of the therapy is attributed to the dog's changing idea of where he stands on the ladder.

At the beginning of this book, we saw that none of this has anything to do with domestic dog reality. The therapy may work, but it's not because of wolves and ranks. If the therapy works, it's for the following reasons:

1) By totally ignoring the dog, you also stop unintentionally rewarding behaviour you don't like, be it with positive attention, be it with negative attention. As you ignore the dog, you also stop punishing him — thus avoiding all the side effects punishment causes. In other words, you stop making beginners' mistakes with your dog, and both of you get a chance to recover a little so as to make a fresh start.

2) The instruction never to approach the dog makes sure we stop walking at a dog when the dog is feeling uncertain about what we're going to do. It shows the dog that we now obey one of the basic canine rules: respect for the other's personal

zone. This makes us less threatening to the dog, and he can start to relax a little. A decrease in stress is good for learning processes. After a while, the dog can be open to learning to have a different, better relationship with those in his surroundings.

3) So now you've stopped approaching your dog when he feels anxious, you've stopped rewarding unwanted behaviour and you've stopped being a source of punishment. At the same time, you've started frequently rewarding the behaviour of sitting or lying down. The dog starts to realise you have interesting things to offer. He starts to learn that it's fun and safe to try to follow a command. The behaviour you are ignoring starts to extinguish, while the behaviour you are rewarding starts to become more frequent. What you witness is, quite simply, the laws of behaviour. These laws operate in every creature with a brain stem. Complicated stories about ranks and status have nothing to do with it.

4) The dog didn't notice you were always eating before he did, and he would not care even if he noticed. He might have thought it was a bit strange that you suddenly started eating dry crackers, since you usually put something on your sandwiches, but aside from that he just got used to waiting a little longer for his food. He may have learned that your eating something is a signal that he will get something to eat soon.

5) By being the first to go through a door, you made sure your dog didn't get run over by a passing vehicle, that he wasn't suddenly eye to eye with a passing pit bull in the mood for a fight, and that he didn't accidentally trip up your elderly neighbour who was just coming home with the groceries.

6) You are now always sitting higher than your dog, which means his teeth are never close to your face anymore. This is a wise measure to take as long as there is still a problem between you and your dog.

7) As you frequently ask him to sit or lie down for a treat, you are teaching him that there are two actions that are always safe and will always be rewarded. Besides the laws of behaviour that operate here, this is a very good thing for a dog with aggression problems to learn. The dog can relax a little. There are now two commands that signal he is not in danger, and has a chance to receive a reward. He now has an alternative for annoying or defensive behaviour. If he wants attention, he can sit, thus getting the reward he used to get by being obnoxious. If he feels anxious, he can sit rather than showing his teeth or biting, since sitting is always safe, and because he knows that, if you approach him while he sits, it's always to give him a reward. He has a new way to defuse a scary situation.

The only useful thing the story about 'ranks' does is to make you feel more confident. It helps you believe in the fact that you can solve a problem with your dog without resorting to confrontations and physical violence. You regain hope, and you start to feel safer with the dog. This diminishes your own stress enough that you can go through a learning process. As you learn, the 'rank' stories keep you from making purely technical mistakes while you do a number of sensible things with the dog. The stories get you to adopt a number of sensible safety measures, for yourself and for the dog.

Fact: Well educated behavioural therapists often do the right things, but this doesn't always mean they understand why they are the right things. In a therapy, this doesn't matter. As long as a therapist doesn't start talking about punishing your dog, you can trust the process. The laws of behaviour operate whether or not anyone knows about them, and even if people ascribe their operation to magical causes.

See also: the text box in Myth 41 about how to find a good therapist.

Myth 98: My vet can tell me all about dog behaviour; after all, she has a university education that was all about animals.

Your vet (who is likely to be a woman nowadays) is a university graduate. So is the physicist around the corner. Because of the field she chose, your vet does know more about animals than the physicist does. This knowledge is mostly about animals' bodies. Unlike the physicist, the vet spends her days with animals, and she does probably learn something about their behaviour. At the very least, she gets to observe distressed and frightened animals, many of them dogs, many times each day. She will have found a way to deal with these frightened dogs so that she can examine them and treat them, despite their fear. However, this does not make her an expert on canine behaviour. After all, most of us manage to cook meals every day, but this still doesn't make us experts on chemistry or nutrition.

When she goes to a veterinary medicine school, a student has about four to six years to master knowledge about the physical workings of a great many animals. Once she's practising, she has to be able to look at a snake, a bird, a turtle, a cat, a dog, a horse, a cow, and even your tarantula spider, and be able to diagnose and treat them then and there. So while she's at college, she has to work hard to acquire all this knowledge about all the bodies and ills of all the various species of animals humans keep on the farm or in their homes. We assume that graduates are capable people who will treat whatever animal you bring in. However, we can't assume that the vet-med student will have time or inclination, in the few short years she has, to immerse herself in the *behaviour* of all these animals as well. Even if she is interested, she still won't have time to do more than attend the odd lecture on behaviour — so her knowledge will be somewhat superficial and patchy. It's just how circumstances and reality are, not at all her fault or failing.

After she's graduated, your vet will feel responsible to keep up with new developments in her own area of expertise. She has to do this in whatever free time she has left after her regular visiting hours at her practice, the operations she has to do, house visits in emergency cases, and her night and weekend shifts. She has to keep up with, for example, the latest bird disease or parasite and its treatment, developments in pain relief in cats, fungus infections in turtles, new diseases that are appearing in dogs in her area (with their symptoms and treatments), new diagnostic tools that are becoming available for animal practices, and so on. The vet just doesn't have time, even after graduating, to gain a second, in-depth expertise in the behaviour of animals, let alone in one particular animal (the domestic dog).

What your vet knows about dog behaviour is, with an exception here and there, what she has picked up out of personal interest — what she reads if she has a little recreational reading time left over after ploughing through her vet-med journals, or what she learns at her local dog club as she trains her own dog (see Myth 95).

Most of the young, recently educated vets understand that animal behaviour is a separate, highly specialised area of knowledge. Nowadays, most vets will refer you to an animal behaviour therapist if there is a problem between you and your dog, just as they will refer you to an orthopaedic or oncological specialist if your dog has a broken leg or cancer. Vets who don't do this are often older ones who grew up when all these other specialists didn't exist yet, and in a day when having a degree conferred a certain demi-godly (thus all-knowing) rank on a human, no matter what area the degree was in. Sometimes medical practitioners can still have a rather misplaced feeling of personal pride, and thus a reluctance to admit that there is something they don't know, or to acknowledge specialisations other than their own.

Besides the whole question of what a vet might or might not know, there is another problem with consulting vets about behaviour. Behaviour therapy requires not only knowledge of dogs, but of human psychology. It's a time consuming process. It can sometimes take hours of interviews and observation before the cause of the problem becomes clear. It is important that the dog's owner receives enough guidance and support once the cause is known — just as much where there's a fear problem as where there's an aggression problem. It's a practical impossibility that a vet can give the concentrated, long-term attention it takes to execute a behaviour therapy safely and effectively. There are only twenty-four hours in any single day.

Fact: Veterinarians are not experts on animal behaviour. Behaviour is not their field and, if they are wise, they will recognise this.

Aiello, S, (ed) *The Merck Veterinary Manual Eighth Edition,* Merck & Co, Whitehouse Station, NJ, 1998.

Askew, HR, *Treatment of Behaviour Problems in Dogs and Cats: A Guide for the Small Animal Veterinarian,* Blackwell Science, London, 1996.

Beaver, BV, *The Veterinarian's Encyclopedia of Animal Behaviour,* Iowa State University Press, Ames, 1995.

Herek, GM, The instrumentality of attitudes: Toward a neofunctional theory, *Journal of Social Issues,* 42: 99–114, 1986.

Hills, AM, The motivational bases of attitudes toward animals, *Animals & Society,* Volume 1 Number 2, 1993.

Katz, D, The functional approach to the study of attitudes, *Public Opinion Quarterly,* 24: 163–204, 1960.

Overall, KL, *Clinical Behavioural Medicine for Small Animals,* Mosby Inc, Missouri, 1997.

Reisner, IR, Erb, HN, Houpt KA risk factors for behaviour-related euthanasia among dominant-aggressive dogs: 110 cases (1989–1992). *JAVMA* 205(6):855–863, 1994.

Sanders, CR, Biting the hand that heals you: Encounters with problematic patients in a general veterinary practice, *Society & animals,* Volume 2, Number 1, 1994.

Personal communications with various young, recently graduated vets; personal experience with various vets 1974–2009; experience with various clients who had received incorrect — and sometimes dangerous — advice from vets.

Myth 99: Scientists know what they are talking about because they study animals in an objective way.

We have seen that many scientists who make statements about dogs have never properly studied dogs. Many of them simply adopted a Nazi Nobel Prize winner's story about dogs, ignoring the fact that the man's speciality was birds. Some just went along with the idea that once you've studied wolves, you don't need to separately study dogs. The scientists who have studied dogs have done so either in highly unnatural circumstances (the lab), or they've only observed them for short intervals. But all the same, they make sweeping — and, as we have now seen, incorrect — statements about the domestic dog, claiming to know what it is and how it works.

We have all been taught to believe that science is able to protect itself from such errors. So the question arises as to why science has been blundering along this way with regard to dogs, producing more fantasy than facts about them. A number of things are behind this.

A huge, almost religious romance has been built up around science. This romance states that science is in the business of constantly turning itself upside down and inside out in the search for Truth. We look at scientists with awe, as if they are a special species and a breed of super humans. The fact is, scientists are ordinary human beings just like the rest of us. And just like the rest of us, scientists have egos. They are subject to pressure to produce, same as the rest of the labour force. Publishing articles fast and frequently helps a scientist's career more than would less frequent (but perhaps more valid) publications. Like us, scientists want to be able to pay the mortgage, keep the kids in private schools and buy a new car next year. Research funding and university jobs are scarce, and there is fierce competition for them. The older generation is ever watchful that the ideas of some young, up-and-coming colleague don't overturn their own, old theories, the ones they've built their senior careers on. It's not so hard to keep some uppity young thing from getting a teaching position, or to prevent a younger colleague from publishing, or at least to delay this, and if that fails, well, they can always manipulate the citation index (see text box opposite).

As a result of all this, science itself is organised in a strictly structured (and enforced) hierarchy — scientists spend their lives moving within a dominance hierarchy they are never allowed to forget, always careful not to step on higher-ranked toes. For example, at scientific congresses, an insider can see at a glance who the Alpha leaders are just by observing the seating arrangements. The closer to the front, the higher the rank. You can ask difficult questions of those sitting behind you, but not those in front. You can interrupt those behind you to correct a mistake, but not those in front. If you disobey these rules, you run the risk of destroying your chances of getting good teaching or research positions, of being cited enough to count, and thus of ever building a scientific career.

In a nutshell, science is partly an honest search for founded knowledge, but it is also partly a complicated ritual dance about ranks and status and to hell with the truth. And of course, the young scientist must, like all young animals, survive in the environment s/he lives in. It is, therefore, not so easy to contradict a Nobel Prize winner (at least not while he's still alive). And when you live and move daily in a world that is organised by the principle of a strict dominance hierarchy and ever-guarded ranks, it's not easy to see when you are projecting this onto others (in particular when the others can't speak to correct you).

THE CITATION INDEX

The fact that both academic career and scientific prestige are so dependent on publishing has led to the churning out of much trivial, irrelevant or even spurious work. Under pressure to 'publish or perish', some scientists have gone so far as to falsify data. Some have even published articles about research that never really took place. In the end, the problem of low quality publications reached such proportions that publication alone was abandoned as a criterion for estimating a researcher's worth. Privately, inside the club, some of the most brilliant scientists openly acknowledge that you have as much chance of finding quality work in the scientific journals as you do on the internet, where any nut (be it a brilliant nut or just a nut) can write and publish as s/he pleases. As both university administrators and the general public began to get wind of this problem, a solution had to be found — some way to more validly estimate the quality of a researcher's work. They came up with the citation index. This is published by organisations that keep track of how much one scientist's published work is cited by other scientists in their footnotes and bibliographies. The presumption is that scientists will tend to use high quality work as sources for their own. This was justified by the fact that Nobel Prize winners turned out, up to 1965, to have been cited about forty times as often as other colleagues (though they published only about five times as much).

But of course, water always seeks the lowest level — and scientists are, just like the rest of us, about sixty percent water. Once the citation index was instituted as a basis for getting jobs and prestige, people immediately began manipulating the index. All you have to do is cite your friends and ignore your competitors whenever possible. Yet again, this has taken such a flight that no one really takes the various indexes entirely seriously anymore. Some scientists openly and publicly ridicule them, while others (guess who) avidly defend them. Everyone recommends, at any rate, not using them as the sole measure of a researcher's scientific worth.

Then there's a second problem with the objectivity of science: most scientists are male. We all know (and it has been proven repeatedly) that men tend to use competitive strategies in dealing with group membership, whereas women tend to use cooperative strategies. As we look at the world around us, we all refer to our own inner experience and motivation as we try to understand and explain it. It can't be otherwise, this is true of all humans. Our personal experience of the world affects which things we find important enough to study, which questions we then pose, which things we think are relevant (and which we count), and how we interpret the results of our studies. Because of this, it's inevitable that the pretty much exclusive presence of men in science has led to some distortions in the way the world is researched and interpreted. This might not be so important when we're looking at non-living things, but when it comes to interpreting the behaviour of living creatures this is a serious failing. This projection of purely male, competitive psychology on to reality has given us many faulty theories about the world of the living. The theory that non-human animals are constantly constructing competitive hierarchies isn't the only one. Freud's theory that incest doesn't occur, that this is just four-year-old girls having fantasies about sleeping with their fathers, came from the same place.

Recent research published by the *Scientific American* has shown that men engage in science in a different way than women do. Men are more preoccupied with career building and tend to be focused on publishing a lot and fast. Women tend to be more concerned with doing really thorough research, even if this slows down their rate of publication. In other words, women tend to do better science than men, but the rules of the game mean that this slows their careers. This doesn't mean that all men are inferior scientists. It means that it isn't always the best scientists who end up at the top of the hierarchy, with the most prestige.

When we are talking about the sciences that study animal behaviour, there is a third factor that gets in the way of objectivity. We now know that science often attracts people who have various autism-related disorders, in particular Asperger's syndrome. This turned out, in 2006, to be the explanation for a small epidemic of autistic disorders among school-going children in the Dutch city of Eindhoven. A worldwide electronics company had established a large scientific research centre in that city, which — as it turned out — had attracted an unusual concentration of parents (scientists employed by the company) who suffered from heritable autism-related disorders. One of the typical symptoms of these disorders is difficulty with social and communicative skills. Those affected often have difficulty conceiving of others as living beings with their own inner world of knowledge, feelings, beliefs and intentions that are not the same as his/her own: they lack the ability to feel empathy. They tend to have difficulty with social and emotional reciprocity. People with these disorders are particularly bad at reading non-verbal language and social signals. Because of this, they often have trouble responding appropriately in social contexts or communicating their own inner world. There has not yet been any large scale investigation into exactly how many scientists have autism-related disorders, nor whether they are concentrated in particular fields of study. Until these questions are answered, it is probably a good idea to be reserved about believing any statements scientists make about the behaviour of animals. First we need to know how many of the observers we have appointed to this task are capable of understanding another's behaviour at all.

When we refer to animals, we mean non-verbal creatures, whose only means of expressing themselves is through body language. Among humans, about seventy percent of the information that is conveyed in a conversation is conveyed non-verbally, by our facial expressions, tone of voice, body postures and positions. Among animals, one hundred percent of the information is conveyed this way. Now of course, not all scientists have autism-related problems with this — but it remains a problem that most scientists are men. Men in general (and this has been scientifically proven) are infamously bad at reading what we call body language; at any rate, they are much worse at it than are women. So it is, yet again, questionable whether we can and should put our trust in what are, evidently, our least capable observers when we want to understand the behaviour of animals.

If we take all of the above together, it may explain why so many scientists still, after some 350 years, embrace Descartes's view of the animal as a machine, a sort of programme-driven automaton that is without feelings, without any kind of thoughts, completely different and separate from humans. It is, in scientific circles, still taboo to contradict this idea. The word 'anthropomorphic' appears instantly as a reproach, and as proof that you must be fairly worthless and quite misguided as a scientist. (Anthropomorphism means assigning human qualities to non-human objects.) This is often still the case even when it's about something as evident as the fact that other mammals feel pain. The accusation of anthropomorphism is usually paired with ridicule and laughter.

Because of all this, science moves only very slowly in correcting the flaws I point out. We know now how similar our anatomies and brains are to those of other animals (and where they aren't similar), including the functions of all kinds of body and brain structures, processes and parts. We know now that we differ genetically from a rabbit only by about fifteen percent — which means that a large number of our own genes are executing the same programmes they execute in other animals. Despite this, scientists are still amazed when, for example, a creature as simple as a crow is able to make plans, to use tools and to complete complicated tasks (a thing any farmer could have told them 300 years ago, had they bothered to ask, and if they hadn't laughed so contemptuously at him). And, after watching the crow make plans, use tools, and do complicated assignments, they still continue to insist that the same crow is unable to feel (for example) pain as we feel it. In a nutshell, science now has to deny many known facts because of adopting an incorrect viewpoint 350 years ago, one which is now very difficult to abandon without great loss of face. But of course, it could be less nefarious. There could be a kind of innocence operating. It could be that scientists are genuinely unable to adapt to changes, preferring to continue their repetitive movements according to their set pattern, because they are semi-autistic and can't understand the meaning of it all, or why it would matter, anyway. The ridiculing laughter may be nothing more than a defensive, autistic panic reaction when confronted with a part of the universe they aren't even able to perceive, let alone understand. This, too, is possible.

Another reason science moves so slowly is the obsession with measurement and quantification. You might *think* you see a thing, but it doesn't really exist until you have measured it. This is something that fits into the pattern of autism, but it is also (to be fair) a kind of honest hope that measurement and quantification will (albeit magically) ensure objectivity. This wouldn't be so bad if scientists had said you don't *understand* a thing until you've measured it. But alas, this isn't what they came up with, and this is a source of huge problems with science. Many aspects of reality are denied as even existing, simply because we can't measure them (yet). The shock at discovering how few genes we have and the conclusion that we aren't so different from other animals as we thought is just one example. Another problem is that the fixation with quantification leads science to focus on things we can measure instead of concentrating on things that are perhaps more relevant. A question that can't be answered with quantitative data and a statistics programme, in an article of not more than seven pages (including diagrams and tables) is set aside — you can't publish it anyway, so why be interested? Even scientists are now complaining that this attitude has led to stagnation in the formation of theory in favour of measuring all kinds of irrelevant trivia.

A final problem is that if you want to measure aspects of living beings, you have to create highly artificial circumstances and situations. This means your measurements no longer reflect the real world, and that your measurements are, therefore, very often irrelevant or even banal. This has sometimes led to surprising results, to the measurement of things that turned out not to exist — things that were a temporary result of the artificial circumstances, which ceased to exist as soon as the artificial circumstances are removed. The dominance hierarchy within a wolf pack is an example of this. Our puppies fighting over a bone in the lab is another one.

Fact: Scientists have forgotten that one of the things they should be observing (if they want to claim objectivity) is their own behaviour. They have forgotten to watch out for how their own psychology determines not only what they see, but even which questions they ask. They have been too unaware that they are, like any other animal, projecting their own inner world onto the outer world and believing that this is the only true reality.

Fact: There are huge unsolved problems in the sciences. Human interests, biases and limitations play a bigger role than we acknowledge, despite sometimes honest attempts to correct these. We would all do well to keep a healthy dose of scepticism as we listen to what the scientists are telling us about dogs. You don't have to (and can't) assume you always know better, but you can — just to be sure — refrain from letting them talk you into doing anything that you suspect may be cruel.

Animals 'projecting'

Most animals do not have the large areas of the brain that give us our abstract cognitive abilities. Most don't seem to have an abstract sense of self and other, nor the ability to think abstractly about themselves or themselves vs. the other. Animals operate within their perception of the world, without being able to stand back and observe themselves. They can't think, 'Maybe the other is living in a different world of perception'.

As a result, many animals will interpret the behaviour of another animal according to their own inner world. When dogs bare their teeth, they are telling the other that they want distance and will use their weapons to get it, if they have to. When chimps bare their teeth, they are telling the other that they feel afraid. Unless the animal has a long learning experience of what it means when we show our teeth, the animal will respond as if our smile means the same thing it means for the animal's own species. When a human smiles at a dog, many dogs take this to mean the human is hostile. When we smile at a chimp, a chimp may take this to mean we are fearful. The animals react to our approach according to the rules that govern their behaviour with their own kind.

Male human scientists are just another kind of animal. They look at an animal and think, 'When I behave that way, it means I have such-and-such a motive, so the animal must have that same motive, too'. And then they tell us to respond according to our human rules, just as any other non-cognitive animal would respond according to its own rules. The fact that scientists are so quick to accuse others of anthropomorphism illustrates how unconscious their own projections are.

Burgoon, JK, Buller, DB, Woodall, WG, *Nonverbal communication: The unspoken dialogue*, McGraw-Hill Companies Inc, NY, 1966.

Carson, G, *Men Beasts and Gods: A History of Cruelty and Kindness to Animals*, Charles Scribner, NY 1972.

Chomsky, N, Language, Politics, and Composition, an interview of Chomsky by Gary A. Olson and Lester Faigley, *Journal of Advanced Composition*, Vol. 11, No. 1, 1991. http://www.chomsky.info/interviews/1991----.htm (accessed 12 January 2009).

Cohen, E, Law folklore and animal lore, *Past and Present* 110: 6–37, 1986.

Dahles, H, Game killing and killing games: An anthropologist looking at hunting in modern society, *Society & Animals*, Vol.1 No. 2, 1993.

Darnton, R, *The Great Cat Massacre and Other Episodes in French Cultural History*, Vintage NY, 1985.

Dawkins, MS, *Animal Suffering: The Science of Animal Welfare,* Methuen, NY, 1981.
Dawkins, MS, *Through our eyes only? The search for animal consciousness* Oxford University Press, 1995.
De Boo, M, Onbereikbare toga; in het Wageningse landbouwereldje kwamen geleerde vrouwen niet aan de bak, *NRC Handelsblad,* 31 mei en 1 juni 2003, Wetenschap en Onderwijs, p.41.
Descartes, R, *Treatise of man* (1629), translated by Thomas Steel Hall, Harvard University Press, Cambridge MA, 1972.
Descartes, R, Animals are machines, in Armstrong, SJ, and Botzler, RG, eds. *Environmental ethics: Divergence and Convergence,* McGraw-Hill, NY, pp 281–285, 1993.
Erwin, J, Deni, R, Strangers in a strange land: Abnormal behaviour or abnormal environments? in Erwin, J, Maple, T, Mitchell, G, (eds): *Captivity and Behaviour,* Van Nostrand Reinhold Co, NY, 1979, pp 1–28.
Engell, J, *The Creative Imagination: Enlightenment to Romanticism,* Harvard University Press, Cambridge MA, 1981.
Finkelstein, JJ, The ox that gored, *Transactions of the American Philosophical Society,* 71 part 2, 1981.
Firestone, S, *De dialectiek van de sekse: Het argument voor de feministische revolutie,* Uitgeverij Bert Bakker, Amsterdam, 1979.
Fox, MW, (ed) *Abnormal Behaviour in Animals,* WB Saunders & Co, Philadelphia, 1968.
Friedman, DF, 'Does altruism produce efficient outcomes? Marshall vs. Kaldor, www.daviddfriedman.com/Academic/Marshal_Pareto/Marshal_Pareto.html, written 27 May 1987, published May 2002.
Goodloe, LP, Issues in description and measurement of temperament in companion dogs, in Voith, VL, Borchelt, PL, eds *Readings in Companion Animal Behaviour,* Veterinary Learning systems Co. Inc., Trenton NJ, 1996: 32–39.
Greer, G, *De vrouw als eunuch,* Meulenhoff, Amsterdam, 1972. (Original title: *The Female Eunuch.*)
Greer, G, *Het lot van de vrouw: De politiek van de menselijke vruchtbaarheid,* Meulenhoff, Amsterdam, 1984. (Original title: *Sex and Destiny. The Politics of Human Fertility.*)
Guerrero, LK, DeVito, JA, Hecht, ML, (eds), *The nonverbal communication reader: Classic and contemporary readings,* Waveland, Prospect Heights IL, 1999.
Hajer, M, Vliegen door verzwavelde rook; de universiteiten moeten zelf hun maatschappelijke onderzoek bepalen, *NRC Handelsblad,* 16 en 17 februari 2002, Wetenschap en Onderwijs p.39.
Hart, BL, Hart, LA, Selecting pet dogs on the basis of cluster analysis of breed behavioural profiles and gender, *JAVMA* 186[11]: 1181–1185, 1985.
Hart, BL, Hart, LA, Selecting the best companion animal: breed and gender specific behavioural profiles, in *The pet connection: Its Influence on Our Health and Quality of Life,* Anerson, RK, Hart, BL, Hart, LA, (eds) University of Minnesota Press, Minneapolis, 1984, pp 180–193.
Hart, BL, Miller, MF, Behavioural profiles of dog breeds: A quantitative approach, *JAVMA* 186[11]: 1175–1180, 1985.
Herek, GM, The instrumentality of attitudes: Toward a neofunctional theory, *Journal of Social Issues,* 42: 99–114, 1986.
Hills, AM, The motivational bases of attitudes toward animals, *Animals & Society,* Volume 1 Number 2, 1993.
Holton, G, Different perceptions: Women approach research with care but their low publication rate crimps their careers, *Sc Am* April 1998.
Icke, V S-baan, *NRC Handelsblad,* 7 rn 8 juni 2003, Wetenschap en Onderwijs, p.36.
Ivy, DK, Backlund, P, *Exploring genderspeak,* MeGraw-Hill Companies Inc., NY, 1994.
Katz, D, The functional approach to the study of attitudes, *Public Opinion, Quarterly* 24: 163–204, 1960.

Koelewijn, J, De Koning, P, De inktwerking van autisme in families; spaghetti met tomatensaus, *NRC Handelsblad,* 7 en 8 juni 2003, p.24.

Koenen, L, De ontmaskering van Nim Chimpsky; profiel van een gedreven wetenschapper, *M: het maandblad van NRC Handelsblad,* maart 2003 pp 24–32.

Kollontaj, A, *De positie van de vrouw in de ontwikkeling van de maatschappij: Veertien lezingen aan de Sverdlov universiteit,* Het Wereldvenster Bussum, 1982.

Kuhn, TS, *The Structure of Scientific Revolutions,* University of Chicago Press, Chicago IL, 1962.

Lattal, KA, A century of effect: Legacies of EL Thorndike's *Animal Intelligence,* Monograph, *JEAB* 70: 325–336, 1998.

Lucas, C, Quantifying complexity theory, http://www.calresco.org/lucas/htm.#t4 (2002).

Maturana, HR, The organisation of the living: A theory of the living organisation, *International Journal of Man-Machine Studies,* Vol 7 1975, pp 313–332.

Maturana, HR, Biology of language: the epistemology of reality, in Miller, GA, and Lenneberg, E, (eds.) *Psychology and Biology of Language and Thought: Essays in Honor of Eric Lenneberg,* Academic Press, NY, 1978, pp 27–63. http://www.calresco.org/lucas/htm.#t4 (2002).

Maturana, HR, and Varela, V, Autopoiesis and cognition: The realisation of the living, in *Boston Studies in the Philosophy of Science,* Cohen, RS, and Wartofsky, MW, (eds.) Vol. 42 Dordrecht: D. Reidel Publishing Co., 1980.

Meijer van Putten B Verzwijgen maakt beter; fibromyalgie verdwijnt als niemand erover rept *NRC Handelsblad* 7 en 8 juni 2003 Onderwijs en Wetenschap p 37.

Mesterton-Gibbons, M, On the evolution of pure winner and loser effects: a game-theoretic model, *Bulletin of Mathematical Biology,*61 1151–1186, (1999).

Midgley, M, 'Gene-juggling', www.royalinstitutephilosophy.org/articles/midgley_gene_juggling.htm, May 2002.

Mulvaney, Becky Michele, 'Gender differences in communication: An intercultural experience'. www.eff.org/Net_culture/Gender_issues/mulvaney.article, April 2006.

Newman, G, *The Punishment Response,* J.B. Lippincott, Philadelphia, 1978.

Nibert, DA, Animal rights and human social issues, *Society & Animals,* Volume 2 Number 2, 1994.

Nicholson, J, *Mannen en vrouwen: Hoe verschillend zijn ze?* Het Spectrum, Amsterdam, 1984.

Phillips, MT, Savages, drunks and lab animals: The researcher's perception of pain, *Society & Animals,* Volume 1 Number 1, 1993.

Phillips, MT, Sechzer, JA, *Animal Research and Ethical Conflict,* Springer-Verlag, MY 1989.

Regan, R, Singer, P, (eds) *Animal Rights and Human Obligations,* Prentice-Hall, Englewood Cliffs, NJ, 1976.

Ritvo, H, *The Animal Estate: The English and Other Creatures in the Victorian Age,* Harvard University Press, Cambridge, MA, 1987.

Rollin, B, Animals in experimentation: Utilitarian objects pets or moral objects, *Anthrozoos* 3: 88–90, 1989.

Royce, JR, A factorial study of emotionality in the dog, *Psychol Monogr Gen Appl* 69: 22 (Whole No. 407), 1955.

Rubin, L, *Vrouwen mannen en intimiteit,* Uitgeverij Maarten Mutinga, Amsterdam, 1985.

Sanders, C, Understanding Dogs: Caretakers' attributions of mindedness in canine-human relationships, *Journal of Contemporary Ethnography,* 22 2: 205–226, 1993.

Sanders, CR, Biting the hand that heals you: Encounters with problematic patients in a general veterinary practice, *Society & animals,* Volume 2 Number 1, 1994.

Sax B, What is a 'Jewish dog?' Konrad Lorenz and the cult of wildness *Society & Animals,* Volume 5 Number 1, 1997.

Shaw, GB, *The Adventures of the Black Girl in her Search for God,* R. & R. Clark, Limited, Edinburgh, 1932.

Shapiro, D, Understanding dogs through kinesthetic empathy social construction and history *Anthrozoos* 3: 184–195, 1990.

Skinner, BF, *The Behaviour of Organisms: An Experimental Analysis,* Appleton-Century-Crofts Inc, NY, 1938.

Skinner, BF, *Science and Human Behaviour,* The Free Press (a division of Macmillan Publishing Co.) NY, 1953.

Skinner, BF, *Contingencies of Reinforcement,* Prentice-Hall Inc, Englewood Cliffs, NJ, 1969.

Skinner, BF, *About Behaviourism,* Alfred A. Knopf Inc, NY, 1974.

Smit, C, *Dierproeven: honderd jaar discussie,* La Riviere & Voorhoeve Kampen, NL 1989.

Smith, WJ, *The Behaviour of Communicating,* Harvard University Press Cambridge, MA, 1977.

Sonnert, G, Advocating women: why should women be encouraged to pursue science the arguments keep changing, *Sc Am* April 1998.

Sonnert, G, Where's the difference? Are women treated differently or are they simply different? *Sc Am,* April 1998.

Strumwasser, F, The relation between neuroscience and human behavioural science, *JEAB* 61: 307–318, 1994.

Thomas, K, *Man and the natural world: A history of modern sensibility,* Pantheon Books, NY, 1983.

Van Delft, D, Heel de schepping op een schoolbord, *M: het maandblad van NRC Handelsblad* januari 2003, pp 40–49.

Van Delft, D, 'Wij Nederlanders hakken terug', *NRC Handelsblad,* 6 en 7 augustus 2005, Wetenschap en Onderwijs, p.17.

Van Hooff, JARAM, Wensing, JAB, Dominance and its behavioural measures in a captive wolf pack, in *Man and Wolf,* Frank, H, ed, Dr W Junk Publishers, Dordrecht, 1987 pp 219–252.

Varela, FJ, *Principles of Biological Autonomy,* Elsevier, (North Holland), NY, 1979.

Varela, FJ, Autonomy and autopoiesis, in Roth Gerhard and Schwegler (eds.) *Self-organising Systems: An Interdisciplinary Approach,* Campus Verlag Frankfurt/NY, 1981 pp 14–23.

Varela, FJ, Thompson, E, and Rosch, E, *The Embodied Mind: Cognitive Science and Human Experience,* MIT Press, Cambridge MA, 1991.

Visser, H, Publieke opinie als chaos; Van Ginneken over snelle meningsverschuivingen, *NRC Handelsblad,* 11 en 12 mei 2002, Wetenschap en Onderwijs, p 37.

Voltaire, F, A reply to Descartes, in Regan, T, Singer, P, (eds.) pp 67–68, reprint from Voltaire, F, *Philosophical Dictionary* 'Animals'.

Worster, D, *Nature's Economy: A History of Ecological Ideas,* Cambridge University Press, NY, 1995.

Myth 100: The author of this book certainly knows better than everyone else.

The truth is, you should never stop reading and thinking critically — not even when you read this book! I mention facts that are just that, a number of which will make some people uncomfortable and even angry — for example, Konrad Lorenz was a convinced, voluntary Nazi, not one of those who joined just to survive. He refused to repudiate his ideas until the end of his life, and those ideas influenced the way he saw and described the world of animals. It's a fact that the idea of a linear hierarchy among domestic dogs is unsupported by evidence or data, and that the whole idea has been abandoned even when talking about non-captive wolves. It is true that punishment has serious side effects, and that it does long term damage to an animal's well-being — without improving behaviour. It's important for you and your dog, in fact for all dogs, that everyone hears these facts.

On the other hand, now that we know dogs don't live in a dominance hierarchy, the discussion is still going among scientists about what dogs do instead. How do they structure their groups, since it's not by dominance? This discussion didn't even get started until a long while after Lorenz died (in 1989), and many of the old guard are still resisting even having it. After fourteen years of watching dogs, it seems obvious to me that the best way to figure out and describe their social systems and behaviour is by looking at them as complex self-organising systems. This model doesn't look at the dog as a static being who only exists on one level. It sees the dog as a complex, learning being, who changes as his life progresses. The social system he lives in, and which he constructs again and again during his days, is a complex system with complex dynamics. Using just a few simple rules, this system is able to find workable equilibriums on many levels simultaneously, from the inside of the dog right on through to whatever (fleeting) social landscape he happens to be in at any given moment. As it seeks this multi-levelled equilibrium, the canine system is able to deal not only with factors playing in the present, but it is even able to take into account things that have happened in the past.

After fourteen years of watching and testing, it's clear that self-organising systems theory (SOS theory) works better as a way to explain what dogs are doing. Instead of pasting labels onto a dog ('dominant' or 'submissive') we take his continuing development and his life-long learning into account. We don't say, 'he *is* this or that', but instead ask how he arrived at this particular behaviour at this particular moment under these particular circumstances. Behaviour is seen as a complex interaction of many variables and factors, as an animal seeks both inner and outer balance. SOS theory acknowledges the role that learning plays. Yet, despite the fact that we now look at dog society as a complex system rather than as a simple hierarchy, the explanation of what is happening is much more simple, elegant and clear.

But it's not only theory. The insights provided by SOS theory turn out to give us better ways of working with what we call 'difficult' dogs. This new way of looking at dog behaviour is interdisciplinary. Instead of looking at a dog from only one viewpoint, we take all of them into our equation simultaneously — genetics, physiology and neurology, are tied into a coherent whole with such changing factors as metabolism, learning and the dog's momentary surroundings. When we combine it all like this, we are much better able to understand behaviour as a complex but coherent whole. We see that both upward causation (molecules → cells → organs → dog → behaviour toward the environment) and downward causation (environment → dog → organs → cells → molecules) are active and interacting.

SOS theory also allows us to see the dog as a living, feeling being. In other words, it corrects the autistic tendency science has had up to now. This doesn't mean we make the dog into a four-footed human. We acknowledge more than previous science ever has that the dog's system has its own rules and dynamics and its own limitations. We recognise that the quality of his life is one of the things that motivate him, and that this quality of life is determined differently for him than it is for us, and is dependent on different factors.

The fact that we now acknowledge all of this takes us a step closer to reality and, being closer to it, we are in a better position to start understanding it. We realise that we can't understand behaviour just by looking at parts of the system, and that it's not about labels. Rather, it's about understanding the dynamics we see when it all interlocks. How do genes, cells and organs, past and present, and the environment the dog is in right now come together to generate the behaviour he is showing?

I can't tell you exactly which genes your dog has, nor how his history has been. Only you know whether he's tired or hungry at any given moment. This means I do not know everything better than you do. My wish is to give you the instruments you need to arrive at your own real *knowing* about your dog. Now that you've read this book, this knowing won't be based on myths and fantasies and foolishnesses, but on real knowledge of what dogs are all about.

Fact: I want everyone to look at their dog with newly opened eyes and to start using the facts they have learned from this book. Your dog will look different to you when you see him as a living system that is constantly developing and changing. Instead of sticking on labels that don't help you at all, you'll be trying to understand the past and present dynamics that are influencing his behaviour. He'll seem different when you understand his limitations, his uncertainty, his searching for a predictable, peaceful balance. You'll understand his behaviour better when you realise it's not only in the dog, but part of a back-and-forth between him and the outside world — and with us.

You can try out what happens if you abandon all the old ideas about power and punishment, forget about being the so-called 'Alpha leader', and start to work in *partnership* with your dog in looking for that predictable, peaceful balance. See how much better your relationship gets once you start obeying the three simple rules that govern his system (see page 52) instead of applying our system rules the way you've been told to up to now. You will understand him much better and, in doing so, will be able to judge for yourself whether what I've said in this book is true.

Epilogue — a final vanity: mankind is dog's best friend.

Now that you've read this book, you know better.

We project all kinds of human qualities onto the dog, while at the same time we deny his pain and his feelings. We lay a Nazi tale on him, then use it as an excuse for demanding that he never have any longings of his own. If he does (which he can't help, after all, he's a living being) we use this tale as an excuse to punish him cruelly for it *without having to feel any guilt for our cruelty.*

The dog gives us a chance to take out all our frustrations and our lust for power on a being who is totally at our mercy and can't resist. Choke chains, pronged collars, electric shocks, kicking him, beating him with a piece of two-by-four or a garden hose... all too many dog owners do it and feel much more of a Real Man because we do. After all, only a Real Man can be the Alpha leader, right?

We call our dog a wolf, but what we actually do is take unfair advantage of his specifically doggy qualities, such as his willingness to look for a compromise in relationships, his reticence about using aggression, his longing to preserve the relationship with us even if we're making it difficult for him — of his willingness to take an amazing amount of bad handling, even violence from us before he finally resists and defends himself. Does anyone *truly* believe you can put a choke chain or a pronged collar on a wolf, or jerk his head upwards with the head halter to get him to sit, or try to bully him into getting into the bath, and survive having tried all this? It's pathetic.

We poison him, we shoot him dead. We shut him up in solitary confinement in our living rooms while we work all day and have a drink after. We chain him, we teach him to lead the blind by punishing him until he doesn't dare do anything else, nay, until he is so beaten down that he stops having longings of his own. We fool around with his genes until we have ruined his dogginess — until he can hardly walk, hardly breathe, or until he loses his capacity to seek compromises and fights to the death without even knowing why he's doing it. We have created dogs who can't even be born except by Caesarean section. We choke him, wound him, answer his friendliness with clumsy and misplaced attempts to 'dominate' him. He doesn't understand why we are constantly showing threat behaviour, but he does his best to accommodate and preserve the relationship anyway. And if he doesn't do this, if he does finally resist yet another beating or portion of abuse, then we all too nonchalantly kill him. 'The problem was in the dog', we say, shrugging our shoulders, then go out and buy another one.

In fact, people who try to dominate dogs must be suspected of being infantile, blind and petty. Infantile because they want a one way street, a relationship that's all taking and no giving, where they don't have to compromise or consider anyone else's wishes but their own, and where they can engage in magical thinking — all of it normal in a child of three. Blind because they don't see how physical relations truly are, not seeing that the dog could hurt the human if he wanted to (the dog doesn't know he'd pay with his life, but this is *not* what keeps him from attacking us back), but that the dog just doesn't *want* to have to hurt us. Blind to how tolerant the dog is, to what kind of creature a dog really is. Petty because they want to base relationships on power, but only dare to do this with a creature who is totally at their mercy, who has no way out, no place to hide, nowhere else to go.

Hope: Happily, not everyone is like this. I hope this book will help us behave towards our dogs as good friends should, without feeling ashamed of it. We will affectionately try to understand and consider his needs and longings, happily seek compromises with him, and thankfully answer his friendliness with the same coin. We will, above all, not punish him, but rather *help* him when he doesn't understand what we want.

SPREAD THE WORD

INDEX